In

Indonesia

third edition

Bruce Grant

MELBOURNE UNIVERSITY PRESS

Melbourne University Press
PO Box 278, Carlton South, Victoria 3053, Australia

First published 1964
Second edition 1966
Revised and reprinted by Penguin Books 1967
Third edition 1996

Typeset in Malaysia by Syarikat Seng Teik Sdn. Bhd. in 10.5 point Bembo
Printed in Australia by McPherson's Printing Group.

National Library of Australia Cataloguing-in-Publication entry

Grant, Bruce, 1925– .
  Indonesia.

  3rd ed.
  Bibliography.
  Includes index.
  ISBN 0 522 84745 5.

  1. Indonesia—History. 2. Indonesia—Politics and government.
  I. Title.

915.98

Contents

Preface   vii
Map of Indonesia   3

 1 Beginnings   1
 2 Nation   18
 3 Leaders   41
 4 Politics   67
 5 Military   87
 6 Economy   110
 7 Culture   124
 8 Land   142
 9 People   155
10 Foreign Policy   193
11 Future   218

Glossary   229
Bibliography   231
Index   237

Preface

FOR THIS EDITION of *Indonesia*, thirty years after the first, I was reluctant to lose the freshness—and the brashness—of the original, yet I found that I could not easily reproduce it. It proved impossible to be as confident (as insouciant!) about Indonesia as I was then. I know so much more about Indonesia now, that in preparing this new edition I have seemed at times to be an amanuensis. Those brave generalizations! Those daring insights! Were they written by me? How could I possibly have known *that*, or thought *that*, or *written* that! Well, I did. And the book that resulted from a young man's enthusiasm was, with all its faults, a good book. It caught the flavour of the time. It was critical and severe, but it was also brimming with sympathy. It helped to set the tone of attitudes to Indonesia for a while, especially in Australia.

So I decided to keep as much of the earlier writing as possible. My motive may also have been personal. *Indonesia* was my first book and I have a particular fondness for it. But the retention of the early material does actually serve a useful purpose. There is always continuity in the history of nations, even if the national protagonists who succeed each other think they are poles apart. In Indonesia, where nationalism remains potent, the elements of continuity are especially strong. It has surprised me how much of the Sukarno era, which is what the first edition was about, has survived into the Suharto era. Indonesian history keeps tagging current events.

I should not have been surprised. After all, Indonesians have a very personal sense of history. I once spent several days with an Indonesian friend and his two daughters visiting their family graves in east Java. An element of ritual was observed, such as flowers, incense and prayers (and while I slept in the nearest motel, they spent the nights at the grave sites) but what I recall now most vividly was the conversation. The young women spoke of their ancestors, some of whom had been dead for hundreds of years, as if they were still alive, remarking on their character, their faults and virtues, their behaviour during some event, as if they were still family members. It should not surprise us that in the Indonesian language verbs have the same form in the past as in the present.

Everything flows. When I opened the preface to the first edition with those words, I did not realize how well they would survive.

Thirty years ago I was not only a young man writing his first book, I was a busy foreign correspondent in the middle of the Cold War. No matter how sensitive you tried to be towards the new nations of the developing world, you saw it as your duty, and perhaps even your right, to keep in mind the big story, which was the strategic and intellectual clash between two global centres of power. The earlier editions of this book have a lecturing tone at times, although fortunately it is a lecture delivered with touches of humour and humility. Today, the visitor to Indonesia is more inclined to accept Indonesia on its own terms.

The last couple of decades have shown that the Western way of doing things is not the only way and not always the best way. Asian countries especially have shown the world that there is a successful model of economic development which does not fit neatly into what Westerners, especially if they are liberal democrats, think is necessary for a developing country. In short, I feel more restrained now in my opinion of how Indonesia should go about its business. But a writer has his or her own values, as much as a writing style, and these values need to be apparent to the reader, just as the style needs to be consistent. Accepting Indonesia on its own terms does not mean that the author has to suspend judgement. You still have to make judgements, because Indonesians themselves are doing so. What are the terms on which Indonesia wishes to be accepted? Whose terms are they? How practical are they?

With the assistance of Melbourne University Press, I have retained the essential format and what I will call mannerisms of the first edition. The anonymous interviews in Chapter 9 created controversy thirty years ago because, although the words were real, the identities of the speakers were deliberately disguised. I have retained and updated the chapter, however. It is important that the words of people who think differently from official Indonesia are included in a book which must properly give weight to the opinion of government and its authorities. The words of ordinary people carry more weight, in the sense that they can be more truthful, if they do not have the consequences which identifying their authors would bring.

The editor and I have also continued to keep the general reader in mind as much as possible, avoiding footnotes and scholarly interpolations. The dreaded acronym has made strides on the world scene since the first edition, and Indonesians seem to have a special affection for it. The rule of thumb adopted here is that if it looks like a word and sounds like a word, it is a *de facto* word and is printed as such, while if it looks like a bunch of initials and cannot be spoken, it is printed in capitals. It's not rational editing, but it seems to work.

I wish to acknowledge that the suggestion for this edition came from Brian Wilder, director of Melbourne University Press, just as the suggestion for the first edition had come from the director then, Peter Ryan. My editor has been Jean Dunn, who I know well from working with her on *Australia's Foreign Relations*. It is always a pleasure for an author to have a supportive publisher and a skilled and creative editor, and I acknowledge this warmly. I wish also to thank Monash University for assisting me to travel to Indonesia in 1995 for research for this edition.

For three years, I was chairman of the Australia-Indonesia Institute. I learned a lot from staff and board members who were involved in Indonesia in direct and practical ways. It has also been my good fortune recently to have been teaching young diplomats. I have been encouraged by the interest in Indonesia from students from the Department of Foreign Affairs and Trade undertaking post-graduate studies as part of their training.

Needless to say, yet needing to be said, what is written is entirely my responsibility.

PREFACE TO THE FIRST EDITION, 1964

Everything flows. Indonesians have often said this to me, adding that the Western anxiety to halt reality and examine its meaning is a cause of unhappiness. It is also, however, a cause of understanding. This small book is dedicated to the proposition that it is possible to halt the processes of a country in order to test them, and, even if this were not possible, that the writer ought to be allowed to try. From an Indonesian's point of view it is therefore an outsider's book.

Indonesians tend to say: 'Oh, you don't understand. You *can't* understand'. What they mean is: 'You can't be me'. This also may be true, but it is a request for sympathy, not for understanding. My sympathies for Indonesia were easily engaged and are lasting. I have wanted in the pages that follow, however, to examine the country more closely than I have been able to do in the past as a sympathetic—and rather hurried—observer.

I went first to Indonesia expecting to contemplate Scott Fitzgerald's 'fresh, green breast of the new world'. When I found that the lovely land had been pawed for centuries, I became absorbed in the political corrective to this sordid affair: nationalism as a form of idealism, nationalism as rebirth. Indonesia did not beckon with a mysterious past, as China, India and Japan do, but writing urgently of what was taking place I was always aware of the country itself, untouched by cabled dispatches, breathing softly in the available distance.

I came to realize that there are three Indonesias. There is an Indonesia, the first, which is defined by political events: what the president says and does publicly, what decisions are taken by the government. In this sense, Indonesia is an important nation with a voice in world affairs, attitudes and opinions concerning the big issues of our time, problems of defence, trade and so on. The second is defined by the resources of the people: their attempts to understand life and death, their humour, their social relations, their style of thought and dress. These things may be uneventful for journalism, but they 'happen' all the time. It is hard to find a national meaning in a beautiful face in the street, the sound of *betjak* bells at night, the sombre colours of a batik sarong, yet they are as much the mark of a country as the insignia of politics. The third Indonesia is defined not by nationalism or culture but by ecology. To the ecologist the reticulated Indonesian rice terraces are more impressive than the artistic galleries of ancient monuments or the edifices of the modern nation. Can Indonesia show that it is a nation able to keep a safe balance between land and people?

This is a book of political interpretation, which means that it is about the first Indonesia. I have tried to use the other two Indonesias, however, to inform and enlarge the study. As much as possible I have tried to keep the information open and dispersed, rather than marshalled in support of a viewpoint in the hope that the book will serve a more general purpose than that of argument. There is a great deal of outside political judgement about Indonesia but very little knowledge of its politics.

As I am not a scholar, this is not a scholarly book. The information is often raw and the judgements made without reference to previous authority. There are no footnotes. On occasions, the main public sources are articles I wrote at the time and I have based myself, without attribution, on them. Sometimes I have used statements made in conversation by leading Indonesians which have not been used before. Generally, however, I have tried to keep the level of source material even and non-controversial.

A special word, therefore, about Chapter 9. I advise readers not to play 'spot the victim' as they will find themselves to have been deliberately misled. The words in these conversations are real; the people are composites designed to lose the scent. The reasons for this subterfuge are obvious enough, although the Indonesian security police is no more active than its counterparts in other Asian countries. There is opposition to the Sukarno government, even if growing weaker, and I wanted in some of these conversations to show the kind of opposition it is. The chapter also shows an acceptance, short of fervent support, for Sukarno. I would not claim any sociological value for it: the people interviewed are English-speaking and Djakarta-based and this gives them a bias. Politically, however, an élite of a few thousand people manipulate Indonesian politics and with few exceptions they live in Djakarta and speak English.

A word, also, about Indonesian names and titles. I have tried to keep the text readable, which has meant sometimes disregarding the refinements and elaborations of Indonesian proper names. Indonesians themselves are casual about this: Dipa Nusantara Aidit is Aidit, Ali Sastroamidjojo is Ali, Tan Malaka is neither Tan nor Malaka but always Tan Malaka. Some, like Sukarno, have only one name. Javanese in particular sometimes change their names to celebrate an event. Wherever possible I have simply followed common Indonesian usage. Titles offer such a technical tangle that I have generally not used them, especially as they are in the process of change. Such aristocratic titles as Raden (Javanese) and Sutan (Minangkabau) are still in fact used, as is the Muslim title of Hadji (for one who has made the pilgrimage to Mecca). Academic titles are doubly confusing to the English reader because they have been inherited from the Dutch. 'Mr'

(*Meester*) is a graduate in law; 'Ir' (*Ingénieur*) is a graduate in engineering, architecture or agriculture; 'Drs' is used by graduates in economics or literature while 'Dr' is reserved for higher degrees in all fields and for medical and dental graduates. The Indonesian president is sometimes called Dr Sukarno but he is more strictly Ir Sukarno. The former Foreign Minister, Dr Subandrio, uses his correct title—as a graduate in medicine. Like most people, Indonesians use the respected title 'Dr' rather loosely.

Many Indonesians helped me to write this book although most were not aware of it at the time. Rather than create an unnecessary mystery over names excluded, or embarrassment—as this is a critical book—for the owners of those included, I have decided not to acknowledge their indispensable assistance. I would like to thank Dr Herbert Feith, of Monash University, Melbourne, who put his enormous mental filing system at my disposal and helped in innumerable small ways. Mr W. E. Purnell, formerly director of the South-east Asia Science Co-operation Office of Unesco in Djakarta (now executive secretary of the Royal Australian Chemical Institute) read the manuscript with a sharp eye. He is the kind of critic who, in addition to a world-wide reference for his knowledge of Indonesia, can say whether it was possible for Shrivajaya to have shipped naphtha to China in the fourteenth century—a handy man to have around. My wife, Joan, did some of the research, edited and typed (at least twice) everything I wrote. As the book had to be completed quickly, her help was much more than that of an assistant: sometimes she seemed to be working harder than I was.

CHAPTER ONE

Beginnings

ON THE PLAINS of central Java stands the pyramid temple of Borobudur. It is one of the great relics of tropical Asia, where only solid stone survives the heat and rain. Mount Merapi rises in the near-distance, but the surrounding land is even, a pattern of shrub-trees and fields of rice and sugar cane. Borobudur does not pierce the undulating landscape like the religious spires of rural Europe. It is an impassive monument, with a contemplative style befitting a Buddhist place of worship. It is set broadly on its base of nearly two hundred metres square, rising solidly at a low gradient to a central stupa shaped like a giant bell. When you stand on the higher terraces watching the steamy morning coming to life in the heartland of Java you may feel that the monument is floating. Sometimes at night, when moonlight falls on the calm-faced buddhas in its galleries, you may catch the spirit that the men who made Borobudur were trying to preserve. It is less dramatic than the relics of its contemporary, Angkor, the ruined Hindu-Buddhist temple civilization of the Khmers in Cambodia, but it is evidence of a standard of art and engineering in Indonesia two centuries before the French produced the cathedrals of Notre Dame and Chartres. (As a matter of perspective, all followed nearly two thousand years after the Egyptian pyramids.)

President Sukarno and other Indonesian leaders of the early nationalist period used often to refer to Borobudur as proof that their country had a civilization of depth and variety. 'We object to the description of ourselves as underdeveloped', Sukarno said. 'Qualify the expression! Call it economically undeveloped or technically undeveloped and, with some reservations, I would agree. But spiritually, mentally, culturally, I disagree wholly and completely.' Today's leaders are more complex in their pride, because Indonesia since Sukarno's time has made advances in economic and technical development, and more circumspect in their politics, but in their hearts many would agree with him.

Borobudur was built between 760 and 820 and among its fourteen hundred bas-reliefs, in addition to serene buddhas, are Hindu gods such as Shiva, and images which spring from the primitive beliefs of the people before the religions of the Asian mainland reached the South-East Asian archipelago. Borobudur embodies the now well-known Indonesian talent for blending religious doctrines—the totality of religious beliefs and practices which in Java is called *agama Jawa*, the 'religion of Java'. It was built just as another religion, Islam, appeared on the scene and was in fact buried by Javanese Buddhists during Islam's penetration of the East Indies. Discovered by an English colonel during the brief British seizure of Indonesia from the Dutch during the Napoleonic Wars (1811–16) it was excavated and restored under the supervision of Sir Thomas Stamford Raffles, then Lieutenant-Governor of Indonesia and later founder of Singapore. When you stand on Borobudur you touch the physical evidence of Indonesia's turbulent history.

An hour's drive away is even more ancient history. In 1891 the bones of 'Java man' (*Pithecanthropus erectus*) were discovered near what is now the city of Solo. We do not know what happened to the Java men, although we have no reason for believing, especially in view of the later reputation of their island-home as a breeding ground for the human race, that they did not multiply. But the evidence of the bones has convinced anthropologists that one of the earliest races of mankind began in this Indonesian island. The direct ancestors of today's Indonesians came to the archipelago hundreds of centuries later, first as a negrito race now found in only a few parts of Africa, southern Asia and Australia, and then in waves of people belonging to the Malay-Polynesian language group. They arrived over an unknown period of centuries before the birth of Christ.

Java has been civilized longer than England, for these people practised complicated techniques of rice cultivation and developed from them forms of social organization. The climate of central Java, with its hot, even temperature, plentiful rainfall and volcanic soil, was ideal for the wet-field method of rice growing, known as *sawah* cultivation, and the society it demanded may explain why the Javanese developed a

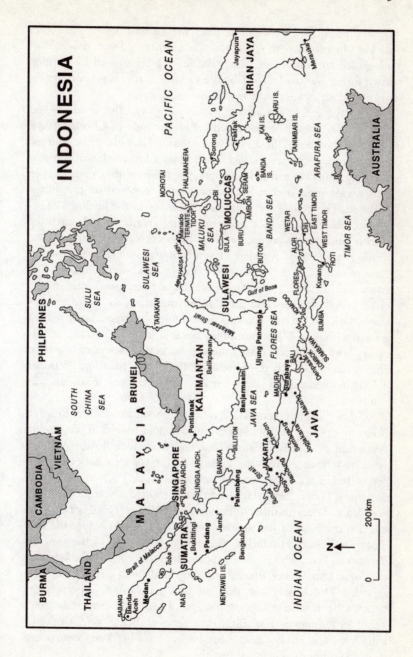

more sophisticated civilization than the inhabitants of the other islands. On islands with less favourable climate and soil, dry-field or *ladang* rice cultivation, in which the fields are prepared by burning down forest, was used. No elaborate social structure was necessary for this simple agriculture, which was also migratory.

The Javanese, at any rate, apparently began to live in towns and cities close to their rice fields well before the time of Christ. Little is known of the lives of these early Indonesians. They grew rice, worked metal—bronze, copper and gold—and had a knowledge of the stars and navigation. They lived in co-operative communities, perhaps even at that stage organized as bureaucratic states imposed on the village headmen. The people were animists, believing in the liveliness of in-animate objects as well as trees and living creatures, and practising ancestor and spirit worship. Terraced hillsides, topped by small stone pyramids and rough wooden or stone figures, which were used as places of worship, have been found in east Java and south Sumatra. The chants and ritual dances which invoked ancestral souls can still be traced in folk masques and plays. Most important, the social and re-ligious duties of the rice-growing communities were gradually refined to form a body of behaviour which became the basis of *adat*, or cus-tomary law. *Adat* has persisted through successive waves of imported religious and social beliefs—Hinduism, Buddhism, Islam and 350 years of Dutch overlordship—and remains today a force in Indonesian culture.

Without written records, it has been difficult for scholars to agree about the strength of this civilization; whether, indeed, it was itself a civilization or merely isolated tribal societies which flowered under civilizing influences from the outside. 'Whoever approaches the his-tory of Indonesia enters into an unknown world', wrote the Dutch historian J. C. van Leur. He nevertheless trenchantly argued, before his death at the age of thirty-four in the World War II battle of the Java Sea, that the basis of Indonesian civilization was laid before the first outside influence, Hinduism, came from India around the time of Christ. Van Leur, who based his approach on the work of the German sociologist Max Weber, fought a running battle with some of the most respected Dutch scholars. But modern scholarship, especially in America, has tended to support him, as, of course, has nationalist sen-timent in Indonesia. The distinction between being 'primitive' and being 'civilized' has become blurred as we have become more aware of criteria other than material wealth.

What is certain is that by the first century trade with other parts of Asia, however motivated and managed, was firmly established. A report in the court annals of the Chinese Han Emperor Wang Mang (1–23) tells of a mission sent to 'Huangtche' or Atjeh, now Aceh, in north Sumatra, to acquire a rhinoceros for the Imperial Zoological Garden. In 166 Indian and Indonesian 'embassies' were in China, at the same time that a representative of Marcus Aurelius arrived in the Celestial Kingdom. Numerous pieces of Han Dynasty ceramics excavated in south Sumatra, west Java and east Borneo suggest that a vigorous trade existed with China in the first century. Apart from rhinoceros horn, prized by the Chinese as an aid to potency, gold and precious stones found their way to China and silk cloth came back. The early trade with India, which was probably more active, involved spices, drugs, expensive woods and exotic birds. In Edward Gibbon's description, it was a trade 'splendid and trifling' and it linked India, China and Indonesia with the ancient world of Greece and Rome.

Religion and culture followed trade. The increasing influence of Brahmin priests in Indonesian courts during the first centuries brought with it the art of writing, which for the first time made the civilization 'vocal'. The oldest works of Hindu art so far discovered, in Celebes (now called Sulawesi) and Sumatra, are statues of Buddha, which date from the third century. The earliest inscriptions, in Sanscrit, are from the beginning of the fifth century in east Borneo. The ruler mentioned in the inscriptions presumably governed a kingdom in which Hindu culture was superimposed on an Indonesian framework of customs and beliefs, because sacrificial animal pillars, common in old Indonesian cults, are mentioned. Another inscription of the same period, at the foot of mountains south of today's Jakarta, is surrounded by two sets of footprints—those of the king, 'the powerful ruler, the illustrious Purnavarman, King of Taruma, whose footsteps are like those of Vishnu', and those of the king's elephant.

But until about 700 information about life comes mainly from Chinese court chronicles, which tell of the tribute offered by 'Kings of the Southern Islands', and from reports of Chinese Buddhist scholars who visited the Indonesian islands on their way to India, adding their influence to the Buddhist doctrines and practices which were already arriving from India. In 414 Fah Hsien, a Buddhist pilgrim, visited the island of 'Ye-p'o-t'i', probably a transliteration of Yavadvipa, or Java, and commented that only a few of its inhabitants were followers of Buddha. A sixth-century Chinese traveller, describing probably a coastal state in the vicinity of Kedah on the Malaysian peninsula, wrote, 'The king half-reclines on a golden bed in the form of a dragon. The nobles in his retinue are on their knees before him, their bodies erect and their arms crossed in such a way that their hands lie on their shoulders. At his court one sees many ... Brahmins who came from India to profit from his munificence and are much in his favour.' I-Tsing, a pilgrim, stayed for four years some time between 671 and 692 on his way home from India at 'Bhoga', a city on an island in the 'Southern Ocean', and found 'more than one thousand Buddhist priests studying and working'.

This island was probably Sumatra, because its early Hindu king-doms, first Malayu and, by the seventh century, Shrivajaya, were cen-tres of Buddhist learning and regular stopping places for pilgrims, as well as being important trading states. The Sumatran coastal state of Shrivajaya was perhaps the first of the great Indonesian commercial sea powers, handling the international trade of South-East Asia under the royal authority of rulers who demanded tribute from overseas depen-dencies and controlled the Strait of Malacca. In Java, on the other hand, Buddhist influence was slighter, and the major central Javanese state of Mataram, which was supreme between the eighth and tenth centuries, remained predominantly Hindu, although its kings were related to Shrivajaya's rulers. Shrivajaya's trade brought it wealth, but Mataram possessed greater manpower, and the two seem to have been both rivals and partners, crowning their partnership with the erection of Borobudur, for which they enlisted the help of artists from India.

At this stage in Indonesia's history, two types of state had emerged. One, typified by Shrivajaya, was coastal and commercial, based on international trade. Smaller, without the reserves of manpower avail-able in Java, these coastal principalities, found mainly in Sumatra, did not build monuments like Borobudur to their greatness. But they seem to have been wealthy and predatory. Van Leur describes the city of Shrivajaya, on a foundation of stilts in the Palembang River like many small towns in the region today, as 'turbulent and cosmopolitan'. In the tenth century, Shrivajaya shipped as presents to the Emperor of China ivory, frankincense, rose-water, dates, preserved peaches, white sugar, crystal rings, coral rhinoceros horn, perfumes and condiments. Glass bottles, naphtha and cotton cloth were trans-shipped; it was clearly a centre on the world trade-routes. One authority supposes that Tamil, Persian, Arabic and Greek would have been heard in its market-place and a twelfth-century visitor described 'eight hundred money changers' apparently busily engaged. Supported by this active commerce, a tight aristocracy seems to have ruled, with a display of warships and warriors. One twelfth-century report describes the funeral of a ruler who is followed in death on the pyre by his retinue. Mercenaries of the Shrivajaya kingdom served as far afield as Persia and Mesopotamia.

The second kind of state was situated inland, especially on the plains of Java, and separated by volcanoes from the sea; Mataram was based on the Solo River region. If the Sumatran coastal principalities recall the Phoenician city states, these inland Javanese states are reminiscent of the mountain fastnesses of early Peru and Mexico. Relying on an agrarian civilization, they were bureaucratic and conservative, already with a marked capacity to absorb and transform the Indian influences. One of east Java's inland rulers had the Indian epic the *Mahabharata* translated into Javanese in the eleventh century. It was later rewritten, using Javanese customs and settings, and introducing new characters such as Semar, originally a clown figure who however developed over time a reputation as a subtle and powerful guardian of the Javanese people and has become one of the major figures in the *wayang* (Indonesian theatre). The written authority used to crush the communists after the abortive 1965 coup is a subtle pun on the Semar character. It is known as *Supersemar*—an acronym for Surat Perintah Sebelas Maret, meaning 'A letter of instruction of 11 March'. The kings of Kadiri, in east Java, stopped using the Hindu title Maharajah and adopted the Javanese title Panji. Temple architecture began to show local forms of design. This is the period when Javanese culture comes into its own, spreading its influence to Bali, where the courts began to use the Javanese language in preference to their own, and to culturally separate Sunda (west Java) where east Javanese styles and titles were imitated.

Kadiri is remembered today for the famous prophecy attributed to its soothsayer King Jayabaya, who predicted in one popular version that 'a white buffalo will come to rule Java, and will remain for a long time; he will be supplanted by a yellow monkey, who will remain only for the lifetime of the maize plant; then, after a period of chaos, Java will come back to its own people'. The sociologist Selosoemardjan in *Social Changes in Jogjakarta* says the prophecies, in which the buffalo was believed to represent the Dutch and the monkey the Japanese, were 'an inexhaustible source of spiritual strength and faith' to the

Javanese during the Japanese occupation of 1942–45, and the sub-sequent military attempts by the Dutch to return. Sutan Sjahrir, nationalist leader and intellectual, mentioned the prophecies during the period before the Japanese occupation in his autobiographical *Out of Exile*; he was unhappy that they should have been so widely believed. Another of Jayabaya's predictions is that momentous events are destined in years whose digits are reversible. Nothing happened as far as is known in 1691 and 1881, but as 1961 approached a ripple of half-believed gossip spread in Indonesia about impending national catastrophes.

When modern Indonesians refer to the glories of their past, they are certain to mention Majapahit. Founded in 1293 with its capital on the Brantas River in east-central Java, it lasted almost a century and is now described in Indonesian schools as Indonesia's Golden Age, comparable with the Elizabethan Age of England and the Tang Dynasty of China. The most powerful personality of its history was not a king but a prime minister or *patih* named Gajah Mada, whose fame as a unifier of Indonesia has made him one of the symbols of the present Indonesian republic. He codified the laws and customs of the kingdom, and the administration he established was so solidly based that it remained essentially the same into the nineteenth century. The name Gajah Mada is said to mean 'an elephant; powerful, impassioned, but with wisdom unswayed by passion'. The university established by the Republic of Indonesia at Jogjakarta is named after him as is one of Jakarta's main streets, in homage to the last man until President Sukarno to unite 'Indonesia' under a single ruler.

Much of the information about Gajah Mada and Majapahit comes from a history by the court poet Prapanca. It is unreliable, being a paean of praise as much as a record of events, but the rise of Majapahit called for lofty phrases. In addition to conquering Bali and establishing a Javanese dynasty on the island, Majapahit's army enthroned a new king, Adityavarman, in Malayu (Sumatra), who actually ruled with relative independence and laid the foundations of the kingdom of Minangkabau. Prapanca includes among Majapahit's vassal states almost all the coastal districts of the archipelago—west, east and north Sumatra, south, west and north Borneo, Celebes, Moluccas, Sumbawa and Lombok. He reports that areas which neglected their tribute were 'visited' by Javanese fleets. Timor sent tribute, and after a fierce struggle the Sundanese kingdom of west Java was conquered. In addition,

Prapanca says that Majapahit maintained regular relations with China, Champa (Vietnam), Cambodia, Annam and Siam. He also describes a royal dinner at which the king sang—'lovable as the call of the peacock sitting in a tree, sweet as a mixture of honey and sugar, touching as the scraping noise of the reeds'—and acted in a masquerade, the king's uncle played in the *gamelan* (Indonesian orchestra), and the queen sang while wearing 'a funny wig'.

By the time Gajah Mada's last king died in 1389, twenty-five years after his prime minister, Majapahit was in decline. The cause may have been malaria and its related fevers, which upset many of these ancient kingdoms. Or it may have been the removal of a strong personal influence, needed to extract support from the hard-worked people and land of central Java for the grand strategies of the courts, with their machinery of officialdom and heavy establishment of priesthood, their armies and their expensive diplomatic habits, such as the gift of pearls (and slaves) to powerful neighbours. The coastal dependencies in north Java rebelled against the administrative hierarchy and began themselves paying tribute to China, taking up arms against Majapahit to support their independence. At this time, too, the first penetrations of a threefold invasion—Islam, Chinese settlers and European explorers—had taken place in the archipelago, and the stage was set for a new and startling development in Indonesia's history.

The first part of the East Indies in which Islam took hold was north Sumatra, where traders from Gujarat (the coastal west Indian state) stopped on their way to the Moluccas and China. Settlements of Arab traders were mentioned on the west coast of Sumatra as early as 674, but religion followed trade at a distance. In 1292 Marco Polo noted that the inhabitants of the town of Perlak on Sumatra's north tip had been converted to Islam, adding, on rather slender knowledge, that it was 'the only Islamic place in the archipelago'. Islam spread steadily; the first Muslim states were Aceh, in north Sumatra, and Malayu. By the time of Majapahit's final collapse at the beginning of the sixteenth century, many of its old satellites had declared themselves independent Muslim states, enriched by their position as trans-shipment points for the growing spice trade with India and China.

The Moluccas had begun their fabled story as 'the spice islands' at the beginning of the twelfth century. They had nothing to offer except their clove and nutmeg trees, which originally grew nowhere else. The trade was monopolized until the fifteenth century by the

Gujarati, who had been introduced to Islam by Persian merchants in the ninth century, but the Moluccas natives were not socially organized and appeared uninterested in the new religion. Another port affected by this spice trade was Malacca, on the Malayan peninsula. Its rulers accepted Islam in the fourteenth century and by the sixteenth century it was the principal port of the region. A European traveller to Malacca in the sixteenth century guessed that more ships harboured there—the large vessels ranging between 200 and 400 tonnes—than in any other port in the world.

A new Muslim kingdom—the last Javanese power—arose in the region of present-day Jogjakarta, calling itself Mataram after the great Hindu state. Also, by the end of the sixteenth century a naval power had risen in the archipelago—the principalities of Makassar and Gowa in south-west Celebes, which had been settled by Malay traders who sailed to Johore, the Moluccas and later to 'Australia'. Manning Clark in the first volume of his *A History of Australia* says that the establishment of a Muslim kingdom at Makassar brought Islam

> . . . to the frontiers of civilization, from which, if they had pushed further . . . they would have moved on into New Guinea and from there across to the north coasts of Australia. They had begun to do this just when the coming of the European ended the spread of Islam, for when Torres first sailed through the strait which still bears his name, in 1607, he met Moors in west New Guinea.

According to missionary reports from Arnhem Land, Matthew Flinders met some of a fleet from Makassar while charting the Arnhem Land coast in 1803. Their ancestors are said to have been visiting the coast for hundreds of years and to have introduced the Aborigines to steel, pottery and tobacco. The Indonesian fishermen who today intrude from time to time into Australia's northern waters still come from this region.

As with Hinduism and Buddhism centuries earlier, Islam was accepted gracefully. It was not the austere religion of the Middle East but a mystic, salvation-conscious variant called Sufism, brought to India from Persia. It seems to have fitted without doctrinal upheaval into the animist beliefs of Indonesia's *agama* and the mystic Tibetan Tantrism into which Java's Buddhism and Shivaism had merged. The syncretic result was tolerant of all the gods. It saw Buddha, Brahma, Vishnu and the Javanese messiah Erucakra as equal principals of order, manifested in kings in the world of men. It was tolerant too, of Islam, which had only one God, not to be reproduced in graven imagery; Islam responded amiably by permitting its sultans to be worshipped as saints after death. Islam at times showed its fire in the Indonesian chapter of its world saga; it was spurred by a holy bloody war with the foreign, Catholic Portuguese and a commercial struggle with the foreign, Protestant Dutch. But its success in adapting to local conditions is one reason why today it maintains at least a nominal hold over 90 per cent of the population.

First reports of Chinese settlements in the archipelago come from the end of the thirteenth century, referring perhaps to the descendants of shipwrecked sailors. In 1382 a fleet of the first Ming emperor found a Chinese pirate ruling Palembang (whom they arrested and took back to China). In the Aceh Museum in Banda is a gift from China, a huge bell cast in 1409. The scattered beginnings of Chinese immigration in Indonesia suggest that the immigrants, usually men, married local women but maintained their own customs and language. They did not play a major part in determining the course of Indonesian history, but they grew in private economic power until, with the tacit consent of the Dutch, they became the middlemen of the economy.

Their clash with Indonesian nationalism is still in process. After independence, many of them took Indonesian names. They have prospered during the long regime of Indonesia's second president, Suharto, who has mobilized their business brains and skills to support his country's economic development.

Marco Polo and a few early missionary-travellers aside, the first Europeans to visit Indonesia were the Portuguese, spearheaded by Vasco da Gama, who came to the east to find the spice islands and to crusade against the 'Moors'. In 1511 Alfonso d'Albuquerque conquered Malacca, which was then paying homage to China, beginning a tradition of terrible European blunders: he captured and looted all Muslim vessels he encountered; he demanded that the Sultan of Malacca let him build a Portuguese fort; when he built the fort, he destroyed Muslim graves for building materials; and he summarily executed the leading Javanese trader. This and subsequent Portuguese behaviour made St Francis Xavier say that their knowledge was restricted to the conjugation of the verb *rapio* (to steal), in which they showed 'amazing capacity for inventing new tenses and participles'.

Not surprisingly, they could not get local support for their ambitions in the spice islands, although until 1641 when Malacca fell in turn to the Dutch they had some successes, building forts on Ternate and Ambon in the Moluccas and obtaining a temporary monopoly of the clove trade and a share in the west Javanese state of Bantam's pepper trade. The Portuguese were surprised at the sophistication and size of Indonesian arms. When d'Albuquerque took Malacca after a long battle, he found 3000 artillery pieces, including 2000 bronze cannon. The Sultan of Aceh was sent skilled artillery troops and guns and ammunition by the Turks to fight the Portuguese.

In June 1596 Holland made its appearance on the scene when four Dutch ships sailed along Sumatra's west coast and anchored at Bantam, on the western tip of Java. The commander, Cornelius de Houtman, concluded a treaty of friendship after finding all of Bantam's trading community kindly disposed. A Dutch account of Bantam at that time gives a lively picture:

> There came such a multitude of Javanese and other nations as Turks, Chinese, Bengali, Arabs, Persians, Gujarati, and others that one could hardly move ... they ... came so abundantly that each nation took a spot on the ships where they displayed their goods the same as if they were on a market. Of which the Chinese brought of all sorts of silk woven and unwoven, spun and unspun, with beautiful earthenware, with other strange things more. The Javanese brought chickens, eggs, ducks, and many kinds of fruits. Arabs, Moors, Turks, and other nations of people each brought of everything one might imagine.

Within three years Dutch ships frequented the archipelago, trading with the Moluccas and finding acceptance everywhere except in Madura and in Aceh, where de Houtman was later killed. Dutch trade expanded quickly because the Indonesian sultans enjoyed the higher prices which Dutch-Portuguese competition brought, and also because Portuguese attempts to drive out the Dutch were thwarted by a British blockade of Lisbon. Indeed, the Indonesian attitude was so unsuspicious that a Balinese king wrote to the 'king of Holland' expressing the wish that 'Bali and Holland should become one' (a Balinese expression meaning they should have a close alliance), and presented a Dutch admiral with a nubile girl. The first Indonesian visit to Holland occurred at about this time, when the king of Aceh, after concluding a trade agreement with the Dutch, sent two ambassadors to the Netherlands.

But unlike the Buddhist-Hindu and Muslim penetrations of Indonesia, which were generally peaceful and left lasting effects, the impact of Europe was violent and had little cultural resonance. Education and language had an influence, because of their professional and commercial advantages, but the Christian religion did not insinuate itself into the customs and beliefs of the people as Hinduism, Buddhism and Islam had done. We are accustomed to speak of the Netherlands' 350 years in Indonesia as if it were an established period; in fact only the beginnings and the end are clear. Throughout the seventeenth century the Dutch East India Company with its superior arms and Buginese and Ambonese mercenaries (who had transferred their service from Java's kings) fought off attacks everywhere in the islands. The Dutch founding of Batavia at the town of Yacatra in 1619 brought a major confrontation between the Company and the Javanese and probably began the Indonesian hostility which ceased only at the end of Dutch rule. This act was the only fruition during his lifetime of the great schemes of Jan Pieterszoon Coen, who had become the Company's 'Governor-General of the Indies' the year before. (His other ideas included the monopolization of the spice trade, the conquest of Manila and Macao using Japanese mercenary soldiers offered by the emperor of Japan, the takeover of spice production by Dutch settlers and colonists from Madagascar, Burma and China, who would be kidnapped if necessary—he preferred Chinese as 'industrious and unwarlike'—and the complete annihilation of Asian and rival European shipping.)

As a first step he ordered the Company storehouse at Yacatra to be secretly fortified, because he thought the English, who were losing their competition with the Dutch for trading advantage in the region, were about to attack his fleet. The prince of Yacatra discovered the fortification, built a battery opposite (by the sixteenth century the Javanese were casting their own cannon and making their own muskets, buffets and powder, though reported not to be very good at their use), and asked the English for help. Coen attacked first, conquering the battery and burning down Yacatra's English trading-post. Then, with a fleet and a thousand troops, he burned down the town—losing only one man—and occupied its land for the Company, building a bigger fort and a small Dutch town complete with today's canals. He called it Batavia after the Germanic tribe the Batavi, who fought the Romans and settled in Europe's lowlands.

Years of warfare followed, with Bantam and Mataram united in their attempt to conquer Batavia. In addition to their muskets, the Javanese foot-soldiers were armed with *kris* (daggers with undulating blades) and shields, and the cavalry used long pikes, guiding their horses with knees and body so as to have both hands free for fighting. The soldiers wore armour of buffalo hide and coats of mail, and marched behind royal banners and pennants which they believed had a magical significance. During the first siege of Batavia, the tide of battle was temporarily turned by the favourite Javanese military tactic of amok-running. During the second siege the Javanese armies spent thirty days trying unsuccessfully to build a river dam to cut off Batavia's drinking water. They also sent the Dutch letters of challenge to battle in traditional form, containing huge exaggerations of the number, strength and imperviousness to wounds of the attackers, describing the terrible destruction to follow and declaiming the greatness of the kingdoms, their rulers and their historical conquests. Gongs, drums and shouting were used during advances as another tactic of intimidation. Finally, Sultan Agung of Mataram called his whole empire to the colours for the third siege, and 'tens of thousands' slowly gathered around Batavia. Unfortunately, this so terrified the sultan of Bantam that he made peace with the Dutch. Sultan Agung continued his preparations, but the troops had to be supplied by sea and the Dutch destroyed hundreds of rice-laden Javanese ships. When the army finally attacked, it was near starvation and was forced to retreat after five weeks of siege.

Some of the above information comes from the *Babad Tanah Djawi*, which was written by Sultan Agung's court poets and revised and enlarged several times during the seventeenth and eighteenth centuries. Its name means 'The Clearing of Java' and it has been called a mixed history and Javanese creation myth. In it, Mataram's defeat at Batavia was transformed into a tale in which the leader of the Mataram armies was a traitor to the sultan, and the Dutch in killing him served the sultan's will, then sending an embassy to the court of Mataram (which in fact they did, after the battle) to thank Sultan Agung for his spiritual leadership. The Dutch historian Vlekke comments: 'The interpretation made Batavia a vassal state of Mataram and it also made further violence unnecessary. The Dutch may have attributed the end of the fighting to their own prowess, but the Javanese attributed it to the fact that their superiority had been acknowledged.' The Babad also turned Coen into a hero of Javanese descent, named Mur Jangkung, whose mother was a princess of the old Hindu Mataram and whose father was a brother of 'Sikender', the Javanese name for Alexander the Great, who symbolized the 'western conqueror'. (The Minangkabau genealogy also incorporates Alexander, as 'Iskandar'.)

'Initially', writes Richard Robison, 'the Dutch were simply one group of traders among Chinese, Gujeratis, Portuguese, Arabs and others—who bought cheap in the Indies and sold dear in other markets'. In the eighteenth century, until its charter expired on 31 December 1899 and its affairs, in a state of deterioration, were taken over by the Netherlands government, the Company was forced to defend its trading privileges against constant attack. Although the Dutch created a close alliance with the west Javanese princes—who were now called regents and appointed by the Governor-General—important areas of Indonesia remained independent, including Bali, Lombok, Aceh and Borneo.

Even on Java the Dutch found the situation by no means easy to control. Unrest continued into the nineteenth century and a revolt was sparked in 1825, turning into a full-scale war when its leadership was taken by Prince Diponegoro, son of the third Sultan of Jogjakarta. Diponegoro had frequented religious schools and meditated on the Koran in sacred caves. As a religious mystic of royal blood he was an ideal Javanese leader and the people told stories of him as a 'Prince Liberator' with a magic sword, who would free them. From the hills of central and east Java Diponegoro conducted a guerilla war, which the Russian ambassador in Brussels described to his government: 'They avoid battles with the troops and have adopted a plan of undermining the strength of the Europeans with the help of the unhealthy climate and fatigue. Such a method of warfare may in the end give them superiority.' The Dutch recruited additional soldiers from Holland as well as troops from Madura, north Celebes and Surakarta (now Solo), but were unable to overcome the rebels, who routed several Dutch attacks. During this period The Hague seriously considered abandoning Java.

After five years of fighting the Dutch captured Diponegoro's closest adviser and the prince offered to negotiate. In March 1830 he went by appointment to one of the Dutch generals and was arrested and deported to Makassar where he died in exile twenty-five years later. There are no official records of the 'Java War' casualties but it has been estimated that 200 000 Javanese were killed as well as 8000 Dutch and 7000 of their Indonesian mercenaries. Diponegoro became not only a Javanese but a national hero and Jogjakarta gained a reputation as a stronghold of Javanese independence—which was upheld by its activities in the post-World War II fight with the Dutch, under the leadership of the present Sultan of Jogjakarta, a direct descendant of Diponegoro. Today one of Jakarta's most elegant streets lined with the homes of government officials and foreign diplomats is named Diponegoro, and the girls' dormitory of Gajah Mada University in Jogjakarta is named after the prince's wife.

In the middle of the nineteenth century piracy was still rampant and the Dutch fought a war in Celebes against a Buginese queen who had ordered her ships to fly the Dutch flag upside-down. Fighting continued to flare up in Sumatra and Java. From 1846 to 1849 a series of expeditions were made to Bali where the Balinese, still independent, had gathered an army of 30 000 with arms purchased in Singapore. The Dutch won several victories but were always forced to retreat, and in 1849 they agreed not to occupy Bali or interfere in its internal affairs in return for an acknowledgment by its rajahs of Dutch 'authority'. There was also a violent war in south-east Borneo, the 'Bandjarmasin War', in which the Dutch bested the sultan.

But the longest and most devastating of all the Dutch wars in Indonesia was the one with the Sumatran state of Aceh, which had remained independent under British protection (Singapore and Aceh had an active trade). In 1871 the Dutch negotiated a new treaty with the British in which England withdrew objections to a possible Dutch occupation of Aceh. In 1872 Acehenese envoys began negotiations with the Italian and United States consuls in Singapore, and the draft of an American-Aceh treaty of friendship was sent to Washington. The Dutch forestalled further developments by declaring war on Aceh in 1873. A Dutch army of 7000 retreated when its commander was killed, and a new expedition twice as large met with no more success. The war went on for thirty-five years, until 1908 when the last guerrilla leaders surrendered. Today's visitor to Banda in north Sumatra can see the results of the war in the old Dutch cemetery. In dated column after column—almost yearly—the names of the dead are carved on white marble at the entrance to the cemetery. You notice the sprinkling of Javanese names among the Dutch.

Between 1900 and 1910 south-west Celebes was occupied by Dutch troops as part of a policy of 'pacification of the outer islands', and more than 250 rulers throughout Indonesia were forced to sign over their rights to Batavia, including those of Bali, which the Dutch finally occupied in 1906. But by this time the first 'nationalist' movements, which were to lead to the Republic of Indonesia, had begun.

From the outside, especially from the colonizing vantage point of Europe, the East Indies were a tropical archipelago of warring tribes which could be subdued or seduced, if not easily, in the great games of trade and religion. To the self-conscious Indonesian of today, however, the responses to these waves of invasion are pointers to a modern nation. Every evidence of organized resistance to the invader is proof of today's national spirit. Evidence of absorption is proof of today's national tolerance. Indonesian leaders refer to the once prosperous empires of Shrivajaya and Majapahit as proof of the material standing and diplomatic sophistication of Indonesians before they were reduced to penury by the Dutch or to Mataram as evidence of a capacity for strategic, military power. It is not surprising, Sukarno told the United Nations General Assembly in 1960 when explaining the traditions behind his ideas for modern Indonesia, that 'concepts of great strength and virility have risen in our nation during the two thousand years of civilization and during the centuries of strong nationhood before imperialism engulfed us in a moment of weakness'. Nor is it surprising that President Suharto, while giving the highest priority to economic development, should often refer to Mataram and persistently argue that a nation that neglects its cultural traditions loses its identity and a nation without an identity is vulnerable, from both outside and inside.

It is hardly surprising either, now that the discipline created by the struggle for independence followed by the Cold War is subsiding, that some of the old ethnic, religious and regional tensions are beginning to surface in modern Indonesia. The territory of the nation we know as Indonesia is, after all—with the exception of east Timor, which is a remnant of Portuguese colonialism—a haphazard construction of Dutch traders and soldiers. Like so many nations created artificially by the European colonial powers, Indonesia had to set about imagining itself as a community after it became independent, in order to create itself as a modern nation.

CHAPTER TWO

Nation

THE FIRST STIRRINGS of Indonesian nationalism are usually dated from the time, about the turn of the century, when the Dutch finally 'pacified' the entire archipelago. It is as if the invader, having laboriously established the outline of his territorial possessions in the East Indies, provided the people for the first time with a definite area by which to assert their rights to national independence. In the world outside—especially as shown in Asia by nationalist developments in India and China and, in particular, Japan's military defeat of Russia in 1905—the time was ripening for the huge shifts of power against Europe-centred and then Atlantic-centred dominance that are still in process today. In the East Indies themselves, various factors provided the groundwork for the slow and by no means confident nationalist movement of the next half century. Islam, as the professed belief of some 90 per cent of the population, became, in effect, a popular gesture of unity against the Christian overlord. The Malay tongue became a national language, having been elevated from the bazaars by the colonial authorities who used it in administration as a means of keeping Indonesians from acquiring the status symbol of Dutch. Improvements in transport and the development of press and radio made it possible for the idea of nationalism to be given an audience, as Sukarno quickly discovered.

There was also the incalculable quality of the Dutch themselves. The spectacle of European colonialism is astonishing in retrospect; the arrogance of the 1494 Treaty of Tordesillas with Portugal and Spain, two sides of a small European peninsula, seriously dividing the world into two spheres of interest, is only a little more unreal to contemplate in today's world than the thought of France's vast possessions or the far flung empire of Britain. But no conquest is more difficult to appreciate than that of the Dutch in tropical Asia. The virtues that made the Netherlands the most ardently-worked plot of land in Europe—thrift, care, cleanliness and attention to detail—were lost in the sprawling plenitude of the East Indies.

Holland is about one-quarter the size of Java, or half the size of Tasmania, and the flatness of its skyline, bringing suburbia within reach of everyone's bicycle, was hardly a preparation for pioneering one of the most mountainous and erratic landscapes in the world. To travel today in Indonesia is to be impressed with the administrative difficulty of running the archipelago from the island of Java. The Dutch eventually did it with sea power, for which they had to thank the industrial revolution and, after the Napoleonic wars, the connivance of the British. But on the land of the islands themselves, they were conspicuously out of place. The tall blond invader strode among the small brown people like someone from another world.

Dutch colonization of the East Indies followed the pattern of Africa rather than Asia, with settlers rather than absentee landlords. Before World War II there were about 250 000 Dutch living in Indonesia and although a probable majority were Eurasian the figure is still high by comparison with the experience of other Asian colonial territories. The number of Dutch in Java, for example, was almost the equivalent of all the British in India. Some Dutchmen and their families came to treat the colony as their homeland, with the unfortunate effect of denying the same emotions to the indigenes. The Dutch in Indonesia did not, as did the Dutch in South Africa after World War II, develop the labyrinthine justification of *apartheid*, perhaps because the Indonesian independence movement nipped it in the bud. When the English writer Geoffrey Gorer visited the East Indies in 1935, he remarked that the Dutch were fortunate in not having developed a 'colour-bar': 'They treat Europeans and Asiatics alike on the basis of economical and social distinctions. That is to say they are willing to associate with, and even on occasion to marry, rich and genteel Javanese; they would no more think of associating with the common Asiatic than with the common European workman.' At the apex of the power pyramid, with the Chinese interposed as economic middlemen, the Hollander ruled indirectly, through the traditional forms of village government. His prejudices were evident but he was not a fanatic, either religious or political. He showed no anxiety to divert the Indonesians from their mysterious spiritual sources nor to convert them from their pre-capitalist agricultural habits, with some regional exceptions. When the great naturalist Alfred Russel Wallace visited the Dutch East Indies in the 1870s he described Java as the 'richest, best cultivated and best governed tropical island in the world'.

But the love that bound the Dutch securely to the islands through three-and-a-half centuries was that of money. It has been said that no colonial power developed its economy to rely on colonial possessions to the extent that the Dutch did in the case of the East Indies. At its pre-war trading peak the archipelago provided an income directly or indirectly to one in every seven Dutch person, when Holland's population was about nine million. Before World War II the Indies were estimated to have supplied 90 per cent of the world's production of quinine, 86 per cent of the world's pepper, 75 per cent of its kapok, 37 per cent of its rubber, 28 per cent of its coconut-palm products, 19 per cent of its tea and 17 per cent of its tin as well as sugar, coffee, oil and most of the world's cigar wrappers. Holland's investment was about US$1422 million in 1940, earning an annual $103 million in interest.

Psychologically, the Dutch dependence on the Indies was considerable. As Herbert Feith makes the point: 'With the Indies, Holland was the world's third or fourth colonial power; without them it would be a cold little country on the North Sea'. Yet for all their skill and perseverance, the Dutch impression on their rich and varied possessions was oddly barren and unexciting. The great Dutch contribution to the art of Europe did not travel well. There is nothing to compare with the romantic literature of imperialist England, and accounts of the Dutch hegemony, though allowing credit for its remarkable pursuit of commerce, all tend to stress the humourless propriety of the colonizers. Money-making aside, the Dutch in the Indies seem to have been noted mostly for the legacy of a cumbersome legal system— and their consumption of food and gin. Manning Clark writes:

> The Portuguese Catholics spoke of infinite merit: the Dutch Calvinists spoke of uncommonly large profit. There was something sensuous and elemental in their discussion of the uses to which they would put the spices from the Moluccas. They wanted pepper for food and for a physic, ginger because it made a man go easily to the stool . . . cloves because they strengthened the liver, the mouth and the heart, furthered digestion . . . preserved sight, and four drams being drunk with milk, procured lust.

Some modern historians see the Dutch, with their Puritan attitude to sex, as spiritual prisoners of the insights of Indonesian women.

The first Indonesian nationalist groups were organized around education, reflecting a desire for social rather than political equality. In 1902 Kartini, the daughter of a Javanese regent, founded a school for daughters of Indonesian officials. In 1908 an organization called Budi Utomo (High Endeavour) was formed; it sought to stimulate a sense of national dignity through education. It received early support from students at the Batavia Medical School; physicians had an unusual influence in the nationalist movement, probably because they were independent and could move among the people, and the number of medical doctors in responsible political positions shortly after independence was noticeable. Budi Utomo quickly gained members, but it was supported mainly by Javanese officials and aristocrats and looked to India for philosophical guidance and for teachers. It never became a mass movement.

A Eurasian founded the Indian Party in 1912 with the slogan 'The Indies for those who make their home there'. He was Eduard F. E. Douwes Dekker, a great-nephew of the Dekker who in 1861 wrote *Max Havelaar*, a novel which exposed Dutch oppression in the Indies and is sometimes described as the *Uncle Tom's Cabin* of nineteenth-century Java. Douwes Dekker's grandparents were Dutch, French, German and Javanese, and not surprisingly the party was multi-racial. It opposed direct Dutch rule, advocating independence and racial equality. Its leaders were expelled from the country.

The first truly mass movement was Sarekat Islam (Islamic Association), which had its origins in a trading society formed in 1909 to protect Indonesians against Chinese dealers. In 1912 it began to expand under the chairmanship of Tjokroaminoto, a Surabaya businessman. Lenin noted the development of Islam in Indonesian nationalism at that time, which suggested to him links with the 1908 reformist Muslim revolt in Turkey and the emergence of an Indonesian capitalist intelligentsia. Sarekat Islam was soon to become the most significant of the early nationalist movements and, although it proclaimed itself to be non-political for security reasons, it quickly attracted support well beyond its outward objectives. Also in 1912, the Mohammadijah, a modernist Islamic society devoted to education and social services, was founded.

In 1914 the Indies Social Democratic Association was created by Henrik Sneevliet, who had been a member of the Social Democratic

Labour Party—later the Communist Party—in the Netherlands. This small Marxist group, which became the Indonesian Communist Party (Partai Kommunist Indonesia—PKI) penetrated the Sarekat Islam and influenced it towards a more revolutionary programme. A showdown came at the 1921 Sarekat Islam congress between the PKI faction led by Semaun and Tan Malaka—two names which recur in modern Indonesian history—and the moderates under Tjokroaminoto. The moderates included Agus Salim, another figure of lasting significance, who took the floor with the argument that Mohammed had preached socialism twelve centuries before Marx. The PKI faction lost and re-signed *en masse*, setting up 'Red' Sarekat Islam branches in opposition.

The communists tried to establish revolutionary conditions along Marxist class lines and by the early 1920s had created unrest in the young trade union movement. Strikes were organized in urban busi-nesses and in sugar factories, leading to revolts on Java in 1926 and among the Minangkabau of Sumatra in 1927. The Dutch suppressed the uprisings with considerable bloodshed and arrested some 13 000 Indonesians, of whom 6000 were imprisoned, detained as political prisoners, or deported.

The failure of the communists, coupled with the tough response of the administration, momentarily turned the nationalist movement away from political activity. The Taman Siswa (Garden of Pupils) movement, established in 1921, aimed at a school system based on a blend of Indonesian and Western culture as Kartini's had been. Politics were forbidden, but the schools were responsible for the education of many who later joined the nationalists.

The Perhimpoenan Indonesia (Indonesian Union) was formed in 1922 by Indonesian students studying in Holland as a nationalist, leftist political group. Some of its members who had returned to Indonesia established the Partai Nasional Indonesia or Indonesian Nationalist Party (PNI) on 4 June 1927. The young Sukarno, who had not been to The Hague to study, was its chairman. The PNI became the most powerful nationalist organization in Indonesia and remains today as the core of one of the three main political groups in Indo-nesia. In 1928 came the 'Vow of Youth', a declaration of support by the second Congress of Permuda Indonesia (Young Indonesia) for the red and white flag, the Indonesian language (Bahasa Indonesia, which is basically Malay) and the anthem 'Indonesia Raya' ('Greater Indo-nesia'), as the symbols of the nation. The Dutch quickly recognized the threat in the PNI's growing strength and in 1930 Sukarno and three other PNI leaders went to jail for the first time. The PNI was outlawed and its membership split into factions. In 1932 two men who were to become famous Indonesian nationalists, Mohammed Hatta and Sutan Sjahrir, returned from university in Holland where Hatta had been president of the Indonesian Union. They joined Golongon Merdeka (Freedom Group)—the name was later changed to Pendidikan Nasional Indonesia (Indonesian National Education Club)—a small group devoted to building up an activist leadership. On his release, Sukarno joined Partai Indonesia (Partindo) which aimed at more of a mass following. In 1933 Sukarno was again arrested and exiled to Flores in the Lesser Sundas; the following year Hatta and Sjahrir were sent to Boven Digul concentration camp in New Guinea. None of the three leaders was freed until the Japanese invaded in 1942.

Sjahrir's book *Out of Exile* remains one of the best sources of this period not only because it is brilliantly readable but because, through the author's isolation, we have an insight into the feeling of some of the men who spent those long years in prison. Sjahrir was only twenty-five when he was arrested on the point of returning to his Dutch wife in Holland, and later sent to a camp for supposed violent revolutionaries. His subsequent career marked him as a moderate with a thoughtful and sensitive mind, and it is not surprising to find him wondering in a letter to his wife what exactly his offence is supposed to have been and where his sympathies lie. He was accused of 'spreading hate and endangering public tranquillity and order' but no precise charges were laid, a typically official imprecision which has not improved with the removal of the colonialists from Asia.

He is appalled at the spiritual disintegration of many of the prisoners at Boven Digul, some younger than himself. He wrote (in 1936 after he and Hatta had been moved to Banda Neira in the Moluccas where his mail was not censored) of an attempted suicide at Boven Digul. The man, a wealthy Christian from Menado in Celebes, had been at the camp for nine years. He was an early socialist and had been a member of Douwes Dekker's Indian Party. Sjahrir describes him as 'a fine and cultivated man with a real humanity in his character . . . I can still see him in my mind's eye, wearing his torn pajamas and digging in the intense heat of his garden'.

In one of the few flashes of bitterness in his book, Sjahrir turns on the Dutch officials at the camp, where he claims a majority of the inmates became mentally ill. It did not have the same degree of brutality as the concentration camps being established in Germany at the same time, but its physical isolation in inland New Guinea and the social distance between the prisoners and their guards provided a different kind of torture. The Dutch had not 'the least idea of the mental suffering they are inflicting. The exiles are simply "trash, scum and criminal"; how could they possibly experience mental suffering? Such suffering is only for Europeans with their more highly developed souls and sensitivities!' At Digul also were the student and youth prisoners 'so completely idealistic, and the only thing with which they could be charged was making propaganda for their ideals'. Of the communists, who were sent to the camp after the uprisings in 1926–27, Sjahrir is surprised at their ordinariness, which he puts down to eight years of intellectual stagnation. 'It is a strange sort of Communism indeed, a mystical Hinduistic-Javanese, Islamic-Minangkabau or Islamic-Bantam sort of Communism, with definite animistic tendencies. There are not many European Communists who would recognize anything of their Communism in this Indonesian variety!' Sjahrir himself was not unchanged by Boven Digul. 'I have acquired a certain hardness . . . the human being of Tolstoi and even of Gandhi, whom I had long held before my eyes, has left me. In reality, man is stupid, vulgar, cruel and brutal.'

With the arrest of its leadership the Indonesian nationalist movement developed a milder exterior and there was more of an effort to co-operate with the Dutch in the Volksraad or People's Council, a local assembly which had been set up in 1917 as an advisory influence on Dutch authority. But as the British diplomat-journalist Bruce Lockhart reported on a visit in 1936, there was an air of repressed nationalism throughout the Indies which contrasted with the amiable atmosphere in Malaya. He notes the heavy jollity of Dutch society in Batavia and the blandness of officialdom. He quotes the Dutch Governor-General, Jonkheer de Jonge, as telling him, 'I always preface my remarks to the nationalists with one sentence: "We Dutch have been here for three hundred years; we shall remain here for another three hundred. After that we can talk."' (Sjahrir quotes de Jonge as saying in a press interview, 'We have ruled here for three hundred years with the whip and the club, and we shall still be doing it in another three hundred years'.) Lockhart records that on a visit to Makassar in Celebes to see the grave of Diponegoro, neither the

Dutch governor nor his Assistant Resident knew that the great Indonesian rebel leader was buried there, although the local Indonesians knew the exact spot with pride.

The reaction of the Dutch, accompanied by the international growth of fascism, caused the most articulate nationalist leaders, including Amir Sjarifuddin and Mohammed Yamin, to establish in 1937 a new party, Gerindo (Gerakan Rakyat Indonesia—Indonesian People's Movement). Gerindo was left-wing but, like the Indian nationalist movement, regarded its struggle as dependent on the outcome of the impending showdown with Germany and Japan. Its members tried to use the People's Council to gain self-government; in 1936 the council had called for a ten-year plan of orderly political development. But despite the efforts of a moderate, Mohammed Thamrin, who was mainly responsible for uniting eight of the major nationalist organizations including Gerindo in an effort to reach solidarity with the Dutch, provided guarantees of self-determination were given, no sign of understanding came from The Hague. Right up to World War II, and even after the Germans invaded Holland, the Indonesian nationalists were given no encouragement to believe that their co-operation was needed or their ultimate aims recognized. Nor was an effort made to increase their responsibility in governing the Indies as they were. In 1940 only 221 of the 3039 top civil service positions in the administration were held by Indonesians.

The Japanese occupation of the Netherlands East Indies in 1942, following the quick Dutch collapse, was carried out at first to the accompaniment of local applause. The red and white flag was flown, Bahasa was spoken, 'Indonesia Raya' was sung; gestures of Asian solidarity were made. Moreover, because all the Dutch administrators were interned, educated Indonesians were rapidly promoted. But it became clear after a few months that the Japanese were not going to be any easier to get on with than the Dutch. Politically they were more flexible but, partly because of the stress of war and also, many Indonesians felt, because of their philosophy, they were extremely cruel. Today the Japanese are welcome visitors to Indonesia, and the yen is much sought as investment currency, but Indonesians still speak privately of the Japanese occupation with horror or contempt.

The nationalist leaders split their forces. Sukarno and Hatta, who were the best known, worked above ground, collaborating with the Japanese. Sjahrir led one underground group and Sukarni, who had worked with the illegal PKI under Tan Malaka in the twenties, led another. Among the members of Sukarni's group were Amir Sjari-fuddin, who later declared his communist sympathies, and Chairul Saleh, whose chequered career brought him finally to power as a militant personality of the Sukarno regime. There was a third body of younger men, often students, including Ruslan Abdulgani and Subandrio, both later prominent in Indonesian politics, who kept in touch with the underground groups. Sjahrir lived at his sister's house in Tjipanas, among the mountains outside Batavia, supposedly because of ill-health; in fact the high altitude was good for radio reception and it was from his secret receiver that the underground was kept informed of the real state of the war. Sukarno, as chairman of various Japanese-sponsored organizations to control Indonesian manpower and enlist mass support for the war effort, and Hatta, in charge of an advisory bureau on relations with the Indonesian nationalists, lived in Jakarta.

The period of the Japanese occupation is important in the development of the nationalist movement, yet it is also obscure and controversial. There is no doubt, however, that the movement gained strength. The Japanese, unlike the Dutch, sponsored mass organizations based on Islam and anti-Western sentiment. Sukarno and Hatta were allowed to travel, addressing gatherings of Indonesians, and Sukarno in particular used the occasions to insinuate nationalist propaganda into respectful addresses celebrating Hirohito's birthday or a Japanese victory. In 1943 they were flown to Tokyo to thank the Emperor for the creation of a consultative body, with Sukarno as chairman, which made concessions to the nationalists. Professor George McTurnan Kahin, whose book *Nationalism and Revolution in Indonesia* is the classic work of scholarship on this period, suggests that the Japanese authorities on Java suspected at this time that Hatta was not playing the game. They proposed that he should be detained in Japan and were greatly surprised when instead he was treated with Sukarno as an honoured guest and returned safely to Indonesia.

As the Imperial Army began to look to recruiting at the end of 1943, the Japanese in Indonesia formed the Volunteer Army of Defenders of the Fatherland, or Home Defence Corps (Soekarela Tentara Pembela Tanah Air—Peta). Given their first opportunity to bear arms for their cause, Indonesians joined in large numbers. Sukarno and Hatta were allowed to address the recruits in the interests of the patriotic spirit and Peta soon became a hotbed of nationalism. In 1944 an armed revolt broke out at Blitar (Sukarno's birthplace) in east Java, and although it was bloodily suppressed by the Japanese a succession of smaller revolts followed. Anti-Japanese activity, especially by students, became more open.

In late 1944 and early 1945, as their military defeats continued, Japanese resistance to nationalist pressures weakened. The Indonesian leaders felt the change and from his Tjipanas hideout Sjahrir pressed the others for an uprising, an unconditional declaration of independence. Sukarno, however, believed that the Japanese might recover, and hesitated. But it was at this point (1 June 1945) that Sukarno made a speech announcing the *Pancasila*, the Five Principles. These principles (faith in one god, humanity, nationalism, representative government and social justice) were the foundation on which Sukarno said an independent Indonesian nation was to be based. This remarkable speech angered the Japanese authorities. But it quickly became the blueprint of the nationalist movement and today still provides the ideological framework for the Indonesian state. It shows Sukarno at his best, as a formulator and expounder of ideas that are only vaguely in the minds of others. Professor Kahin comments, 'Probably in no other exposition of principle can one find a better example of the synthesis of Western democrat, Modernist Islamic, Marxist and indigenous-village democratic and communistic ideas which form the several bases of the social thought of so large a part of the post-war Indonesian political elite'.

In introducing the *Pancasila* Sukarno did not define precisely the boundaries of the new Indonesia, and he brought into prominence problems of nationalism which his leadership throughout the years of independence failed to solve. He said:

We will establish an Indonesian national state . . . This is what we must all aim at: the setting up of one National State upon the unity of one Indonesian land from the tip of Sumatra right to Irian!

. . . the national state is only Indonesia in its entirety, which existed in the time of Shrivajaya and Majapahit, and which now, too, we must set up together . . . let us take as the first basis of our state: Indonesian Nationalism. Indonesian Nationalism in the fullest sense.

. . . But—undoubtedly there is a danger involved in this principle of nationalism. The danger is that men will possibly sharpen nationalism until it becomes chauvinism, and think of 'Indonesia uber Alles'. This is the danger. We love one country, we feel ourselves one nation, we have one language. But our country, Indonesia, is only just a small part of the world.

. . . do not let us say that the Indonesian nation is the most perfect and the noblest whilst we belittle other people.

. . . We must proceed toward the unity of the world, the brotherhood of the world. We have not only to establish the state of Indonesia Merdeka, but we also have to proceed toward the familyhood of nations.

The *Pancasila* speech was made to a group of Indonesian leaders gathered by the Japanese to form a constitution for an independent Indonesia. Called the Body for Investigation of Indonesian Independence (Badan Penjelidik Kemerdekaan Indonesia—BPKI), the group was at this time discussing the territorial boundaries to be claimed from the Japanese, who were still in control not only in the East Indies but throughout South-East Asia. After lengthy debate the sixty-six Indonesian members of the BPKI voted by secret ballot on the correct territorial definition of their proposed nation. There were three plans and the voting was as follows: 1. Former territories of the Netherlands East Indies and the territories of North Borneo, Brunei, Sarawak, Portuguese Timor, Malaya, New Guinea, and surrounding islands (39 votes); 2. Former territory of the Netherlands East Indies (19 votes); 3. Former territory of the Netherlands East Indies combined with Malaya and omitting New Guinea (6 votes); two votes were informal.

The debate as recorded by Mohammed Yamin, a close colleague of Sukarno's, in a book published in 1959 shows Sukarno as leader of the Greater Indonesia faction, while Hatta supported the second plan and was prepared even to drop New Guinea. Sukarno championed the cause of Pan Indonesia even to the extent of technically including the Philippines; he recognized, however, that as an already independent country it should have its sovereignty respected. Yamin felt that Indonesia's boundaries should be based on the German concept of culture and soil (*Kultur und Boden*) and defined the area by references to the old empires of Shrivajaya and Majapahit. Sukarno also showed special interest in Malaya, producing to one of the meetings some Malays who had come to offer allegiance. He argued that Indonesia could not be secure unless both sides of the Strait of Malacca were in her hands. In spite of the majority feeling of the meeting the Japanese seem to have influenced the nationalists to accept the second plan, but the discussions are important for the attitudes they reveal and for the glimpse of a historical point in time when 'nationalists' had to think precisely of the 'nation' they intended to liberate.

By August 1945 Tokyo was prepared to promise independence and Sukarno and Hatta went to Japanese regional command headquarters in Dalat (in southern Vietnam) to receive the news. When they returned they found the underground movement determined not to wait but to rise against the Japanese. Sjahrir, with his radio tuned to outside reports of an armistice, urged a revolutionary declaration of independence, but Sukarno and Hatta still hoped for a peaceful transfer of power. In the early morning of 16 August a group of impatient students kidnapped Sukarno, his wife and children, and Hatta, and took them to a stronghold outside Jakarta. The two leaders learned that the Japanese had surrendered the day before and as mere agents of the Allies could not grant independence. After an all-night discussion on the text of a declaration a small group gathered at 10 a.m. on 17 August at Sukarno's house, 56 Pengangsaan Timur in Jakarta. The red and white flag was hoisted and the Republic of Indonesia was proclaimed.

Several versions of the 'kidnapping' episode exist. One creates the impression that Sukarno was more or less forced at pistol point to declare Indonesia's independence. The other, which was later outlined by D. N. Aidit, the PKI leader, in an interview with Arnold C. Brackman, American journalist and author of *Indonesian Communism*, is that a form of 'consultation' took place; Aidit stressed the caution of Hatta rather than Sukarno. But common to all versions is the conflict between the 'underground' and the 'collaborators'; traces of this conflict remained long after the issues they reflected had been resolved.

After Sjahrir had sounded out the feeling of the people and had become convinced of the genuine popular loyalty towards the Sukarno-Hatta leadership, the anti-Japanese underground groups swung their support behind the republic. Sjahrir was its first prime minister, Sjarifuddin its second. The republic had a constitution, a national committee of 135 men, which later became a legislative assembly, and a cabinet responsible to the president who was, of course, Sukarno. Hatta was vice-president. For six weeks the Indonesian Republic, with a government of sixteen ministers formed on 31 August, sparred with the Japanese authorities. Intermittent fighting took place as rearguard nationalist army units tried to arm themselves from the Japanese, but when the first British troops landed at Jakarta on 20 September the situation was calm, with the republic's administration in effective control of most parts of the country.

The task of the British (and Australian) troops, who began arriving throughout the territories from October onwards, was barely practicable. They had to disarm the Japanese and return them to Japan. At the same time, they had to deal with the Indonesian nationalists until the Dutch, still recovering from German occupation, could return to assert their 'lawful' sovereignty over their old territories.

It is sometimes said by Indonesians now that the fighting which followed would have been reduced if the British had not used the Japanese army to recapture towns, such as Bandung, held by the Indonesians. But the real confrontation, which was with the Dutch, would not have been materially altered. Heavy fighting broke out in Java, especially at Surabaya, which the British, with Indian troops, took after ten days of bitter resistance by armed Indonesian youth. There was also resistance in Bali and south Celebes, where the Dutch brought in Captain 'Turk' Westerling to restore order. The Western military alliance against Indonesia, the brutality of Westerling and the heroism of the Indonesian civilians and guerrillas who fought for the infant republic in those days has become part of the folklore of Indonesian nationalism. This is the period of high endeavour, when the capital was transferred from the dubious safety of Jakarta to Jogjakarta, the cultural centre of Java, where the patriotic Sultan refused to cooperate with the Dutch; when Nasution, later to become the nation's first military leader, learned his lessons in guerrilla warfare; when Sukarno was a knight in shining armour, rather than a skilful politician; and when the people of Indonesia proved their worth.

Today, nostalgia lingers for the 'Jogja Days', when the nation lived perilously and the national motto, 'Unity in Diversity' was not just a slogan, but a reality. Still today, an Indonesian, who happened, say, to have been a member of the contingent of armed youth which marched from Jogjakarta to relieve Surabaya, can hold the floor at a party, by common consent. As he tells his story, it becomes evident that the episode is national property. His audience prompts him at well-known incidents and adds small, secondhand stories of its own. Some members of the student army TRIP (Tentara Republik Indonesia Pelajar) recruited from east Java were as young as fourteen. They fought not only the Dutch but also the British, and probably killed Brigadier General Mallaby, leader of the British forces who had just arrived in Indonesia and whose death sparked the battle for Surabaya.

For four years, until the Republic of the United States of Indonesia was recognized by the United Nations in 1949, a state of intermittent war and political bargaining continued. The nation already existed as far as its parent nationalists were concerned, and for some friendly midwives like Australia, the United States and India, but at times it seemed unlikely to survive. In the negotiations with the Dutch, Sjahrir led a cautiously pro-Western government, opposed to the more violent leftists and nationalists. An abortive attempt by the national-communist Tan Malaka to stage a *coup d'état*—the so-called 'July 3rd affair'—took place in 1946.

In November 1946 the government negotiated the Linggadjati Agreement which Sukarno and Hatta approved a little ahead of Sjahrir, who was prepared to press for more concessions. The agreement achieved for the republic *de facto* recognition in Java and Sumatra and proposed by 1949 a federal Indonesia within a form of union with the Netherlands. But both sides began to undermine the agreement, Indonesia by seeking diplomatic recognition for itself, the Dutch by technical quibbles. The first of the two Dutch 'police actions' followed in July 1947, representing the fact that the Dutch then had 150 000 soldiers in Indonesia. Sjahrir's government fell and the Renville Agreement, signed on an American warship in Jakarta harbour in January 1948, recognized the advanced military position of the Dutch in Java and Sumatra.

It was a hard time for the nationalists. Hatta had taken over the prime ministership from Sjarifuddin, and the communists, reacting against Hatta's moderate leadership and playing on disorder and unemployment, staged a revolt in September 1948 at Madiun in east Java. Sukarno appealed by radio:

> I call on you ... to choose between Musso [the communist leader] and his Communist Party, who will obstruct the attainment of an independent Indonesia, and Sukarno-Hatta, who, with the Almighty's help, will lead our Republic of Indonesia to become an independent Indonesia which is not subject to any country, whatsoever.

The effect of this stand may have been important in bringing Western opinion into more open sympathy with Indonesian nationalism. Also, the Dutch forced the issue by launching the second 'police action' in December 1948, when the Madiun revolt, a stab in the back to the nationalists, had barely been suppressed. The republican capital of Jogjakarta fell and Sukarno, Hatta and the other top leaders were captured and exiled. The Dutch expected the republic to collapse but it resisted vigorously with an effective scorched-earth policy. As world opinion swung strongly against the Netherlands and it became clear that the war against the republic could not be won without a sustained campaign, Dutch policy changed.

The Netherlands decided to sacrifice political sovereignty in the hope of protecting Dutch investments in Indonesia, and this is the course negotiations took. The Round Table Conference at The Hague ended on 2 November 1949, with an agreement transferring sovereignty to Indonesia. Moscow called the 'Sukarno-Hatta clique' traitors. Sukarno returned to power in triumph.

The nation was incomplete, however, both in letter and spirit. West Irian was missing. Moreover, the Republic of the United States of Indonesia (RUSI), as the sovereign state was called, was a federation of the former republic and fifteen autonomous states created by the Dutch, mostly in the outer islands, between 1945 and 1949. These states would have numerical control of the proposed house of representatives and senate. In addition, special guarantees to Dutch investors were provided and RUSI undertook to consult with the Netherlands on aspects of financial policy affecting Dutch interests. The republic balanced these losses by gaining effective control of the armed forces. The compromise did not succeed. Within seven months the Indonesian government, under nationalist pressure and suspicious of Dutch intentions, had violated the Round Table Agreement by dissolving the constitution. The new 1950 constitution, establishing a unitary state, was proclaimed to the ominous accompaniment of armed revolt in Makassar and Ambon.

By now the outside world had formally recognized the victory of Indonesian nationalism but the nationalists were themselves divided on the extent to which a victory had been won. The new constitution gave greater power to the centre, but less to its executive. The cabinet was no longer responsible to the president as in 1946, but to a parliament. Parties proliferated (to as many as forty-three) and political deals for cabinet seats increased the rate of government turnover. There were seventeen cabinets for the period 1945–58, an average of a change every ten months. After the Japanese occupation and the guerrilla war against the Dutch, the economy was in urgent need of repair. Instead, the game of politics occupied everyone's attention. This is the period of Mochtar Lubis' depressing novel *Twilight in Djakarta* and of one of the major works of scholarship on Indonesia, Herbert Feith's

The Decline of Constitutional Democracy in Indonesia, in which the gradual rise of the 'solidarity-makers' at the expense of the 'administrators' is traced.

The chief solidarity-maker was President Sukarno, who was determined not to be cut off from power by parliament and who was sustained in that ambition by the Javanese masses, for whom he had become a father figure or, to use their mythology, a messianic 'just prince'. The president's tendency to interfere when cabinets decided on a policy he disliked helped to speed the deterioration of constitutional democracy, especially in parliamentary control of the army. The government of Prime Minister Wilopo (April 1952–August 1951) collapsed over an issue on which the president opposed it—the eviction of squatters from the concession of a foreign tobacco company in east Sumatra, so that the acreage under production could be increased.

Frequently postponed elections helped to aggravate instability by prolonging what was in effect a continuous election campaign, and when elections were held in 1955 they were not decisive. No party gained more than 25 per cent of the seats; short-lived coalition governments continued. The elections did show, however, a dramatic decline in the fortunes of Sjahrir's Socialist Party (PSI), which captured only 5 seats (compared with 14 in the provisional parliament), while the Communists (PKI) jumped from 17 to 39 and the Nahdatul Ulama (Muslim Teachers' Party—NU), a traditional Muslim group strong in Java and little influenced by modern ideas, leapt from 8 to 45. The Nationalists (PNI), regarded as Sukarno's party, topped the poll, gaining 57 seats. Masjumi, whose modern Islamic ideas on economics were close to the rational, pro-Western socialism of the PSI, also won 57 seats with less of the popular vote, but was surprised by the rise of the NU, a breakaway group. Partai Kristen Indonesia (Parkindo), the Protestant party, received 8 seats, the Partai Katolik, the Catholic party, won 6, and there were many smaller groups, like the League of Upholders of Indonesian Independence (IPKI) which had a following among army officers (4), and Partai Murba, the national-communist party (2). With a total of 257 seats, the scope for parliamentary manoeuvring was again limited more by the power situation outside parliament than by the strength of the parties within.

By 21 February 1957, when President Sukarno proclaimed 'guided democracy' to bring 'liberal, Western-style democracy' to a close, the Indonesian leadership was in disarray and the new nation was in danger. Hatta had resigned from the vice-presidency on 1 December 1956, breaking the Sukarno-Hatta duumvirate which many non-Javanese (especially Sumatrans) saw as a balance of the Sumatra-born, Muslim, West-leaning Hatta and Java-born, polytheistic, Soviet-leaning Sukarno. Regionalists, served in the field by several army commanders outside Java and with the moral support of the Masjumi and PSI, were critical of the merry-go-round of Jakarta politics, and the burden of inefficient and corrupt administration on the rich exporting areas of Sumatra and Sulawesi.

The regionalism which had been preserved by the Dutch was intensified at this stage by Java's declining share in the export trade. The foreign earnings of the other islands, which had the mineral deposits and the staple export crops, were used to import rice and consumer goods for Java's increasing population. As the effects of the Korean War boom wore off and Jakarta's discordant politics wore on, regional feeling grew stronger. Army commanders organized smuggling of copra and rubber on a large scale and, in a series of bloodless coups between December 1956 and March 1957, they took over from several Jakarta-appointed civilian governors in Sumatra and Sulawesi.

After protracted negotiations failed, the regionalist group declared itself (on 15 February 1958) as the Revolutionary Government of the Republic of Indonesia (Pemerintah Revolusioner Republik Indonesia —PRRI) in Padang, central Sumatra. The north Sulawesi arm of the revolution called itself Permesta (Overall Struggle). It was a revolution of economists and colonels—a significant comment on the weaknesses of the Jakarta regime. Its prime minister was Sjafruddin Prawiranegara, a Sundanese member of the Masjumi who, while minister for economics, had taken over as prime minister of the republic in 1948 when the Dutch in their second 'police action' captured the leadership at Jogjakarta. His speciality was taxation and he had been governor of the Bank of Indonesia, urging harder work and government economies. With him in revolt were Dr Sumitro Djojohadikusomo (PSI), a brilliant, frustrated economist who had served in several cabinets as trade and finance minister, and two former prime ministers, Mohammed Natsir and Burhanuddin Harahap, both Masjumi. Among the dissident colonels were some of the most promising in the Indonesian army.

Although it has been described as an unnaturally civil war, it was in its early stages a threat to the unity of the nation, especially as the rebels received supplies from outside, air-dropped and smuggled from Singapore and Manila. It ended with the return of the defeated rebels to 'the fold of the republic' on mild amnesty terms. But in the three years of the rebellion the shape of domestic politics had been radically altered. In 1960 the Masjumi and the PSI were banned and some of the old nationalists were discredited. (Sjahrir and others were placed under arrest in 1962.) The army, led by General Nasution who had proved his loyalty to the Sukarno regime by taking up the fight against the rebels, many of them his personal friends, had gained administrative authority throughout the country because of the war emergency regulations. The communists had strengthened their position and were helped by the rebellion to erase the memory of Madiun.

Most important, Sukarno had transformed the machinery of government and was now able to exercise almost unchecked legal power. In 1959 he abolished the 1950 constitution and ordered a return to the republican constitution of 1945. It was a return not only to a presidential cabinet secure from parliamentary control, but to the '1945 spirit', sometimes called the 'rails of the revolution', before the nationalist movement was forced to 'compromise'. In March 1960 the elected parliament was dissolved by presidential decree, to be replaced shortly afterwards by a parliament of 281 members appointed by the president as follows: 130 representatives of 10 political parties (the others being dissolved) and 151 representatives of 'functional groups' —the armed forces, peasants, labour, women's organizations and so on. It had no authority over the president and enacted laws subject to his agreement. The task of electing the president and vice-president (the latter post unfilled since Hatta's resignation) was taken over by the Provisional People's Consultative Congress (Madjelis Permusjawaratan Rakyat Sementara—MPRS) which was required to meet once in five years to determine the broad outlines of policy. Called the highest authority in the state, as an embodiment of all the people, it was composed of the entire parliament plus 94 regional delegates and 241 representatives of functional groups, a total of 616 members.

Much of the former authority of the cabinet passed to the Supreme Advisory Council, a body of 45 members including the president, who appointed the others. Its proposals did not bind the government but it became the chief policy-initiating body, submitting proposals to be discussed by the parliament and carried out by the cabinet. The cabinet or Council of Ministers (called *kabinet kerdja*, or work cabinet, to signify its non-party nature) comprised the president as prime

minister, a first minister, two vice-first ministers, and eight deputy first
ministers in charge of sectors, as well as numerous ministers in charge
of departments. After the death of First Minister Dr Djuanda in November 1963, three vice-first ministers were appointed—Dr Leimena,
Dr Subandrio and Chairul Saleh.

A mass organization called the National Front was installed in
September 1960. Intended to 'mobilize the revolutionary forces of the
people' it had a 70-member central executive board, presided over by
the president. It became a useful adjunct to government in organizing
'demonstrations' such as sacking embassies.

The changes were intended to give the president real power. As he
said: 'What is the use of being called President, Supreme Commander
of the Armed Forces, Prime Minister, Chairman of the Supreme
Advisory Council and even the Great Leader of the Indonesian Revolution, if my commands are ignored?' To mesh this apparently un-
wieldy machinery with the concept of guided democracy, Sukarno
abolished the Western parliamentary form of voting (called 'fifty per
cent plus one democracy') and introduced the traditional Indonesian
techniques of *gotong royong* (common, voluntary effort by the community, whether for its own benefit or that of some member), *musjawarah*
(deliberation among elders) and *mufakat* (decision by unanimity, a
form of veto).

Under its new-style leadership, the Indonesian nation turned toward the completion of its territorial boundaries. The issue of West
Irian had never been allowed to rest. In 1957 the Dutch estates had
been confiscated and in 1960 diplomatic relations were severed. With
the negotiation in 1960 of an arms agreement with the Soviet Union
costing about US$1000 million, Indonesia began a diplomatic and
military 'confrontation' of the Dutch position in its sole remaining territory. The military task was under the command of today's president,
then Brigadier General Suharto. An agreement was finally reached on
15 August 1962 under the auspices of the United Nations, by which
administration of the territory passed to Indonesia on 1 May 1963.
Now the nation was complete from 'Sabang to Merauke' for the first
time, although the requirement that the Papuans in West Irian be
given the opportunity by 1969 to decide if they wanted to remain
with Indonesia or become independent was criticized by some ex-
tremist elements. Sukarno stood by the agreement, however, and
called his 17 August (Independence Day) speech in 1962 'A Year of
Triumph'. The civil war was over; West Irian had been 'regained'.

Now the third task of the revolution—*sandang pangan*, or food and clothing for the people—could be fulfilled.

But, before the year was out, Indonesia embarked on another test of her national strength, the 'confrontation' (*konfrontasi*) of the new nation of Malaysia on her northern boundaries, and fresh sacrifices were being asked of the Indonesian people.

It took nearly three years for confrontation of Malaysia to run its course. Although the military conflict tied up 50 000 British, Australian and New Zealand troops in Malaysia, it was never a serious threat to the security of Indonesia's neighbour. There were occasional spectaculars, like the paratroop landings on the Malayan peninsula in September 1964, but the critical effects on both sides were political and economic. In Indonesia confrontation gave full reign to Sukarno's romantic conception of nation-building—that an idea, such as driving British power from South-East Asia, would unify the Indonesian nation more effectively than the provision of food and clothing. But, unlike the West Irian issue, it proved too ideological to be sustained against the effects of the deteriorating economy and the sense of isolation which Indonesians felt as the policy alienated Western nations, failed to arouse the neutrals and, especially after January 1965 when Sukarno ordered Indonesia's withdrawal from the United Nations in protest against the seating of Malaysia in the Security Council, came to depend more and more on the support of Communist China.

This was at the height of the Cold War in South-East Asia. It was the year the Americans took fateful military decisions to escalate the war in Vietnam. Sukarno had become such a master at manipulating the political forces in Indonesia—the communists on one side, the military on the other and the nationalists in between—that many assumed this uncharacteristic lurch to one side would be corrected by a flurry of activity in another direction. However, an unexpected event in Jakarta swept all the manipulative politics of Sukarno's era to one side—and Sukarno himself with them.

A communist-led attack on the army leadership in Jakarta in the early morning of 1 October 1965, killing six generals, changed the situation almost literally overnight. The reaction to this abortive coup became a defining moment in Indonesian history. A wave of anti-communism, including the massacre and imprisonment of communists on a massive scale, followed, and while Sukarno adjusted to his changed circumstances, it was obvious that, without the PKI, he could no longer keep the army in check. Also, he was suspected by army leaders of being half-involved with the coup, or at least sympathetic. The removal of ministers like Subandrio and Chairul Saleh and the rise of Major General Suharto, the commander of the Army Strategic Reserve Command (Komando Candangan Strategis Angkatan Darat—Kostrad), underlined the president's failure to get support. So did the rise of student groups, mainly Muslim and Catholic, which early in 1966 set the pace for government reforms aimed at curbing Sukarno's authority and reviving constitutional restraints on the executive. When Sjahrir died in April 1966, Hatta emerged from retirement to place the blame for his death on their old nationalist comrade. Eventually Suharto displaced, then replaced, him.

Sukarno died in June 1970. The new men in power, administrators rather than solidarity-makers, set about achieving that which, after more than twenty years, the Indonesian nation still had to give its people—a demonstrable improvement in living standards.

One more territorial crisis remained before the nation which we know today as Indonesia took final shape. The western half of the island of Timor, being Dutch, had passed to Indonesia with the succession. The eastern half, being Portuguese, had not. Post-colonial India had also been faced with a Portuguese enclave, Goa, in the midst of another empire and had resolved the issue simply by gobbling it up. The Indonesians had not been so strategic. Preoccupied elsewhere, they had paid little attention to East Timor and were now faced with a colony in revolt on their doorstep. What followed was a mixture of what happened in Goa in 1961 and in Bangladesh ten years later.

In April 1974 a leftist military group in Lisbon seized power from the dictator Marcello Caetano. The young military officers wanted to modernize Portugal, which meant ridding Lisbon of the colonies held in Africa and Asia since the sixteenth century. (The military coup in Portugal is credited, incidentally, with beginning what Samuel Huntington called 'the third wave' in the historical evolution of democracy, because in the fifteen years after the change in Lisbon some thirty countries in Africa, Asia and Latin America moved towards democratic systems of government.)

Three political groups sparred for ascendancy in East Timor during 1974. The Timorese Democratic Union (Uniao Democratica Timorense—UDT) wanted federation with Portugal. The Timorese Social Democratic Association, which became the Revolutionary Front for an Independent East Timor (Frente Revolutionaria de Timor-Leste—Fretilin) wanted independence. The Association for the Integration of Timor into Indonesia, which became the Timorese Popular Democratic Association (Associacao Popular Democratica Timorense—Apodeti) wanted integration with Indonesia.

At first Indonesia disavowed any special interest in Timor, saying that it was every country's right to be independent if it wished. But another view developed in the army and then in the government— that an independent Timor could become 'a Cuba on the doorstep' and be used by unfriendly powers as a base to subvert or put pressure on Indonesia. The two key figures in developing this position were Major General Ali Murtopo, who was head of the secretive, if not secret, Special Operations Unit (Operasi Khusus—Opsus), and Brigadier General Benny Moerdani, head of the military's intelligence operations. During 1974, they gradually took charge of the Timor operation.

Early in 1975, in the face of Indonesia's increasing support for integration and therefore of Apodeti, the two other political groups, UDT and Fretilin, combined, with a policy of total independence, rejecting integration with anyone. But the Fretilin radicals and the UDT landowners could not trust each other, and in May the coalition collapsed. On 10 August UDT launched a coup in Dili, the administrative capital of East Timor. Fretilin announced 'armed insurrection' in response and by September was in effective military control, forcing thousands to flee into West Timor. The Indonesian political and propaganda campaign having failed, commando units infiltrated East Timor in support of what was now called an anti-communist alliance of Apodeti, UDT and some smaller groups. During the fighting in October, five Australian journalists were killed. Indonesia claimed they were killed in crossfire between the Timorese factions, but a counter-claim is that they were killed by Indonesian commandos.

Fretilin on 24 November called on the United Nations to demand the withdrawal of Indonesian troops. On 28 November it declared East Timor's independence. UDT-Apodeti then called for integration with Indonesia. A formal invasion by Indonesian troops took place on 7 December. The United Nations in a series of resolutions disregarded by Indonesia condemned the invasion. On 17 December a provisional government was formed in Dili under an Apodeti official. In May 1976 hand-picked delegates of a people's assembly voted for integration with Indonesia. On 17 July 1976 President Suharto declared East Timor to be Indonesia's twenty-seventh province.

Until 1982 the United Nations conducted an annual debate on East Timor, resolving that Indonesian troops be withdrawn and that the Timorese people be given the right of self-determination. Since 1982 the secretary-general's office has arranged a series of talks between Indonesia and Portgual to try to find an acceptable solution. At the time of writing, that is still the position.

Unrest continued in East Timor and the military presence required continued to be out of proportion to the territory's size and importance. On 12 November 1991 at a service in Dili for a student killed in a previous encounter, troops scattered the mourners with gun fire. It was a massacre, not crowd control, and it was condemned internationally. It drew attention not just to the unsettled status of East Timor but also to the role of the military in Suharto's Indonesia. The Indonesian authorities admitted a tragic mistake. But troubling questions remained. The original estimate of 19 killed was eventually changed to more than 50, but credible accounts persisted that the real figure was much higher. One well-attested count was 273.

The Indonesian nation was now defined and secured, but what kind of country was it? Or could it become? The campaign for West Irian had been exhilarating. The conflict over Malaysia had seemed unnecessary—foolish and reckless. The incorporation of East Timor was mismanaged. In particular, as the nation celebrated a half century of independence in 1995, the issue of the succession was hotly debated. The transition from Sukarno had been managed, but it had been bloody, and it had consolidated the role of the military in Indonesian public life. Indonesians were now asking themselves what role the army would play in the next presidential succession and whether the transition from Suharto would be more peaceful than it had been in Sukarno's time.

The nation became preoccupied with its internal development—the economy, of course, but also the system of government, especially its capacity for democracy.

CHAPTER THREE

Leaders

IN THE FIRST half-century since independence, the Republic of Indonesia has had only two presidents. The first was romantic, charismatic and instinctively drawn to the arts and the company of women. The second is shrewd, pragmatic and cautious—the discarded child of poor, rural parents who became the head of perhaps the richest family in modern Indonesia.

Sukarno and Suharto seem like chalk and cheese. They share little except the similarity of their names and the presidency of Indonesia. Part of that difference is that they have served Indonesia at strikingly different times, the times needing—and finding—the man appropriate to it, and the man in turn adapting himself to his time. The mismanagement and excesses of Sukarno during the turbulent early days of the republic demanded a corrective which Suharto knew he had to provide. He did it with a dogged pursuit of political stability and economic development.

But, whatever the differences, they are both unmistakably Indonesian. Both were of Javanese ethnic origin (Sukarno from east, Suharto from central Java) and born in the same month, June; both touched by mysticism and the intense inner life of traditional Java. Both relished the opportunity to serve their country and, in their different ways, enjoyed the use of power. Both made their mark abroad, Sukarno as the *enfant terrible* of the turbulent Cold War period, Suharto as the *paterfamilias* of a New Order of restraint and sustainable development.

Indonesia has been fortunate in its political leadership. When you compare the experience of other post-colonial territories which became nations in the rush to independence after World War II, Indonesia stands out as having produced two political leaders of unusual quality and lasting effect. However, having changed leaders only once in half a century (and in circumstances both dramatic and traumatic), the method of succession is not firmly established. Also, the political system puts enormous power in the presidential office and depends heavily on the penetration of the military into the everyday life of Indonesians. Neither fits comfortably with the development of a market economy, which is part of the broader development of a civil society in Indonesia. So the succession after Suharto has become a critical issue and the system itself is under scrutiny. Because such power is now concentrated in the presidency, the succession has become a personal test of Suharto's political leadership. After thirty years in power, his achievements are considerable, but will he be remembered for holding on to power too long, thereby threatening these achievements?

As for Sukarno, political leaders who are lucky enough to be the founders of their nations have a head start in the historical stakes, and Sukarno is no exception. There is a revival of 'Sukarnoism', now that he has been dead for a quarter of a century. The silly things he did when he was alive have been forgotten. He is seen, especially by young people, as a visionary, the architect of Indonesian nationalism and a leader who represented all the people, including the marginal and dispossessed. He loved unwisely, but he died poor, which in today's Indonesia, where fortunes are being amassed as security for the future, is seen as a mark of integrity. His grave in the mountain town of Blitar in east Java, where he was born, has become more popular year by year as a tourist site, and the anniversary of his death on 20 July has changed from a simple family occasion to one of national homage. Sukarno is now in the early stages of the idolatry that flows irresistibly to those political leaders, not just Indonesians, with a zest for life. It is the people's way of keeping hope alive for themselves.

SUKARNO (1901–1970)

As early as 7 a.m., when the tropical air was still cool enough for them to wear scarves and sweaters, crowds of people were making their way to an open field, the equivalent in Indonesia of the town square. It was Heroes' Day in Jogjakarta and Sukarno was to speak. The people came, astride hundreds probably thousands of bicycles; in *betjaks*, the brightly painted, three-wheeled pedicabs; on foot. The car-loads of important persons would come later. They laughed and chattered as if they expected to enjoy themselves. They did not give the impression of having been forced to come. Rather this was a great show, like the *wayang*; a public holiday. Seeing and hearing Bung (Brother) Karno had become one of the folk traditions of the new Indonesia.

A Colombo Plan conference was in progress and the city was decked out with flags and streamers, slogans stretched across the streets. The flags of all the Colombo Plan countries were flown, but the red and white bi-colour of Indonesia, represented in hundreds of thousands of miniature paper flags, created the dominant effect. Jogjakarta is a university city and many of the early morning bicyclists were students. Some of them sang as they pedalled abreast in small groups. They were Western-dressed in casual fashion and they seemed relaxed and carefree.

After the Asian Games in August 1962 the president spoke on big occasions in Jakarta in the main stadium, which seated one hundred thousand and was the equal of the best in the world. Some of the atmosphere of the open-air gathering was lost. The president did not face the crowd directly, as he did from an open-field platform but, speaking from one side of the stadium (the side sheltered from the sun), he half confronted, and was half-surrounded by, his audience. The stadium was also noisier. The murmuring of the audience rose to fill the huge saucer; the roars of the crowd boomed and rebounded. The top of the stadium was spaced with flags; the tiered balconies were hung with slogans and the groups, identified by placards (national front, youth organizations, and so on), were organized like cheerleaders. They sang and stamped at appropriate moments. A helicopter dropped leaflets, an electric board announced messages, sirens wailed, guns saluted, balloons were released. In the great structure of steel and concrete (especially if the armed services were on display in the arena), a modern, military nation was on show. For a Westerner, the link with the European dictatorships was easily made as the president stepped on to the rostrum.

But Sukarno was not a violent orator, in the tradition of the great European mob-rousers. His style was friendly, coaxing and confidential. He began quietly and slowly. 'Sisters and Brothers . . .' His voice, a slightly throaty baritone, played with each word, sometimes skipping quickly over two or three, sometimes repeating a word or a phrase three or four times with a rising sharpness; but generally the tone was low. Dressed smartly, either in a sparkling white uniform, with ribbons, swagger stick and *kopiah* (black velvet cap) or in a modest grey uniform (but always in uniform) he moved quickly into his speech. He stood lightly, leaning slightly forward, using the microphone discreetly, like a nightclub entertainer rather than an orator. His figure was the trim indication of a younger man. Occasionally he punched the air, languidly, as if exercising a tired shoulder.

> Do you and you and you and you . . . do you consider yourself as Bearers of the Message of the People's Sufferings? Are you really aware that you are Bearers of the Message of the People's Sufferings, do you really feel to the marrow of your bones that you are Bearers of the Message of the People's Sufferings? [No answer from the crowd, which is quiet and attentive.] It is this social consciousness of the Indonesian people which is the basic element of the Message of the Sufferings of the Indonesian People. The Message of the Sufferings of the Indonesian People is thus part of the social consciousness of mankind.

In rising tempo:

> Thus the Message of the Sufferings of the Indonesian People is part of the Message of the Sufferings of the whole of mankind! Thus our Message of the Sufferings of the People is not just a national idea or a national ideal. Our Message of the People's Sufferings is interlocked with the Message of the Sufferings of Mankind, the Message of the Sufferings of Mankind is interlocked with our Message of the Sufferings of the People. The Indonesian Revolution is interlocked with the Revolution of Mankind, the Revolution of Mankind is interlocked with the Indonesian Revolution.

The speech, repetitive and emotional, usually took on great occasions at least two hours to deliver. People who know the language well say he handled it adroitly, sometimes brilliantly, occasionally beautifully. The English translation loses the flexible use of Indonesian words and the startling bursts of foreign languages—Dutch, English, French or German—with which Sukarno spattered his speeches. In declaring 'It is an entity of social consciousness like a burning fire', the words 'like a burning fire' will be spoken in English, for no apparent reason. Some thought the president liked to show off his languages, using frequently phrases like '*l'exploitation de l'homme par l'homme, de nation par nation*' or '*socialisme a la Indonesie*' not because the phrases had an exact meaning which Bahasa is not able to convey, but because they suggested to the people an image of Sukarno's intellectual familiarity with the world. Others said he just liked the sound of the words:

> Oh yes! I know that I am often ridiculed by people who do not like me for being a 'man of feeling'—'*gevoelsmens*'—and that in politics I have too much of the character of a 'man of the arts'— that I am too much the *artist*. How happy I am with these derisive remarks! I express thanks to the Almighty that I was born with traits of sentiment and artistry, and I am proud that the Indonesian Nation is also a 'Nation of Feeling'—'*gevoelsvolk*'—and a 'Nation of Artists'—an '*artistenvolk*'.

Molly Bondan, who had the job of putting Sukarno's speeches into English, writes:

> Bung Karno's style of oratory was very much influenced by the narrative style of the *dalang*, the puppet master of the *wayang* plays. Repetition of the content for the sake of clarity or emphasis, frequent asides, remarks addressed to individual persons present, the spacing out of the syllables of words for emphasis, allusions to characters or situations in the *wayang* plays, exclamations, humour, poetic phraseology and an appreciation of the rhythm of sentences were all part of his speeches and were reflected in his writing . . . It was not always possible to reproduce this . . . in English . . .

Sukarno stressed in his speeches the non-material, lofty aims of the Indonesian revolution. He often claimed that it was bigger and more complex than the French, American and Russian revolutions because it embraced all aspects—social, political, economic as well as spiritual —of Indonesian life. It was 'many revolutions in one generation', a phrase he used in its English form. It would create a 'new Indonesian man', a man of feeling like himself, demanding justice, humanity and dignity as his due:

> Therefore, all you people of Indonesia, keep your heads high! Do not retreat, do not stop, put your feet firmly on the ground! If there are times that you feel confused, if there are times that you

almost despair, if there are times that you do not quite understand the course of our Revolution which indeed sometimes resembles a vessel at sea tossed in a raging storm—return to the source of our Message of the Sufferings of the People which is congruent with the Social Conscience of Man.

The intimacy and mysticism of Sukarno's approach grew noticeable with the years. He described each 17 August as:

dialogue . . . a two-way conversation between myself and the People, between my Ego and my Alter-Ego. A two-way conversation between Sukarno-the-man and Sukarno-the-people, a two-way conversation between comrade-in-arms and comrade-in-arms. A two-way conversation between two comrades who in reality are One!

I become like a person possessed. Everything that is non-material in my body overflows! Thoughts overflow, feelings overflow, nerves overflow, emotions overflow. Everything that belongs to the spirit that is in my body is as though quivering and blazing and raging, and then for me it is as though fire is not hot enough, as though ocean is not deep enough, as though the stars in the heavens are not high enough!

He also used these occasions to affirm his determination to serve his country, however great the demands might be, 'until the Almighty calls me home to my source'. Sukarno made the pilgrimage to Mecca several times. He claimed that the Trikora (a three-fold plan to take West Irian issued by him in December 1961) was a 'vision' from God. References to his increasing age and decreasing strength, to humility in the face of the great responsibility which he carried as Great Leader of the Revolution, Mouthpiece of the Indonesian People, Main Bearer of the Message of the Sufferings of the Indonesian People—as well, of course, as President, Prime Minister and Supreme Commander of the Armed Forces—became increasingly frequent. Sukarno, who had become personal psychiatrist to a whole nation, increasingly showed concern with his own health.

Yet his speeches continued in the romantic, hopeful mould of his youth. There was always something new around the corner, even if it was as unpoetic as 'self-propelling growth'. Usually, the imagery was more conventionally mesmeric—the Dawn, the Rising Sun, the

New World were awaiting. The triumph, however, was elusive and Sukarno's object in his long, rambling discourse, was to prepare the Indonesian people to struggle for it. He appeared unhappy about the present, except as a vehicle of change. For a 'fighting nation' there was no journey's end. 'I am one of the people who is in love with the Romanticism of Revolution; I am inspired by it, I am fascinated by it.'

> If, for example, at this moment, an angel were to descend from the heavens and say to me: 'Hi, Sukarno, I shall grant you a miracle, to give the Indonesian people a just and prosperous society as a gift, as a present', then I would reply: 'I don't want to be granted such a miracle, I want the just and prosperous society to be the result of the struggle of the Indonesian people!'

When he said, 'Hi, Sukarno', there was a ripple of laughter. Indonesians enjoy cockiness. Angels descending from heaven are part of the Javanese mythology (one of the restaurants at the Hotel Indonesia in Jakarta is almost exclusively decorated with the story of such a visitation) and Sukarno enjoyed the role of gamin in the play. His humour was usually deflationary, appealing to ordinary people; it was not sophisticated or elaborate, although he would use it to overcome a political difficulty.

For example, on the troublesome question of a Nasakom cabinet —Nasakom is an abbreviation of Nas (nationalist), A (*agama*, or religion) and Kom (communist), the three political streams whose support he claimed—Sukarno said:

> There are still persons who suffer from the communist-phobia. Because they have the communist-phobia, they have the Nasakomphobia! Whilst I have explained hundreds and hundreds of times that revolutionary national *gotong royong* ways cannot possibly be affected without Nasakom at its hub—Nas-A-Kom—the three objective groupings into which the Indonesian People's political consciousness falls, I have also often explained that to be anti-Nasakom is the same as being anti the 1945 constitution, the same as being anti *Pantja Sila*, the same as being anti the concentration of forces . . . the same as being . . . soft in the head!

The crowd murmured a laugh, but they were no wiser on the issue of whether communists would be included in the cabinet.

Or, taking account of the difficulties Indonesia had found in getting development in West Irian under way:

> In West Irian, for example, a whispering campaign is being spread that 'under the Republic the situation is deteriorating as compared with what it was under the red-white-blue flag.' Deteriorating? Deteriorating in what things? If we ask such a concrete question— 'deteriorating in what things?'—then it turns out that the problem is: there is not enough canned beer in West Irian now! . . . Sisters and brothers in West Irian! You there, sisters and brothers in West Irian! Sisters and brothers in Kotabaru, in Sorong, in Merauke— sisters and brothers on the slopes of the Trikora Mountain, the Sukarno Mountain, the Sudirman Mountain, the Yamin Mountain!—the Republic has never indeed promised canned beer to the people in West Irian! The Republic has promised and is building schools, the Republic has promised and has brought independence, the Republic has promised and is bringing Clear Rays and Brightness.

Sukarno's speeches were not wholly tendentious. Often, he took a point of some complicated matter of principle or policy and produced a masterly summary. His ideas on economics were often so human and simple that they were misleading. But perhaps no crowd could possibly survive a sincere and expert analysis of Indonesia's economic problems, if a leader could be found to deliver it. When Sukarno said that his ideas on the 'economic question' boil down to this: 'If nations who live in a dry and barren desert can solve the problems of their economy then why can't we?', he was posing the problem in essentially realistic terms, although he might not have liked the answer some observers would give.

On great occasions he was a stickler for correct procedure, as it affected the prestige of the president of the Republic of Indonesia. He kept his correct distance ahead of others. His face was held in a severe and disdainful pose. When he tried to be militant, raising his voice or making strong gestures, he ran the risk of looking foolish. Sometimes he played the clown. While waiting for the delayed arrival of Nikita Khrushchev at Jakarta's airport in 1960, Sukarno sat on a rolled-up red carpet, a lopsided umbrella shielding him from the rain, grinning broadly. He still held his swagger stick under his arm, but his cap was slightly askew. He looked like an actor who had been called in to play a head of state.

As president, Sukarno's performance was often criticized privately by Indonesians, however careful people were not to reflect on the dignity of the position of head of the Indonesian State. Sometimes, even before the outbreak of opposition early in 1966, the criticism was public. In August 1963 a teacher in the east Indonesian island of Flores was given fifteen months' gaol for having said that the president was 'a good orator' but had 'an empty head'. The sentence—indeed the judgement—seemed harsh until compared with what it might have been in the England of Elizabeth I or Henry VIII. Most heads of state, including some in politically advanced countries today, are overweight with solemnly accepted virtues which do not exist.

In the *wayang*, of which President Sukarno was an avid and intelligent follower, one of the stock characters is Gatutkacha. He stands for courage—compared, say, with Puntadewa, who stands for integrity and modesty, and Bima (Gatutkacha's father) who stands for a strong will. He can also fly, is very popular, and cannot bear injustice. Gatutkacha was Sukarno's favourite, and it may be that the Indonesian president modelled himself on his hero.

There was something of the effortless charisma of leadership in Sukarno's life. The short list of candidates when Indonesia became independent was impressive. Hatta and Sjahrir were men of sterling capacities, and there were several others who, if fortune had smiled the other way, might have been preferred to Sukarno. But he always managed to create in the minds of those around him—whether Indonesian, Dutch or Japanese—an impression of having been chosen to lead the Indonesian nation in its first entry into the world. Irresolute compared with the decisive Sjahrir or flippant beside the serious Hatta, he retained his position while they faltered.

Sukarno was born in Blitar, near Malang in east Java on 6 June 1901. His mother was a Hindu Balinese and his father, who was a schoolteacher and a member of the Theosophical Society, was a Muslim Javanese. His zodiacal sign of Gemini convinced Sukarno, he once said, that he was to serve as a meeting point of all the world's philosophies. His father's profession and the support of several prominent friends, including the father of Ruslan Abdulgani, a long-time political associate of Sukarno's who became minister for information, helped the young Sukarno to get the kind of education reserved for

Indonesians privileged under the Dutch. He spent some of his early youth with his grandparents at Tulungagung (east Java) and, according to his official biography, was spoiled. At school he was good at languages, but did not shine in class. As a lively youngster he earned the nickname 'rooster'. He could climb higher on trees than his friends and he stage-managed their games.

At fourteen Sukarno went to Surabaya High School. During his five years at high school, he lived with the family of the founder of the Sarekat Islam, Umar Said Tjokroaminoto, a Surabaya businessman, at whose house he met early nationalists like Agus Salim, Alimin, Musso and Semaun. He joined the youth organization Young Java where his liking for oratory first showed, and he contributed editorials (signed 'Bima'—the strong-willed prince in the *wayang*) to Tjokroaminoto's newspaper *Utusan Hindia* (the *Indies Messenger*). In 1920 he went to the Bandung Technical Institute to study civil engineering. The official biography notes that after two months he broke off study to earn money for the family of Tjokroaminoto, who had been arrested. Sukarno worked in the state railways. He is also said at this time to have become a member of Sarekat Islam, but while studying he developed 'a more definite and concrete system of political ideas of his own'.

The Dutch claim that Sukarno failed twice in 'Theory of Structures' and never graduated. The official version is that he graduated in 1925 with a thesis about harbour construction, earning a civil engineering degree and the title 'Ir' (Ingénieur), although his particular study was architecture. He set up as an architect in Bandung and became known for a modernized style of hut design. He also helped to design a mosque.

Already known to the Dutch authorities as a fiery speaker, he became chairman of the Bandung Study Club, the members of which formed in 1927 the Persarikatan Nasional Indonesia (Indonesian Nationalist Organization) which became in 1928 the Partai Nasional Indonesia (Indonesian Nationalist Party—PNI). The party's aim was complete independence for Indonesia and it urged non-cooperation with the Dutch authorities as the means of achievement. Sukarno was active at this time in developing a philosophy which he called *Marhaenism*. He used '*marhaen*' to describe not only the peasantry and proletariat but a kind of pauperized mass of 'little people', wager-earners and small farmers, and developed from this constituency a theory of a kind of socialism suited to Indonesia. It was useless waiting for 'an aeroplane from Moscow or a caliph from Istanbul', he said in speeches at this time, urging self-reliance and unity of the nationalist movement.

In December 1928 a step toward unity was taken when, on PNI initiative, six groups came together in a federation, Permufakatan Perhimpunan Politik Kebangsaan Indonesia (National Union of Political Associations—PPPKI) and elected Sukarno as chairman. By 1929 the PNI had over 10 000 members and the Dutch were becoming concerned at its growing influence. In December the authorities arrested Sukarno and three others for allegedly planning a rebellion. After eight months detention they were brought to trial at Bandung. The trial lasted four months and enabled Sukarno to make a now famous defence plea, 'Indonesia accuses', in which he spoke of the poverty of the *marhaen*. He received the longest sentence—four years, later reduced to two.

Sukarno's long exile began, with his wife, mother-in-law and adopted daughter, on the island of Flores. Unlike many Asian and African nationalists who continued their political writing during imprisonment and later wrote about their time in detention, Sukarno has been reticent about his years of enforced isolation and it is a difficult period to document. But after four years on Flores his health broke down and he was transferred to Bencoolen, in south Sumatra. During this time he wrote several pamphlets on Islamic law and theology. As the Japanese advanced, the Dutch moved him to Padang, in central Sumatra, reportedly with the intention of taking him to Australia. He assisted in the evacuation of Dutch civilians and, perhaps fearing Japanese reprisals for pamphlets he had written attacking their ambitions in the Pacific, he 'managed to escape', as the official biography phrases it, 'appearing' later at Bukittingi. According to Sjahrir, Sukarno was treated 'rather roughly' by the Japanese and he regarded them as 'pure fascists'. He worked for them in Sumatra as a translator, then, on the initiative of Hatta and Sjahrir who some months earlier had decided on tactics to be pursued under the Japanese, he was taken to Batavia (later Jakarta), under the assumed name 'Abdul Rachman'.

Sukarno's reputation as a 'collaborator' with the Japanese was utilized by Dutch propaganda after World War II, when the Netherlands was anxious to show that the republic was a Japanese creation rather than a product of genuine nationalism. The criticism was picked up by the communists in the early post-war years. The leader of the 1948 Madiun revolt, Musso, attacked Sukarno as a '*romusha* dealer', a reference to the *romushas* (slave labourers) conscripted by the Japanese, most of whom perished. (Sukarno was chairman of the People's Manpower Centre—Pusat Tenaga Rakyat, or Putera—created by the Japanese in March 1943.) Yet in reality Sukarno seems to have behaved no differently from many Asian nationalists who were forced suddenly to cope with the unknown Japanese after the colonial power had retreated. With Hatta, his role was pre-arranged, and whether he was 'actively pro-Japanese' or 'anti-British and American' as has been claimed is beside the point, which is that he tirelessly used his position under the Japanese authorities to strengthen Indonesian nationalist sentiment.

It may have been that Sukarno was more impressed with the Japanese than were some of his colleagues, who had been educated abroad and had seen the civilization of Europe. Sukarno at this stage had never left Indonesia except to visit Japan and the Japanese headquarters in Vietnam, and his chief source of comparison with the Japanese was the Dutch, against whom his prejudices were natural enough. His caution about declaring independence, dealt with earlier, seems to have been mistaken, though understandable in the confusion of the period, and it provides an early glimpse of a capacity for self-preservation which proved remarkable.

Like many romantics who enjoy pleasure, Sukarno developed essentially withdrawn and protective attitudes to his leadership role. He was rarely seen informally among the people, except when he toured Java or one of the islands. He did not play games, as many Asian leaders liked to do, enabling them to mix casually on the golf course or the tennis court. He was informal at parties, but in a proprietorial way, more a matter of style than of sentiment. On these occasions he treated the services of diplomats—including their ability to sing their native songs, like 'Home on the Range' or 'Waltzing Matilda'—as his private property, behaviour reflected in his attitude to paintings or pretty ankles that caught his eye. In Jakarta he lived in his heavily guarded palace, one of five he inherited from the Dutch governor, flying by helicopter to the palace at Bogor or, when forced to travel about the city, moving in a motorcade of great noise and size—eight motorcyclists, eight jeeps, with several staff cars following the president's own black limousine; all with sirens wailing.

Part of his seclusion was, of course, inevitable. An Indonesian friend who accompanied me to the president's palace at Merdeka Utara in Jakarta one day in 1963 said, as we approached the gate sentry: 'It is better to take off your sun-glasses. The guards like to see your eyes.' This mysterious message was translated later: the guards had orders to shoot first and ask questions afterwards. A trick of would-be assassins is to conceal the tell-tale emotional flicker of the eyes seconds before they act. Perhaps my friend was an unusually cautious man, or perhaps he had something to hide; but as five attempts had been made on Sukarno's life it is not surprising that the crack regiments that guarded his palaces were sensitive to strangers. (They were also sensitive to political corruption, as the ambiguous role of the Tjakrabirawa Regiment in the 30 September 1965 affair showed.) His escapes from assassination may have confirmed his right to leadership in the people's eyes, as proof that the magico-historic royal quality of imperviousness to weapons was his.

Like all political leaders, Sukarno in private had moments of relaxed charm which surprised visitors. The image of inhuman self-possession which the cabled reports of Sukarno's official activities necessarily created was upset by the spectacle of a balding man in shirt-sleeves, with a battery of vitamin pills and other stimulants on the breakfast table. But Sukarno was not warmly regarded by his close associates. One of his colleagues expressed his feelings in oblique fashion: 'Sukarno has strong personal views which, as head of state, he must be prepared to defend and justify'. A head of state with strong personal views is not a person to be easily trusted; personal matters can be elevated into affairs of state.

Nor did Sukarno manage to create in the minds of most Indonesians a great awe or fear. Many Indonesians would react against personal criticism of him, especially if it was made by foreigners, but they did not seem to walk respectfully in his shadow, even to the extent that Indians did with Nehru. Sukarno was a very human leader and was regarded as such by his people.

Visiting foreigners were regaled with gruesome accounts of his latest sexual exploits, his irreligious flirtation with Marxism, his personal saturation of flattery and deceit and his insensitivity to economic conditions. But despite these criticisms he became more generally accepted. It was as if the Indonesians had changed their view of him for the third time—first, the revolutionary, nationalist leader; second, the controversial nationalist leader, and then, the controversial head of state. The same Indonesians who worried about Sukarno's faults also wondered whether these faults were not in some way attuned to the deepest instincts of the Indonesian people themselves.

No other Asian leader so keenly offended the puritan values of the West. Abstinence, monogamy, balanced budgets and other virtues

believed to justify the pleasures of success were conspicuously under-
valued by the Indonesian president. By claiming to be a believer in
God and a Marxist, Sukarno added insult to injury, confusing his foreign friends and confounding his enemies. Within Indonesia, these
human failings amounted to little. Especially among the Javanese, the
ability to hold apparently contradictory beliefs at the same time was
considered merely as evidence that the soul is marvellously flexible. Of
all the qualities required in an Indonesian leader, many of them possessed by Sukarno and none of them accountable to puritan values in
personal life, Sukarno's notorious liking for women was on the whole
an advantage for him in Indonesia. The defiance of recognized rules
because of magic power, possessed so strongly that it cannot be controlled, is an ancient Javanese mark of leadership, springing from
animist beliefs.

One day Sukarno appeared at a press conference attired correctly
except that he was not wearing shoes. Curious correspondents asked
why. He explained that an electric storm was brewing and he had been
told by his *dukun* (medicine man, although sometimes used to mean a
masseuse), that he was so full of vitality that he would attract lightning
(and presumably without shoes an electric charge would be conducted
away). Western correspondents found this episode to be more evidence of Sukarno's lack of rationality, but Indonesians expressed no
surprise. Sukarno's energy, whether in dancing all night, or in political
musjawarah (discussion) that lasts perhaps ten hours, was a badge of
leadership. He was not expected to be a good family man, faithful to
his wife in the tradition of Western politics. The siren of his outrider
escort, which sped him through the town, was popularly called, without malice, his 'mating call'.

Sukarno's first marriage was to a 15-year-old daughter of Tjokroaminoto. It is said the marriage was never consummated, and it ended
in divorce in 1922. The next year, while in Bandung, he married Ibu
Inggit, a widow from a well-off Javanese family and twelve years older
than him. Their marriage, although childless, lasted seventeen years.
During his detention by the Dutch in the southern Sumatran town of
Benkulen, he met Fatmawati, a village girl in her late teens. They were
married in 1943. They had five children, one of whom, Megawati, is
the president of the PDI, effectively the successor to her father's old
party, the PNI. Fatmawati proved herself a popular first lady after
Sukarno became president, and there was criticism when in 1955
Sukarno married Hartini, the former wife of a minor Shell Oil

Company official, by whom she had had five children. The women who objected when Sukarno took Hartini were not complaining about his being unfaithful to Fatmawati. They complained at Fatmawati's loss of social position, by being excluded from the palace and the functions as first lady. They would not have objected to Hartini becoming a mistress, which is a common enough pattern in Indonesia, as in most Asian—and some Western—countries. Intelligent and socially astute, Hartini was a competent partner for Sukarno as president. Their marriage produced two children. In 1963 Sukarno secretly married a Tokyo bar girl Nemoto Naoka, who was renamed Ratna Sari Dewi. They had one child. Sukarno took another wife, Hariarti. All his wives except Hartini divorced him before his death in 1970.

Sukarno achieved much for Indonesia. His influence was important in the establishment of a secular, rather than an Islamic, state; the advantages of this are probably more apparent to a non-Muslim than to a Muslim, but it does seem generally true that the removal of religious tests from the operation of government improves stability. He promoted national unity. It is arguable whether a unitary state is more suited than a federation to Indonesia's peculiarly varied needs, but Sukarno proclaimed the unity of the people of Indonesia 'from Sabang to Merauke' with such persistence that a national awareness became the badge of modern Indonesia. Sukarno also awakened in his people a sense of pride in their own achievements, after centuries of being regarded by the Dutch as hopelessly second-class and improbable human beings.

Much of Sukarno's flamboyance and apparent radicalism was camouflage for an essentially hesitant man, who was also an expert politician. As president, Sukarno wove an intricate web of authority. Even at the peak of his power, he was not a dictator in the sense that he had a party behind him to force, in the name of its leader or an ideology, actions which could not be taken in the name of the state. He dictated through persuasion of conflicting forces, and his rule was relatively free of the brutality of conventional dictatorships.

SUHARTO (1921–)

It is June 1995 and President Suharto is explaining the intricacies of the country's foreign debt. It is true, he agrees, that Indonesia's foreign debt has reached the psychologically disturbing figure of US$100 billion; it is a burden that all have to share, including the next generation. There is public concern, he acknowledges; fears are often expressed to him that Indonesia would not be able to repay its loans. He wants to reassure everyone that the debt is well managed and within Indonesia's capacity to maintain sensibly and repay, and that being in debt is just another way of building up assets for the future.

The president is briefing a small gathering of ministers, provincial governors, regents and executives of non-government organizations in his main presidential office, but what he says is also on national television. He is seated at a small, ornate table, with two vases of flowers helping to conceal the microphones, wearing the official black cap and a tweed jacket, with a shirt open at the neck. The camera concentrates on the president's face and upper body. Sometimes, but not often, it moves to his audience, which is sitting in serried rows, attentive but expressionless, except that they appear in nervous awe of the speaker.

The president's address goes on and on; I did not time him, but it seemed that he had been speaking for as long as an hour. He talks about exports, the national economy, the capacity of industry, interest rates, the sale of state assets, the appreciation of the yen, long-term loans and soft loans. His manner is that of the head of a family explaining simple matters of domestic housekeeping which everyone is expected to understand. He does not refer to J-curves or use any of the slick language of the financial markets. Sometimes he uses crude imagery to make a point, such as a reference to food passing through the body in contrast to loans which build national assets and infrastructure, but for the most part his language is sensible and unexciting. When he jokes, his eyes become mischievous. He screws them up to make a point, twists his lips. His features under the black cap are mobile, almost clownish at times—a shrewd, peasant's face which has experienced life and knows how things work.

He explains that the state's assets are appreciating in value and, if sold, would wipe out the foreign debt. Also, the assets of the private sector, which had accumulated about 40 percent of the total foreign debt, were appreciating strongly and business leaders were confident that according to their own requirements—not the same as government's—their debts were manageable. At this point, the president assumes his most reassuring and confidential manner. Indonesia could, if it wished, wipe out the foreign debt by selling state enterprises (he does not use the term 'privatization'), but why should the state divest itself of valuable assets when the money which made up the debt had been borrowed on such beneficial terms? Nearly half the loans were long-term and carried interest rates under 3 per cent. Why pay them off when you have such a good deal? The mobile face is alive with cunning satisfaction.

On Indonesian television, which might otherwise rate among the less demanding in the world, the president's address is a *tour de force*. It is a masterly performance, totally different from the platform oratory of Sukarno yet in its own way just as effective. Suharto prides himself on being a simple, uneducated person who has risen by the grace of God and the will of the people to the highest position in the land, but his self-effacing manner conceals or rather, in the intimate focus of the television camera, reveals strength in reserve. He speaks without notes in a low-key conversational manner, fatherly and reassuring, chuckling to himself with pleasure on a point he has made well, completely at ease in the medium, confident, clear in his mind about what he wants to say. He is no orator, no visionary. He casts no spells. No hearts beat faster at his appearance. But his personality shows authority, un-mistakeable and deliberate, not to be trifled with. He is resourceful, discreet, sagacious. He stoops to conquer.

Suharto was born on 8 June 1921 in the small village of Kemusuk, west of Jogjakarta. Two events in his early life are significant—a disturbed childhood and his discovery of a new family in the form of the army.

Passed from family to family in a poor farming community during the difficult economic times of the 1920s, his character was formed in the crucible of traditional Javanese peasant wisdom. Among farmers in the Javanese heartland the boy Suharto learned to read the Koran, and to fast every Monday and Thursday, and heard for the first time the stories of Indonesian heroes like Kartini and Diponegoro. He learned the three 'don'ts' which as president he says are his guiding philosophy —'Don't be easily surprised, don't be overwhelmed by anything, and don't overestimate your own position'.

As a small boy, Suharto was moved among relatives and family friends after his parents divorced. Staying with one of his father's relatives, he cleaned the house before going to school, bought food at the market, sold handicrafts, even sometimes cooked in the afternoons. He tells the story of having to change schools because of a regulation that students wear short pants and shoes, which his parents could not afford. As a child he wore a sarong and went bare-foot. 'I became a worker', he writes, 'someone who could stand on his own feet if necessary. And I knew I could learn many things quickly'.

Unlike Sukarno, who imbibed the sentiments of urban anti-colonialism as a teenager, Suharto seems not to have been caught up in politics at the Muhammadiyah high school in Jogjakarta to which he cycled each day from his village. He writes:

> In Jogja, I heard that protests were being levelled at the colonial government. There were stories about political leaders organizing public meetings. Even at school students talked about the issues that were raised at public meetings. However, I was not impressed by all that talk. I concentrated on my studies and finished school in 1939.

He had difficulty getting a job before being employed briefly as a bank clerk, then joined the army in June 1940, aged nineteen. It was the Dutch army, not the Indonesian army, and Suharto seems to have taken to it with enthusiasm. He became a sergeant before the Japanese invaded, and undertook an officers' training course under the Japanese in 1944. Success in the army seems to have affected him in much the same way as has Colin Powell's success as a black man in the United States army. The army, especially the Dutch army, represented power, authority, status, not to mention a secure wage—all the things which in the poor rural villages of Suharto's boyhood belonged in another world. He frequently acknowledged later the importance of his army training. The army represented efficiency and organization, as well as success and power in the world beyond. The minds of the Dutch and the Japanese were dramatically different from the humanism and mysticism of the rural elders. Although he clung to his original beliefs, Suharto learned as a successful soldier how to deal with the political forces that were shaping the new Indonesia.

The army also provided him with a new family. Observers detect a wistful quality in Suharto's attitude to family matters. In some interpretations he was abandoned as a child, passed from inlaw to inlaw in a state of near, if not actual, poverty. Some say this accounts for his complex emotional attachment to the Habibie family, whom he met while on a posting in Sulawesi, and for his reluctance to rein in his own children. The army was for some years his extended family—as the whole nation is now. In February 1967, when he took the decision to become acting president as the first step in removing Sukarno, it was to a meeting of 500 senior military officers that he first explained his decision before announcing it publicly. He began his own family, after marrying a local girl Siti Hartinah, in 1947; they would have six children, three girls and three boys.

When the Japanese left, Suharto rose quickly in the newly formed Indonesian army. He took part in the 1949 offensive against the Dutch to retake Jogjakarta, and his army career proceeded steadily, without being brilliant. It suffered a setback in 1959 when he lost his command of the Diponegoro division in central Java. He was moved by Nasution as part of an anti-corruption exercise. Many senior officers at this time were engaged in business or took a cut from state corporations. In his detailed study of the army and politics in Indonesia, Harold Crouch notes that Suharto claims that he was moved because he was too 'anti-communist' for Sukarno, but Crouch finds it hard to believe that this would have been the reason for Nasution to act. He notes that several sources stated in interviews that Suharto had been involved in a sugar smuggling scheme. Suharto deals with the incident in his autobiography, in which he describes a sugar/rice barter operation carried out by Indonesian businessman Bob Hasan through Singapore, admitting that it was legally risky but disclaiming any personal benefit. He was sent to the army staff college in Bandung and did well, being promoted to brigadier general and placed in charge of the campaign (code-named Mandala) to wrest West Irian from the Dutch. On his return to Jakarta, he was promoted to major general and given the prestigious command of Kostrad, the army's élite strategic reserve, which is where he was when his career was transformed, literally overnight, in 1965.

Listening to Suharto now, as the wise and experienced leader of his people, one is struck by his certainty. He has the courage to use his own understanding of things, which is a powerful quality in a leader. He listens to others, but his mind is making its own picture of reality and he will act upon it, in his own way and in his own time. He is secretive, and Indonesians who have to deal with him say that in private he is different from his fatherly 'bapak' performance on television. He adopts a poker face, concealing his thoughts and feelings. He gets his information from many sources. If a source becomes known, he ceases to use it. It is unwise to state at the outset of a discussion what one's preferred position is, as he will almost certainly not adopt it. You need to 'guide' him skilfully through several options, and it is useful to know to whom he will turn for advice after you have left the'room.

All politicians are suspicious (as they have good reason to be). But Suharto's wariness is not just politics: it is part of his personality. The three 'don'ts' are a homespun version of the balance between external and internal control which is the essence of Javanese good form, but it is also the strategy of a cautious man. He knows his enemies. He does not confront them. He strikes when they least expect it. His ability to put down rivals is legendary. Take, for example, his comments in his autobiography on Ali Murtopo and Sudjono Humardhani, two generals who were highly influential during the 1970s:

> Some people thought that Ali Murtopo was the man who decided everything. When I was about to take a decision to increase the price of gasoline from four rupiahs to sixteen rupiahs per litre in 1967 or 1968, Ali Murtopo was very upset. He even cried before me when he advised me not to take that decision.'If you do this', he said,'the people will revolt and the government will fall. We want to save you, Pak Harto', he went on. 'If you insist on taking the decision to raise the fuel price, it will destroy the New Order government.' This is what the supposedly rational Ali Murtopo said at the time . . . At that time people were willing to pay twenty five rupiahs for a litre of bottled tea; twenty five rupiahs just for a few sips of tea. So why should they not be willing to pay sixteen rupiahs for a litre of gasoline, which could be enjoyed by so many people on a drive for so many kilometres? Why should we be afraid of a possible revolt? I was quite sure nothing would happen and I did not yield. For the sake of development I decided to raise the gasoline price, contrary to Ali Murtopo's advice. And nothing happened.

Humardhani was the president's economic adviser as Murtopo was his political adviser, and with Murtopo founded the Centre for Strategic and International Studies (CSIS) which was a think-tank for the New Order government in its early years. Of him, Suharto wrote:

> I had heard people say that he knew more about mysticism than I did . . . It is true that Djono used to come to see me with a book full of notes. He believed in spiritual teachings, and in that capacity he often gave me advice. I just listened to make him feel

good, but did not take in everything he said . . . If it was reasonable, if it made sense, I would accept it. If it didn't, I would not follow his advice. So those who thought that Djono was my guru in mysticism had it wrong . . . He would ask me about it, not the other way around. He himself once said, 'I learn from Pak Harto'.

As Sukarno discovered, Suharto's deference conceals a stubborn ego and is itself a perverse kind of authority. Suharto tells of an encounter with Sukarno at the height of the tension following the coup in 1965. At this stage the real power was in Suharto's hands, but Sukarno was still president. Sukarno said to him (in Javanese, which Suharto considered significant), 'Harto, just what are you going to do with me? I am your leader.' Suharto replied, 'Mr President, I come from a poor farming family. But my father always reminded me to respect my elders.' He used two phrases, *mikul dhuwur* (respect for parents) and *mendhem jero* (not to call attention to shortcomings), to which Sukarno nodded approval. 'I have always respected you as I have my parents', said Suharto. 'To me you are not only our national leader, but I consider you as a parent. I'd like to regard you highly, but unfortunately, you do not wish this.'

This is deference inside a ring of steel. The two men were locked in disagreement, especially on the question of banning the PKI. Sukarno regarded the attempted coup as a ripple on the surface of the Indonesian revolution, a foolish escapade, and he refused to issue the order to ban the communists. They would only go underground, he argued, and Indonesia's international reputation would suffer. Suharto saw the coup as an act of treason and infamy. He was morally outraged by it and day after day, week after week, he held out against the president's wishes like a person under orders from a higher authority than either of them. He neither disobeyed nor obeyed his president. He acknowledged Sukarno's position, both as president and as nationalist leader, while insisting that his understanding of the situation they were in as a result of the attempted coup was faulty.

No doubt Suharto was affected by the grisly deaths of his colleagues. He tells how he felt horror and shame after viewing the bodies of his fellow officers recovered from the well at Halim, and then uneasiness when shortly afterwards, at a meeting at the Bogor palace attended by PKI leaders Lukman and Nyoto, Subandrio and others, the atmosphere was 'filled with laughter'. Sukarno did not attend the funeral of the assassinated generals, which deepened Suharto's distrust.

Yet Suharto was a soldier, used to death, and capable of acting with decisive brutality himself. His attitude to Sukarno is consistent with what the scholar Benedict Anderson described as the idea of power in Javanese culture—concrete, homogenous, constant in quantity and morally undifferentiated. Both men had some of that power. Suharto had decided that Sukarno, while not being responsible personally for the coup, had encouraged the communists and would continue to do so. His strategy was to persuade Sukarno that he was mistaken or, if that was not successful, to persuade him to hand over power. Sukarno refused to admit he was mistaken; so he was forced, in a hand-over of power that proceeded in stages and took until March 1968 to complete, to surrender his position.

Suharto later wrote about the period 1965–67: 'If you are too forceful with someone who is out of sorts, he will only become angrier. But if you face him with wisdom and an attitude of respect, he will be subdued.' Sukarno was subdued.

Suharto's ego is not grandiose, demanding to be the centre of attention. Nor does it seem to be an abnormally envious ego which cannot tolerate fame or fortune elsewhere—unless a person is being promoted as a potential rival. A joke doing the rounds in Jakarta in mid-1995 involved his grandson. Asked what he would like to be when he grew up, the boy said, 'President'. 'Ssh', the family around him said, 'keep your voice down'. Some presidential watchers have decided that Suharto's ego is that of a small boy who still needs reassurance and cannot bear to be left out of the action. But as Suharto's stature has grown in the presidency, the voice of the small boy shouting to be heard has taken on the resonance of wisdom and experience.

Suharto is helped by the simplicity of his beliefs. His spiritual beliefs are clear. He believes in a formless God, and is impatient with people who ask 'Where does he live?' and 'What does he look like?' God is Goodness, and everyone should try to control their lives so that they draw as close as they can to God's nature. God sent his prophets, like Muhammad and Jesus Christ, to particular parts of the earth where the people were not living according to his wishes (not to Java, of course) but the message they brought was for all mankind. Everything the president says about religion—and he says a good deal—comes back to the fundamental principle of *Pancasila*, which is that God is the creator of the world and the author of all religions and that religious tolerance is an obligation, indeed a civic duty, of all Indonesians. This is an acute political message in a country like Indonesia, nominally

Muslim but containing strong Hindu, Buddhist and Christian streams and traditions. The president states it, however, as a self-evident spiritual truth.

Similarly, young people should respect their parents and learn from them. Suharto shows none of the Western, especially American, tendency to enlist youthful support by encouraging them to follow their own star. Indeed, at times youthful indiscretion and rebellion seem to Suharto to be uncomfortably close. There are elements of special pleading in this. The electoral system is stacked so heavily in favour of hierachy and authority that the president does not have to seek the youth vote. Also, his accounts of his own family life ring falsely at times.

'I consider "free love" to be wrong', he writes. 'I have been able to control myself in this regard.' Or, 'None of my children has been pampered. Not one. And thank God, so far not one has done anything improper or out-of-bounds of human decency, let alone been influenced by crime or drugs . . . On the contrary, they take a low profile and do not feel or act as if they are the children of a President'. There is an air of piety and rectitude about these pronouncements which is not convincing, especially as the Suharto children's business behaviour has become such an issue. They have also been involved in some human scandals, including drugs. In any case, intelligent political leaders have learned that, on the question of 'family values', it is wise not to cast the first stone.

At times, his explanations are so simple that they are almost simple-minded. In his account of how Indonesia came after the 1971 elections to reduce the number of political parties from nine to two—with a supposedly non-political organization Golongan Karya (Functional Groups—Golkar) which somehow manages nevertheless to win all elections—the president explains:

What, in fact, were our ideals in life? . . . As a nation that believed in the One Almighty God and in the life hereafter, we should be concerned with both worldly matters as well as the hereafter. So the basic question was how could we live harmoniously together as human beings, outwardly and inwardly, materially and spiritually, in this world as well as in the hereafter? If this were our approach, I said, then let's devise a program of action for our life in this world, which also considers our life after death, because the two cannot be separated.

So he proposed two parties—one with a material-spiritual programme and one with a spiritual-material programme. The Christian parties decided to join with the PNI and other nationalist groups in the material-spiritual party, Partai Demokrasi Indonesia (PDI). The Muslim groups formed the Partai Persatuan Pembangunan (PPP) or United Development Party, which would deal with the spiritual side of life (but because Suharto would not allow it, Islam is not mentioned in the party's name).

Suharto lays all this out solemnly in his autobiography. One wonders what the politicians around him made of it. Suharto says that whenever he explained his ideas, he would joke and there would be 'much laughter'. 'Pak Harto has lured us into a fish trap!' But he would explain that, unlike fish in a trap which are taken out and cooked, we were there to 'eat together' and the trap was none other than the *Pancasila* state. Or he would say that there were too many vehicles on the political highway and accidents might happen. His suggestion was for each of them to park his own car and ride in the two or three provided—Golkar, PDI and PPP. Someone said, 'Fine, so we park our own cars and hitch a ride in another. But what about the Armed Forces?' Suharto answered, 'Just let the Armed Forces become the military police and use their own car while regulating the traffic'.

So Indonesia's present political system was devised with much good humour, and harmony between the spiritual and material aspects of life was preserved. Suharto notes that outside the meeting there was heated discussions and lobbying, but inside, consensus ruled. The reader can be forgiven for thinking that before the meeting began the shape of the consensus was already inside Suharto's political brain. Like Sukarno, Indonesia's political leaders were eventually subdued, or perhaps just worn down.

As Indonesians took stock of Suharto's presidency after nearly thirty years, he was widely acknowledged for three achievements. He has presided over an expanding and modernizing economy. Almost from the beginning of his presidency, an unlikely alliance of senior military officers and expert economists held sway in Jakarta. The experts have become less influential and the senior military officers less dedicated, but the results are nevertheless there. Because the Asia-Pacific region has become an economic powerhouse—and has remained peaceful—living standards in Indonesia would probably have improved anyway, but we do not know for sure and, in any case, having presided over the improvement, Suharto is entitled to the credit.

Family planning is the second achievement. Suharto took control personally in 1970, when the two main family planning organizations were merged. He and his wife have been active in the programme, which internationally is regarded as sensible and successful. It is interesting that such a sensitive and contentious policy area is one in which Suharto, a cautious and conservative politician, should have taken a stand. The policy was typically a blend of his own religious instincts (against abortion) and the technical advice of advanced international thinkers, like the head of Unicef, James P. Grant, who stressed improvement of social and economic conditions to reduce child mortality. Economic growth and a hold on surging population numbers have together provided the basis of the success story of the New Order.

And Suharto refashioned Indonesia's foreign policy. Like many newly independent nations, Indonesia had been both insecure and combative, and Sukarno had taken the country to the brink of conflict. Suharto knew that his first priority, economic development, needed political stability, and that political stability within Indonesia depended on conditions within the region. He dismantled 'confrontation' of Malaysia and set Indonesia on a steady course of regional co-operation, both through the agency of the Association of South-East Asian Nations (ASEAN) and later in the wider Asia-Pacific through the forums of Asia-Pacific Economic Cooperation (APEC) and the Asean Regional Forum (ARF).

His personal control of negotiations leading to the security agreement with Australia in December 1995 was typical of his cautious, constructive approach. Australia had shown by the reorganization of its own defence and by its commitment to APEC and ARF that it was no longer an outpost of either British or American interests. It had an obvious interest in security co-operation with Indonesia, but what interest did Indonesia have in security co-operation with Australia? Suharto's thinking, which seems to have surprised all his ministers except State Secretary Mordiono and Minister for Foreign Affairs Ali Alatas, was that the agreement with Australia would complete a circle of co-operative security around Indonesia. The agreement with Australia would, because of Australia's similar agreement with Papua New Guinea and because of Indonesia's existing relations through ASEAN with the ring of states to its west, north and east, put Indonesia at the centre of a benign regional security environment, protecting it from whatever cold winds might blow from the north.

Always in the international headlines during Sukarno's time, Indonesia since Suharto became president has been subdued and conciliatory on international issues. Even on such difficult questions as East Timor, when Indonesia has had to withstand severe international criticism, Jakarta has kept the level of disputation as low and as diffuse as it could, within the bounds of maintaining sovereignty.

CHAPTER FOUR

Politics

INDONESIANS, who are among the most syncretic, flexible people in the world, have absorbed into their political system a little of everything while retaining something which is unmistakably Indonesian.

Politics in Indonesia followed a post-colonial pattern. In half a century or so of hectic liberation from various forms of colonial control, a variety of governments emerged on the world scene. Having gained the freedom of the nation, the nationalists usually sought political freedom also, choosing a form of democracy, but concessions to the demands of nation-building often proved too much for democracy. Some became democracies, like India. Some were communist states, like Vietnam. Many were single-party states or military regimes. Indonesia became a three-party state in which the government party, backed by the military, always won elections—and always reappointed the president.

In the 1950s Indonesia tried genuine multi-party parliamentary democracy, which was discarded by Sukarno for what was called 'guided democracy' after a succession of unstable governments. The pattern set by Sukarno has been followed by its second president, Suharto—strong leadership, in the form of the presidency, and a controlled system of representative government based on traditional, indigenous ideas of consultation, discussion and unanimous decision-making. Under Sukarno, the military, although powerful, was deliberately held in check by the president. Under Suharto, the military has become pervasive. It reaches into every aspect of Indonesian life as the guardian of national security and the protector of the new Indonesian national identity. Occasionally, the president himself has become concerned over the power of the military and checked it, but he can do this only by becoming more powerful himself.

Democracy has not been discarded in contemporary Indonesia, but it has been so tamed that its vital spark has gone. Its formalities—like elections and legislative assemblies—have been adopted, but they have no life of their own. They sustain a system that has become centralized, arbitary and increasingly personal to the president, with the military hovering in the background as a kind of secret police. Indonesian elections are a foregone conclusion. The only uncertainty about the result is whether Golkar's winning vote has gone up or down. The People's Representative Council (Dewan Perwakilan Rakyat—DPR) has no substantial political role. In theory it can initiate legislation, but has never done so.

Indonesia is not a dictatorship in a legal sense, but the law is uncommonly restrictive and alternatives to what the president wants, or the authorities think he wants, are not widely known, because the process of public debate is constrained by fear of the consequences of stepping out of line. It is sometimes done, but only at personal risk. Opportunities for 'openness' arise mainly when there is a rift between the president and the military, which is less a recipe for transparency than for instability.

In keeping a closer watch on political activity than in Sukarno's time, the authorities draw also on colonial experience. Any gathering of more than five people must have a permit. In mid-1995 several seemingly innocuous discussion groups were broken up by the police, including one in which the speaker, an American academic specialist on Islam, Robert Hefner, was interrogated for several hours. Also the government has a blacklist of people whom it prevents from travelling abroad and from speaking and writing on political matters. While no-one seems sure of the source of this authority, it is constantly in use. The government also takes political activists to court. Following the banning in 1994 of three news magazines, the Asosiasi Journalis Independen (Association of Independent Journalists—AJI) was formed as a protest against the timidity of the official journalists' association. The group behind the AJI was declared an unlawful organization and charged with various consequential offences.

Adnan Buyung Nasution has conducted a sustained campaign for human rights in Indonesia. He was one of the founders in 1969 of the Indonesian Legal Aid Foundation (Yayasan Lembaga Bantuan Hukum Indonesia—YLBHI) and was jailed for two years in 1972. Still active, he sees promise in the courts being open to two-way traffic, although obviously the flow is not the same both ways. Goenawan Mohamad, the former editor-in-chief and columnist of one of the banned magazines, *Tempo*, took the government to court, claiming that the withdrawal of the licence to publish was illegal; he has been successful in the tribunal system set up to test administrative decisions, although the government could appeal to a higher court.

Freedom House, the American organization which monitors political rights and civil liberties around the world, has three main categories—Free, Partly Free and Not Free. Freedom is difficult to quantify and needs time to practise, as the Americans have themselves discovered, but the Freedom House categories are a rough-and-ready guide to the state of democracy around the world. Indonesia is Not Free (like Brunei, while Indonesian neighbours Thailand, Malaysia, Singapore and the Philippines are Partly Free). Moreover, the annual survey by Freedom House for 1994–95 shows a decline in freedom in Indonesia, due mainly to strong-arm enforcement in East Timor, Irian Jaya and Aceh, labour riots and the suppression of three news magazines.

In fifty years of independence, the identification of the political leadership with the people has inevitably changed. The instinctive emotional unity of the people and the nationalist leaders against the Dutch overlord was quickly lost, but something was retained by Sukarno in his campaign against the new colonialists of the Cold War period. Under Suharto there was for a time a bonding of leaders and people in the task of getting the economy on its feet. This done, and as Suharto's presidency inevitably nears its end, the system has come under strain. Disappointed expectations, corruption and nepotism in the scramble for the spoils of success, racial and religious tension under the surface, restive workers and the dashed hopes of the middle class for a more open political system were some symptoms.

The politics of discontent and resentment were widespread, not just in Indonesia, perhaps reflecting that curious phenomenon *fin de siècle*, explicable only by the fact that the century one has lived in is ending. They have gathered pace in Western countries, especially in the United States, although there they are the politics of individualism, suspicion of government and an emphasis on rights rather than duties. In Indonesia, alienation is not resentment of power as such. It is resentment that the power is not being used wisely.

In one respect Indonesia shares the politics of resentment with several other countries—a mounting concern over corruption in high places. Political leaders and their families and associates in countries as disparate as the United States, Italy, Mexico, Philippines, India, Japan, China, Taiwan and South Korea defended themselves in the 1990s against a diverse array of corruption charges. It is a reflection partly of the rise of economic issues to the top of the international agenda and the triumph—and elusive nature—of the private sector. Corruption in Indonesia has often been treated as a disguised form of social wage, like tipping, necessary in order to grease the cogs of the economy and keep it turning smoothly. This kind of corruption is so small and widespread that it is not corruption at all, it can be argued. Also, Suharto seems to regard it as his patrimonial right, indeed his duty, to distribute the spoils of office to those on whom he can rely for support, which includes his family and its business associates. He is not alone among the world's political leaders in that. The problem lies in the fact that the kind of corruption now discussed in Indonesia is not at the small and universal end of the scale, but at the large and exceptional end, at the level of the Pertamina scandals of the 1970s, involving amounts so big and sectors so important that, if true, the corruption has become dysfunctional. The issues revolved around members of the president's family and their close business associates and the effect their remarkable success was having on the climate of economic reform and business efficiency in Indonesia.

This has exposed the lack of institutional restraint on power in Indonesia. It was always thus. This comment (in Chapter 9) was made thirty years ago on the Sukarno regime:

> What worries me . . . is that there is no structure of restraint. Take the US president, for example, perhaps the most powerful, single political leader in the world. He is surrounded by a framework of critical restraint—press, pulpit, opposition parties, and a whole public philosophy to which his critics and advisers can refer in restraining or urging him. Even in communist countries, where power is more naked, there is a sufficient structure of restraint in Marxism-Leninism, which can be refined and revised . . . Here, in Indonesia, we have no such restraints by which the satisfaction of power can be controlled. Everything—education, law, even religion—can be used in Indonesia to sanctify power.

Suharto, like Sukarno, has made much of indigenous Indonesian, especially Javanese, political ideas to combat the liberal democratic values of the West. However, there are democratic as well as anti-democratic elements in Javanese culture, as there are in Islam. It depends how democracy is defined, and on political will. What is obviously not democratic is Suharto's particular view of politics, in which dissent is seen as disloyalty to Indonesia and a real political contest becomes a threat to the stability of the state. What is anti-democratic is the military's inclination to shoot first and ask questions afterwards. Crude answers to complex problems of stability, slackening economic reform and a lazy, authoritarian attitude to democracy have become the marks of Suharto's later leadership. Indonesia is thus at a crucial stage of its political development. If it is to hold on to a system which subdues the vitality of the people's voice in favour of the stability of a military-authoritarian regime, the regime will need to manage successfully the transition from Suharto to a new leader. But one of the issues in that succession is democracy itself; whether the people, through the electoral process, will have a say in choosing the candidates for the presidency.

While Suharto remains president without an apparent successor, the political culture is trapped in a contradiction. It cannot manage Indonesian politics without Suharto, yet it needs a new leader to take it forward. It cannot manage Indonesia without a Javanese-style king as its ruler, yet it cannot join the modern world with one. Some people are reassured by Suharto's presence and the prospect that he will remain at the helm for some time. But other people (and sometimes the same people) are anxious about the future because the succession is not clear. If the succession after Suharto is orderly, which in practical terms means the vice-president Try Sutrisno becoming president, the system, which has evolved through Sukarno's 'guided democracy' and Suharto's disciplined 'new order', will remain essentially the same, especially its military component. If the succession is dramatic, changes could well result—but they could bring less rather than more democracy, less rather than more accountability.

In the early 1990s an impression of mounting change gained pace in Indonesia as elsewhere, but it faded. It faded because the authorities and the president particularly became concerned at a loss of control. Events seemed to be getting out of hand, as evident from the Dili massacre in 1991, signs of social and intellectual rebelliousness, indifference and sometimes independence in the media to the interests of the government. Adam Schwarz writes:

On a trip through Central and East Java in 1992, many Indonesians I met spilled over with frustration and anger in contesting the power of government. The grievances varied—from inadequate compensation for appropriated land, to the business advantages given to relatives and friends of local bureaucrats, to low wages, to the cost of subsidising Suharto family monopolies on the distribution of cloves and television licences—but the underlying theme was the same: the fear that any complaints by *orang kecil*, the little people, would be met with military intimidation or arrest. In a typical comment, one farmer in East Java resignedly told me: 'If I say anything they will just call me a communist.'

The president moved to close down the 'openness' that was beginning to glimmer in Indonesian politics, because such resentments had become widespread and alarming. He has contrived such a finely balanced and tightly structured form of government, with himself at the centre, that any crack in the system, no matter how small, threatens the whole.

There are now two views among those Jakarta political insiders who otherwise agree that it is in the nation's interest for the president to prepare to step down and not to seek another five-year term (which would be his seventh). One view is that the president should be made to feel secure, so that he does not feel the need to seek re-election. The other is that he should be presented with an agreed successor, as he was presented with a vice-president he did not want in 1993, or that there should be several candidates for the presidency, requiring a vote, which was almost what happened for the vice-presidency in 1988.

The first group is essentially military, and would want Suharto to be succeeded by the present vice-president, Try Sutrisno, former army chief of staff and armed forces commander. Their thinking is that the president has to be reassured about national security issues, including regional security, as well as the future of his children in business, before being willing to step down. Some high ranking officers are said to have agreed for this reason to the security agreement with Australia, although they regarded it as compromising Indonesia's traditional non-aligned stance. The second group is more concerned to strengthen democracy within the Indonesian political system, which they see as hamstrung by the pervasive idea of 'consensus'. They want to encour-

age the belief that variety is healthy, that dissent from political authority is not disloyalty to Indonesia, and some of them believe that the
military should get out of government and return to barracks. While
they have some support within the armed forces, they would obviously
prefer a civilian to succeed Suharto. Their difficulty would be in finding a candidate on whom they can agree.

One group taking this position was within ICMI (Ikatan Cendekiawan Moslem se Indonesia—Indonesian Association of Muslim Intellectuals), whose candidate would presumably be the Minister for
Science and Technology Dr Bacharuddin Jusuf Habibie. Habibie is a
clever, energetic minister, and he has an unusually close relationship
with Suharto, but he lacks the kind of presence most Indonesians feel
the presidential office requires. He is the quintessential boffin or
'backroom boy'. On economic policy, he is sympathetic to state intervention and big projects rather than market forces and small industry
as a way of maintaining the momentum of Indonesia's national development, which has brought him into conflict with the technocrats and
the finance ministry. He is distrusted within senior ranks of the military. Educated in Germany, where he began his career in engineering,
he stands out from the Indonesian political scene as a modern innovator, who has given Indonesia the beginnings of an aircraft construction industry. Perhaps his most controversial project is for nuclear
power stations on volcanic Java. His purchase of virtually the entire
east German navy was opposed in the finance ministry: it was the sur-
facing of that issue in the weekly news magazine *Tempo* that caused its
closure.

Habibie has loyally and visibly supported the president, whatever
he chose to do. Another civilian sometimes mentioned is the National
Planning Minister, Ginanjar Kartasasmita, who has wisely kept his
ambitions to himself. The president's oldest daughter Hardijanti
Rukmana (Tutut) and his son-in-law Prabowo Subianto are also on
the gossip list. President Suharto remained inscrutable. Politics in
Indonesia, as elsewhere, is, like love and war, not for those with generous temperaments, transparent motives or a weakness for self-denial.

In pre-dawn raids on 1 October 1965, six Indonesian army generals
were taken from their homes by soldiers from the palace guard and
killed. Their bodies were dumped into an unused well at the edge of
the Halim air force base outside Jakarta. The six generals represented

the army's top echelon, including its commander, Lieutenant General Achmad Yani. The nation's leading soldier, General Nasution, who was defence minister, was meant to be included, but he escaped over the wall into the garden of the Iraqi ambassador next door. (His five-year-old daughter was mortally wounded and an aide, a lieutenant, was abducted instead of Nasution, and later killed.)

This bald account can be almost endlessly elaborated and refined, but its essentials provide the moment which divides the political history of Indonesia after independence between the Sukarno and Suharto eras.

Even today, argument persists over the nature of the Thirtieth of September Movement. It exposed factions and personal rivalry within the armed forces. The air force commander, Air Marshal Omar Dhani, was prominent in his support. It exposed naivete and opportunism among the communists. Several low-level emissaries of Aidit, the leader of the Indonesian Communist Party (Partai Kommunist Indonesia—PKI) scurried back and forth among the plotters.

Ganis Harsono, who was a deputy foreign minister under Subandrio and who spent nearly eight years in custody (1966–1974) as a result, had some special insights and knowledge. In his book *Recollections of an Indonesian Diplomat in the Sukarno Era* he documented mounting tension between Aidit and Sukarno, culminating in a showdown on the evening of 28 September 1965, two nights before the coup, during a communist student rally at the Istora Sport Palace. The rally called for the government to ban the Islamic students' union Himpunan Mahasiswa Islam (HMI), which Sukarno would not do. According to Harsono, Aidit spoke wildly and personally about Sukarno, who was present, warning the students against fake leaders who appropriated public funds and had several wives. By this stage, according to Ganis Harsono, Sukarno was openly favouring Nyoto, third in the communist hierachy, over the leader, Aidit.

Josef Ishak, a journalist of the Sukarno era and publisher of Pramoedya's novels, who was also detained after the coup, now says the evidence points to Aidit as the architect and the PKI's Special Bureau (Biro Khusus) as the instrument. He points to a mysterious communist called Sjam (whose real name was Kamarusaman Bin Ahmad Mubaidah, born in 1920) as the central figure in the Special Bureau, which was a secret organization under Aidit's control, set up to infiltrate the armed forces. Sjam went underground after the coup, was captured in 1967, served as a key state witness in the trials of the coup leaders and was himself executed in 1986 for his part in the coup. An underground figure, his political history is obscure and Ishak speculates that he might have been a double agent. But he provided the authorities with a clear connection between Aidit and the coup leaders.

But if there is still argument about the coup, especially over the role of the PKI, there is no argument over the result: as an attempted coup, or half-coup (as it was directed against the army leadership rather than the state) it was a fiasco, and its failure closed off an era in Indonesian history.

On the news the morning after the coup, it was announced that the 'Thirtieth of September Movement', led by a Lieutenant Colonel Untung, a battalion commander from the president's palace guard, had acted to forestall a coup against President Sukarno by a 'Council of Generals', sponsored by the American Central Intelligence Agency (CIA). The president was safe, it was announced, under the protection of a Revolutionary Council, which would continue his 'active and independent' foreign policy.

Later that day other decisions were announced, including membership of the Revolutionary Council. Its forty-five members included two of the three deputy prime ministers (Subandrio and Leimena), the commanders of the air force, navy and police, as well as lower-ranking army officers and representatives of all the main political parties. Its chairman was the hitherto unnoticed Untung, who may have been personally responsible for another decision announced that day—that all military ranks above his own had been abolished. Also, non-commissioned officers and privates who joined the movement were promised promotion.

The most important general not on the list of those to be abducted (at his trial, Untung denied he intended to kill the generals—the soldiers had panicked, he claimed, when the generals resisted) was Major General Suharto. His exception gave rise over the years to the suspicion that he might have expected to benefit from the coup. He seems to have known some of the plotters and had been present the year before at Untung's wedding. However, the fact is that Suharto acted decisively against the coup leaders, whereas his superior, Nasution, prevaricated. As soon as he learned of the deaths of his colleagues, Suharto took over effective leadership of the army, refusing to acknowledge Sukarno's appointee, Pranoto Reksosamudro. Without a shot being fired he won over two key battalions which had been stationed in Merdeka Square, controlling the palace and the adjoining radio station and telecommunications centre; he publicly announced that he intended to crush the coup and set about organizing an attack on its headquarters at Halim air force base. Sukarno retreated to his palace at Bogor and the coup, lacking his support, collapsed.

Suharto's decisiveness broke the nexus that had governed Indonesian politics since the collapse of parliamentary democracy. The PKI needed Sukarno to keep the army from its throat and Sukarno needed the PKI to maintain his revolutionary spirit. Sukarno needed the army to keep the new nation of Indonesia intact and the army needed Sukarno to apply the brakes on populist democracy, in which the PKI might prosper. The most vulnerable factor in this neat balance of interests was the army's need of Sukarno, which owed something to Nasution's personal sense of propriety. The coup exposed this weakness and thrust an army leader into the presidential office, destroying the PKI.

The People's Consultative Assembly (Majelis Perwakilan Rakyat —MPR), purged of its communist members, ratified the moves against Sukarno. It deprived him of his life-time presidency, dismissed his supporters and promised elections. Sukarno made an emotional defence of his policies, urging national self-reliance and warning against foreign aid; his address was received in silence. General Nasution, who had been active in the army's campaign against the communists and was subsequently dismissed as minister for defence by Sukarno, was elected chairman (a post formerly held by Chairul Saleh). The MPR confirmed Suharto as executive head of government.

It took Suharto about eighteen months to get rid of Sukarno. It was done with great politeness, as befitting a subordinate who with a sense of Javanese propriety would not humiliate an elder, and with great ruthlessness, as befitting a rival who knew that power had passed to him. Essentially, Suharto loyalists in the army did his work for him. When they encountered resistance, they adopted the simple expedient of arresting whoever stood in the way. Eventually, Sukarno found himself confined to his palaces; slowly it became apparent that he was in fact under house arrest. Announcements were made that he was not entitled to use the title of commander-in-chief of the armed forces, nor use the presidential flag. His photographs disappeared from government offices. He was not permitted to use the title of president, although it was not for another year—in March 1968—that Suharto was formally appointed his successsor.

Why, then, did the PKI act to break an arrangement that seemed to serve it well? The foolishness was so patent—and the attempted coup itself so inept—that some observers could not believe that the PKI had had anything to do with it. The PKI seemed to have accepted the Sukarno regime as the most tolerant any communist party in Indonesia was likely to get. It could not seize power without the arms to withstand the army in a civil war, surrounded as it was by anti-communist neighbours like Australia, Malaysia and the Philippines, who were perhaps only too anxious to support breakaway govern-ments in Sumatra, Sulawesi, the Moluccas or West Irian. On this reck-oning it was more profitable for the PKI to expand its influence slowly and unobtrusively through official channels. Given legitimacy by the president, it could build its power in the country at large in prepara-tion for Sukarno's death or disablement.

The degree of PKI planning and participation in the abortive coup is still debated. It is clear that the PKI did not plan and execute the event as a revolutionary *coup d'état*. Only a very few PKI leaders seem to have been aware of it and the rank-and-file knew nothing until they heard the news on the radio. None of the resources of the PKI, es-pecially its mass organization, were used. On the other hand, the PKI gave support to the coup, notably in an editorial in its party newspaper, *Harian Rakyat*, on 2 October, describing the 'September 30 Move-ment' as 'patriotic and revolutionary'. The editorial also described it as 'an internal army affair'. This suggests that the PKI did not see Untung as the leader of a *coup d'état*, but as a potential army leader who might be sympathetic to the PKI. The coup, in other words, was not directed at the state but at the anti-communist army leadership. In Untung's first statement on the morning of 1 October, he described his movement as 'solely within the army' directed at the so-called 'council of generals' which was supposed to be plotting Sukarno's overthrow. But he then went on to set up a Revolutionary Council—of mixed civilian and military, and almost all shades of politics—and spoke of corruption and the need for general elections. All enlisted men who supported him would immediately be promoted one grade; those who took a direct part in the 'purge' on 30 September would be promoted two grades. The style was reminiscent of another colonel, Nasser, and a Laotian captain, Kong Le, who led coups of lasting political significance.

Nor was Sukarno's own role immediately clear. Did he encourage Untung, believing the story of the generals' plot against him? There seems little doubt that he knew of the plan to remove the generals, but at what stage and in how much detail? The uncertainty concerning the motives and many of the actions of the major participants has encouraged speculation. A plausible version is that the coup was another clever manoeuvre in the hothouse of Jakarta politics. Both Sukarno and Aidit knew of Untung's intentions and both went along with him. Each stood to gain from a change of army leadership, but neither could openly support a coup until it was seen to be successful. (Observers have been puzzled by the absence of Sukarno's name from the list of Untung's Revolutionary Council. It is hard to believe that the exclusion was made on Untung's initiative.)

Had the coup succeeded, the alignment of forces post-Sukarno would have changed in the PKI's favour. It would not have been faced by an anti-communist army leadership. The party might also have expected to have been rewarded politically by the president for its patriotic support of Untung's movement, perhaps in the form of the long-awaited Nasakom cabinet. If 30 September is seen not as a *coup d'état* but as a half-coup designed to break the anti-communist leadership of the army, the long-term advantages to the PKI, without loss of the immediate benefits of Sukarnoism, become clearer. The Special Bureau looks like a classic communist exercise—secret members designated to infiltrate the armed forces, under the direct control of the leader operating outside the party organization. Then, as now, the Indonesian armed forces, especially the army, was rife with factionalism, creating a micro-world of politics. In the feverish atmosphere of Jakarta at the height of the Cold War, a half-coup designed to change the army leadership on the pretext that it was planning a real coup with American support might have seemed a smart ploy to Aidit, a useful opening to a leftist colonel like Untung and a necessary step to Sukarno.

Unlike their action at Madium in 1948, the PKI did not fight this time. Aidit went quickly to central Java, leaving Lukman and Nyoto to watch developments in the capital. The PKI leaders evidently believed that Sukarno would be able to hold the balance; Aidit advised his followers against resistance. But on 4 October a joint statement by Muslim and Christian organizations for the first time blamed the PKI for 'masterminding' the coup and called on the president to ban the party and its mass organizations. In the weeks and months that followed, it seemed that Sukarno had decided that the PKI had over-reached itself and needed to be checked. PKI members and sympathizers were hunted down by the army and by mobs throughout Indonesia. By

December a fact-finding committee established that 87 000 had been killed, but this was a conservative figure. Sporadic killing went on into 1966 and observers put the number of dead as high as 200 000 or 300 000; some put it much higher. In addition, a wave of anti-communism swept Indonesia. The party and its affiliates were banned and its membership of all instrumentalities of government suspended. Thousands of PKI members and sympathisers were arrested or detained. Its leaders were all killed, arrested or in hiding. Aidit and Lukman were among the dead, as were many other PKI leaders.

Whatever the PKI's role in the coup, the effect on its fortunes was more devastating even than Madiun. President Sukarno had said, 'You can't abolish Marxism', but it was evident that as a party the PKI would not be a force again in Indonesian politics for many years, if ever.

Moreover, the crushing of the PKI established the credentials of the new men in power in Jakarta and what was to become President Suharto's New Order. It enabled Suharto to start afresh. Although it is never possible to break entirely with the past, especially in a country with such an intimate sense of history as Indonesia, he needed to sever the intricate balance of forces that had hamstrung Sukarno and he did this by shifting power decisively to the state, including the armed forces. The crushing of the PKI was also a warning to any successor to the PKI wishing to challenge the supremacy of the new élite that it would have to reckon with the use of massive force against it.

The history of the PKI is a story of frustration and a corrective to the view that populist or utopian politics are irresistible in countries with many mouths to feed. Except where it gained power by arms, as in China, communism had little success in Asia in the years of colonialism's retreat. Only in Vietnam did the departing colonialists trade national sovereignty with the communists. In the rest of Asia, nationalists moved into the vacant seats of power, as happened in Indonesia.

Over the years of the Cold War, Moscow and Peking created a bewildering assortment of theories to assist local communists to deal with the phenomenon of bourgeois Asian nationalism. In the 'two-camp' doctrine of 1947, Moscow called on the Asian nationalist leaders to take sides—to declare for the communist camp or be declared lackeys of the imperialist camp, led by the United States. Another theory was that of 'national democracy', adopted by a conference of eighty-one communist parties in Moscow in November 1960. This new term was created to satisfy both the Russians, who did not want to lose their good relations with such leaders as Nasser, Nehru and Sukarno, and the

Chinese, who wanted something stronger than the diplomatic wooing of the non-committed nations that had become standard Soviet practice after Stalin's death. A 'national democracy' was the communist model for a transitional form of government between bourgeois nationalism and communism. In essence, it meant a government which allowed freedom of action to local communists and gave them some say in determining policy, which rejected military relations with the West, accepted aid from the communist bloc and worked for social and economic reform, especially land reform.

The PKI worked hard to bring Sukarno's Indonesia towards this model. Sukarno responded, apparently believing that the split between Peking and Moscow would enable the PKI to operate as a truly Indonesian party. Formed in 1920, it was the oldest communist party in Asia and the biggest outside the Soviet Union and China. By 1965 its membership was three million. It had penetrated the apparatus of government in great detail, except for the inner cabinet. It controlled the biggest trade union organization, the Central All-Indonesian Workers' Organization (Sentral Organisasi Buruh Seluru Indonesia—SOBSI), and the largest peasants' group, the Indonesian Peasant Front (Barisan Tani Indonesia—BTI), and had influence in the major mass organization, the National Front. The membership of its affiliates was between fifteen and twenty million. Moreover, the foreign policy of the Indonesian government, especially after 1963, moved Indonesia closer to Peking and farther from Washington than the republic had ever been. In domestic affairs, however, especially social and economic reform, the PKI remained dissatisfied with Sukarno's grandiose blueprints. It wanted closer control of the administration of policy. It pressed also for the workers and peasants to be armed in self-defence units. The pressure increased during 1965 amid other signs that tension between the PKI and the army was sharpening.

An Indonesian folk-song, written at another time of national emergency in the nineteenth century, summed up the PKI's dilemma under Sukarno:

> *We have lived to see a time without order*
> *In which everyone is confused in his mind*
> *One cannot bear to join in the madness*
> *But if he does not do so*
> *He will not share in the spoils*
> *And will starve as a result.*

When the Cold War collapsed in 1989, it became difficult to maintain that communism was still a residual threat to either the internal or external security of Indonesia. Some signs of relaxation became apparent. After nearly thirty years in detention, Subandrio and Omar Dhani were released (although shortly afterwards two lesser known detainees were executed). The offensive letters 'ET' (Ex-Tahanan Politik—former political prisoner) were removed from identification tags, although not from police records. But some Indonesians in positions of authority continued to see the PKI (or if not the PKI, communism, or if not communism, non-specific forms of dissent and criticism, described as 'formless organizations') as a threat to the good government, welfare and prosperity of the Indonesian people. They maintained that communism was still alive and well in Asia (China, Vietnam, North Korea) and, as communists and ex-communists made a political come-back in elections in Poland and in Russia in 1995, they became more assertive.

Originally formed in 1962 by the military to oppose the PKI, Golkar (Golongan Karya—Functional Groups) is now the official civilian party, to which all civil servants must belong. It is is officially designated as a functional group or community organization, not a political party, which gives it advantages over its rivals. These include additional funding and the ability to campaign widely—in the countryside as well as in the towns, to which the political parties are limited. Its titular head is the Minister for Information, Harmoko, and one of its four executive directors is the president's daughter, Siti Hardijanti (Tutut). Both the State Minister for Research and Technology, Dr B. J. Habibie and the president's son-in-law, General Prabowo Subianto, are influential in Golkar.

Partai Demokrasi Indonesia (Indonesian Democratic Party—PDI) was created by a forced presidential merger in 1973 of five parties considered 'nationalist' in character—the PNI, Sukarno's original party; IPKI (in which Nasution had been active); Murba (Adam Malik and Chairul Saleh were leaders) and the Protestant and Catholic parties, Parkindo and Partai Katolik. Also formed under presidential pressure after the 1971 elections was Partai Persatuan Penganunan (Development Union Party—PPP) comprising Muslim groups, Nahdatul Ulama, the scholarly and orthodox Islamic organization, which later withdrew; PSSI (successor to Sarekat Islam); Parmusi (replacement for the modernist ideas of Masjumi); and Perti (a social welfare group originally from Sumatra).

These political groupings are not only disadvantaged by official favouritism of Golkar. Government and army persistently intervene in the affairs of PDI and PPP, whether on behalf of the Suharto government or of Golkar is hard to determine technically but the distinction is probably unimportant. Interference is clearly intended to favour some persons and groups against others and it is present at all levels of the political process. Electioneering in Indonesia is restricted by the fact that members of parliament do not represent actual constituencies. At election time, a slate of candidates is presented to the authorities before voting takes place. These authorities, headed by State Secretary Mordiono, can rearrange the order of precedence of the party's slate of candidates, effectively excluding some by placing them low on the list. If elected, they become members of parliament but not representatives of particular constituencies, so that the link between the people and the legislature is not strong and intimate as it is in a democracy. Members of parliament are always vulnerable to official persuasion, not to mention corruption, because they depend on government approval.

Election results (expressed as a percentage of the vote) show the dominance of Golkar in New Order politics.

	1971	1977	1982	1987	1992
Golkar	63.2	62.1	64.3	73.2	68.1
PPP	27.3	29.3	27.8	16.0	17.0
PDI	9.5	8.6	7.9	10.9	14.9

(The 1971 elections were contested before the merger of parties, so the figures show the combined results of the four parties which became the PPP and the three which became the PDI.)

General elections are held every five years in the year preceding the election of the president. Election of the president and vice-president is formally the responsibility of the People's Consultative Assembly (Majelis Permusyawaratan Rakyat—MPR) which has 1000 members—half from the House of People's Representatives (Dewan Perwakilan Rakyat—DPR) and half appointed by the president, according to the results of the general elections the year before and including representatives from the regions, appointed by the governors. The DPR, which is the nation's parliament, has 500 members, 425 of whom are elected at the general elections and 75 (reduced from 100 in 1995) appointed by the president from the military, who are not permitted to vote at elections. Only the three authorised political groupings contest the 425 seats—Golkar, PPP and PDI.

In Sukarno's time, it was the communists (PKI) which laid a claim to being the party of the people and it was the military which kept an eye on them, suspecting that their notion of how to represent the people of Indonesia was not in the best interests of the Indonesian state, as the military leaders saw them. In Suharto's time, it is the Muslims, with their passion for justice and equality, who come under the watchful eyes of the military. The resentment felt by the '*marhaen*' or little people in Sukarno's day because the promised new bright day never dawned is now felt by workers struggling to survive on no more than an Australian dollar or two a day, while the president's family grows insatiably rich and the families of those with government connections become wealthy and secure.

It is remarkable that Islam has not become a political force in Indonesia. Like communism, its history in Indonesia is a study in frustration. During the Dutch colonial period, Islam was understandably suppressed, but it was also jostled out of the main game after independence by both the PNI and the PKI, not to mention the army. Sukarno's Nasakom concept did include *agama* (religion) but it was the balance between the nationalists and the communists that caught everyone's attention and the stand-off between the army and the communists which preoccupied Sukarno. Islam was given a political role in the New Order in the form of the PPP, but without any prospect of breaking Golkar's grip on government or having an influence on the way national development was being undertaken, PPP has declined in electoral importance, while PDI, operating under the same constraints, has improved its position. Yet Islam continues to be an important influence in the lives of ordinary Indonesians. Indeed, its influence has probably recently increased, reflecting both the rise of Islam abroad after the oil-price hikes of the 1970s, and the traditional ethical and nationalist concerns of Muslims in Indonesia about some of the symptoms of rapid economic growth—corruption, high living in Jakarta, Chinese dominance of the big conglomerates, for example. It is not surprising, then, that the most interesting developments in Islamic politics have not been within the PPP, but outside the electoral system—the Council of Muslim Scholars (Nahdatul Ulama—NU) which withdrew from the PPP in 1984 and under the leadership of Abdurrahman Wahid since has been critical of the Suharto government, and the Association of Indonesian Muslim Intellectuals (Ikatan Cendekiawan Muslim Indonesia—ICMI) which was established in 1990, as an adjunct to government under Habibie's leadership and as a rival think-tank to the Christian, ethnic Chinese and American-influenced CSIS.

The relative failure of Islam as a political force in Indonesia is usually attributed to the division between 'abangan' (or nominal) and 'santri' (or devout) Muslims. That 90 per cent of Indonesians are Muslim is one of those statistical facts that have little meaning, because the majority are 'statistical Muslims' only. Islam as a political force has thus always had in Indonesia the contradictory quality of a minority movement. Almost everyone pays homage to it and historically it was the first unifying force of nationalism against the Dutch, but when it comes to the political crunch it is treated with suspicion.

'Co-optation' was a technique of the Dutch, as it was for other imperialists, and they brought into the colonial administrative service the priyayi élite and the abangan court culture and its followers, which pushed the santris into radical opposition. Since independence, and under two seemingly different presidents, the struggle between abangan and santri has continued, with the former on top. In Sukarno's day, both the PKI and the PNI drew on abangan support, and many accounts of the killings of 1965–66 depict the aggressors as santris in the grip of moral anger (including anger over land reform). Many Indonesians expected the post-Sukarno period to be more sympathetic to Islam, but Suharto, even more than Sukarno, adopted the style and authority of the pre-Islamic Javanese aristocracy. Ruth McVey described the New Order in 1985 as 'a rich mixture of western consumptionism, abangan mysticism, damn-the-public capitalism, technocratic elitism and bureaucratic politics. Culturally, politically and economically, the New Order élite is considerably more distant from the mass of population than were its indigenous predecessors'. Suharto seems to have realized that the forces which destroyed the PKI could also destroy the New Order. Islam was safely packaged in the PPP, which was not allowed to call itself Islamic, and neutralized in the Pancasila, in which Islam was only one of five recognized religions and Indonesia was designated a secular state.

It is against this background that ICMI and NU have become rival forces of contemporary Islamic politics. Each has leaders—

Abdurrahman Wahid and Bacharuddin Jusuf Habibie—who are, to say the least of them, unconventional. Each represents a major departure, suggesting that the containment of Islam by the Indonesian political system had been effective, but was either ending or needed a new approach.

Founded in 1926 to counter modernism and to defend the interests of orthodox Muslims, NU was a political rival of Masjumi in the early days of the republic. Its base is east Java, although it has spread to the outer islands, especially Kalimantan, with a programme of social welfare, education and small business. In the *santri* tradition, it works from the local *pesantren* (Muslim school), but since Abdurrahman Wahid became chairman it has developed a following in the towns and cities also. A buoyant, idiosyncratic personality, Wahid has created more controversy lately than any public figure. He has been sharply critical of Suharto for holding on to power, ardent about democracy (he formed Democracy Forum in 1991), fulsome about *Pancasila*, friendly with some army leaders, contemptuous of ICMI. He even negotiated a community bank for rural areas which charged interest and whose partner was an ethnic Chinese and a Christian. In the *Monitor* case in 1990, when the Christian editor of the tabloid published a popularity poll of his readers in which the Prophet Muhammad came a disappointing eleventh, Wahid denounced the Muslim activists who demanded the editor's removal (who was gaoled for five years). With so many adversaries, inside and outside NU, Wahid has led a charmed life. Part of his strength is his family history. His grandfather was one of the founders of NU and his father a respected leader. With his wit and charm, Wahid runs the risk of being only controversial, but he also has a serious core of purpose, which is to strengthen the capacity of ordinary Muslim people, ordinary Indonesians, to live in the real world, inside and outside Indonesia. This social and educational purpose has given NU a massive following, claimed to be as high as thirty million.

ICMI has been just as controversial, although it works in the opposite direction. Its strength is its association with government; its weakness is the suspicion that it is run by opportunists who profess to be serious about Islam because that is the flavour of the moment. So an established Christian newspaper like *Kompas* is deliberately offset with *Republika*, CSIS with the Centre for Information and Development Studies—CIDES. The impression a visitor gained on a visit in 1995 to ICMI headquarters and CIDES was of a hive of excited industry, somewhat like its illustrious patron Habibie, without any of the suave competence and aesthetic excellence of its rival CSIS. In a round-table debate, the issues were democracy, social and economic development, human resources. The chairman of CIDES, Adi Sasono, who has a credible record on human rights, passionately advocated the president's early retirement.

ICMI is syncretic Indonesian politics at its most obvious and active —balancing, accommodating pressure, grafting on to government whatever seems to be growing. NU seems to be heading in another direction, equally traditional but also more radical—the awakening of the broad mass of Indonesians and, if necessary, passive disobedience.

CHAPTER FIVE

Military

INDONESIA'S MILITARY FORCES have become, by the contingencies of politics and history, an integral part of government. There is widespread agreement among political élites that no major change can occur in Indonesia without the military's consent, but the armed forces have become resistant to political change, and especially suspicious of democratic reforms which take away their power. The coupling of state authority and national unity, which worked for the military in the past, has now come up against the need for economic efficiency and competitiveness, and the growing demand for human rights and a more just society, defined in part as less inequality of wealth. As Indonesia slowly develops the elements of a civil society, which looks beyond the government and the forces of law and order for the ingredients of stability and peaceful change, the armed forces are being asked to take a less authoritative and intrusive role.

Instead of being part of the answer to political instability, as the military claims for itself, it has become in the eyes of some Indonesians part of the problem. After its success in removing the communists, it became adept at intimidation as a way of preserving law and order, and safeguarding its own position. It became entangled in the authority of government without having the political and economic skills required for modern administration and management of a market economy. As the world after the Cold War experienced flurries of transnational interdependence, the military mind in Indonesia remained focused on traditional concerns like internal security, control of the nation's territory and the spoils of government.

A glance at the organization of the Armed Forces of the Indonesian Republic (Angkatan Bersenjata Republik Indonesia—ABRI), shows how extensive its penetration of everyday life has become. It controls the nation's élite intelligence agency (latest title Badan Intelijian Negara—BIA), which is concerned with political surveillance. It runs the Body for Coordinating National Stability (Badan Koordinasi Bantuan Pemantapan Stabilitas—Bakorstanas) which was established in 1988 to replace the Law and Order Restoration Command (Komando Operasi Pemulihan Keamanan dan Ketertiban—Kopkamtib) the national security network Suharto set up in 1966 to eradicate the PKI. This permanent body deals with situations of martial law as they arise, so that in emergencies it can immediately facilitate military action. It is headed by ABRI's chief of staff, and includes the chiefs of staff of the army and police and the attorney-general. The office of chief of staff for social and political affairs in ABRI also has a key non-military role; it is the military's link with Golkar, PPP and PDI and the various legislatures. Another organization, staffed by the military, is located in the ministry of Home Affairs; it supervises political activites in regions and districts. In addition, the ten military territorial commands throughout the country monitor, supervise and direct a range of political and civilian activities in their areas. ABRI is also instrumental in press censorship and the education of civil servants on security issues through courses at the National Defence Institute (Lembaga Pertahanan Nasional—Lemhannas).

When you take into account that military officers are appointed to senior positions in government ministries and state enterprises, as regional governors and vice-governors, district heads and ambassadors, as well as to Golkar and to seats reserved for them in parliament, the extent of ABRI's all-pervasive presence is clear.

The police are part of the armed forces. They have their own command structure, as does the army, the navy and the air force. But because the army is dominant in ABRI and the ABRI commander, who has operational control of all four services and also holds the position of minister of defence and security, has always been from the army, the police have not developed a separate policy, nor a culture, on internal law and order. Police in, say, Korea and Japan, India and Israel, have methods of dealing with rioting which do not involve major loss of life—the use of batons, shields, tear gas and rubber bullets are just some of the means used to restore order. In Indonesia, riot control has been a military responsibility, sometimes with disastrous results.

The army has had a political role in Indonesia from the beginning. As a guerrilla force between 1945 and 1949, it was vital in gaining the country's independence. At the time, there was distrust among army units in general toward the political leadership. Seen from the field, the diplomatic agreements which the republic's government negotiated with the Dutch compromised the nationalists' military position. The official *History of the Armed Forces of the Republic of Indonesia* describes the Renville Agreement, 1948, as 'a very detrimental step'. Republican troops were withdrawn from areas they controlled and the Dutch were given greater scope to launch their later attacks. Every member of the armed forces was 'deeply hurt' by the humiliation, the history recites. It goes on to complain generally: 'We had to sacrifice repeatedly our military position for the sake of diplomatic interest; however diplomacy had repeatedly experienced failures.'

As early as 1946 the army had become involved in politics by giving sectional support to Tan Malaka's 'no compromise' campaign against Sjahrir, who was then prime minister. Tan Malaka, ordered to be arrested, was released by General Sudirman, and Sjahrir was himself kidnapped one night at Solo by regular army troops. Sjahrir was later released by another army unit, while other troops tried to kidnap the minister for defence, Amir Sjarifuddin, who was believed to be plotting against Sjahrir. Eventually the army leadership withdrew support from the Tan Malaka 'national-communists', but according to Sjarifuddin, as quoted by Professor George Kahin, the left-wing People's Democratic Front in July 1948 controlled about 35 per cent of the armed forces. The figure may be high. The Madiun rebellion at the end of 1948 did not show army support to anything like this degree for the communists. But it is clear that in the years before the republic was internationally recognized in 1949, the army was militant politically and was inclined to trust its own fighting spirit rather than the devious techniques of diplomacy. The armed forces' history comments:

> Basically it was the armed forces and militant government officials, the Indonesian youth and the people in the villages which formed the last bulwark of the Republic of Indonesia. If this last bulwark fell, the political position of the Republic of Indonesia in the occupied cities as well as at the sessions of the Security Council and later also at the negotiations . . . would have been entirely lost.

The nation's leading soldier and later Defence Minister, General Nasution, formulated in 1957 what he called the 'middle way', which saw the army as a kind of watchdog or umpire, explaining the rules and intervening when necessary. But with the collapse of the parliamentary system and the introduction of martial law, senior army officers openly took on political and economic functions, like running the former Dutch estates and enterprises when they were nationalized in 1957–58. After Suharto replaced Sukarno, ABRI developed consciously a 'dual role' (*dwifungsi*) for itself, which included both military and social-political responsibilities. This has enabled it to permeate the everyday life of the country and the everyday affairs of its citizens.

The army regards itself as having won the right to be protector not just of the physical security of the Indonesian nation but also of the integrity of its national identity and the patriotism of its citizens. It is self-appointed promoter and guardian of Indonesian nationalism. Its authority to interpret what is good and bad for the nation, combined with the effect of having its tentacles in everyday life, is what gives it unique political power.

When the President talks about national awareness, for example, as he does each year on 17 August, Indonesia's national day celebrating independence, it is military leaders who decide what his words really mean. These unexceptional remarks from Suharto's 1991 address were followed speedily by the Dili massacre in November:

> Nationalistic awareness must be continuously awakened, preserved and developed, so that every citizen and group can feel safe and protected and enjoy equal opportunities to develop their creativity . . . With the kind of nationalism that is both healthy and responsible, every Indonesian citizen should continue to unite the country. This is not only in spirit and with determination, but also in every effort and means necessary with which to face the future . . . we are watching with concern that a number of nations are undergoing a critical disintegration process . . . [In Indonesia] we are grateful not only because we are able to preserve our unitary state, but to develop it as well . . . Although the law is not yet being upheld as we all wish, we do sense that the authority or power of the law is being more keenly discerned . . .

ABRI's pervasive presence in Indonesian life has, however, weakened it. Being such an important part of the political system, inevitably it has become a miniature reflection of that system. It has always tended to be factionalized, in the tradition of *aliran* (or streams). Now it is fragmented in other ways as well, being drawn into business ventures and presidential family politics. A crisis might be expected to pull the troops into line, as happened in 1965–66. But it should be remembered that before that crisis was resolved (at great cost), the PKI had succeeded in infiltrating parts of the army and the loyalty of the air force was in doubt. Today, there are again several factions in ABRI, reflecting the objectives and ambitions of individuals and groups both within and outside the armed forces.

The role of ABRI in enforcing law and order in crisis situations— such as the Dili massacre in November 1991, or the Tanjung Priok riots in 1984 or the Malari incident in 1974—is well-known, but its political, social and economic role as part of *dwifungsi* is equally important. The twenty-ninth congress of Nahdatul Ulama (NU) in December 1994 in Cipasung, west Java, and the case of Marsinah, a 25-year-old worker in a watch factory outside Surabya, who became involved in a strike at the factory in May 1993 and was murdered, show how intrusive the Indonesian military has become.

The NU congress was notable for an attempt by the Suharto government to unseat the chairman, Abdurrahman Wahid, who was standing for a third five-year term. It failed, but the vote at the end, 174 to 142, was close enough to be uncomfortable. Wahid's brilliant, controversial leadership of NU had created opponents within the organization, but the main source of the campaign to remove him came from outside—the president himself, his daughter Tutut, who was deputy chair of the Golkar board, the Golkar chairman and Minister for Information, Harmoko, Minister for Research and Technology Dr Habibie and ABRI's head of social and political affairs, Lieutenant-General Raden Hartono (who later became ABRI chief of staff). A veritable cavalcade of authority descended on the local *pesantren* (Islamic school) in which the five-day congress was held. The president opened the congress, the armed forces commander, General Feisal Tanjung (who has cabinet rank) and ten ministers spoke and the vice-president closed proceedings. There was no doubt in anyone's mind that the Suharto government considered the congress to be of the highest significance. (After the congress, having lost, the president showed his displeasure by refusing to grant an audience to the new NU board, making plain that they would have to live with the consequences of their independence).

What is interesting about ABRI's role, as expressed on this occasion by Feisal and Hartono, is that it did not have the support of other senior ABRI officers, including the Defence Minister, General

Edi Sudrajat. Indeed, most senior officers were probably supporters of Abdurrahman Wahid, regarding him as an ally in their struggle against ICMI, which they saw as the use of Islam by Suharto and Habibie to counter the influence of the armed forces. Nevertheless, ABRI's resources were extensively used against Wahid at the congress. Before the delegates left for the congress they were summoned by local government and military officials and told how the government wanted them to vote, and Hartono openly dispensed funds to Abdurrahman Wahid's opponents. Here you have the military, or a section of it, being used by the government, or the president and his political allies, to interfere in the affairs of an organization which was not even a political party, NU having withdrawn from the Muslim political group PPP.

Similarly, the army successfully used its influence within PDI against Guruh, Sukarno's son and a popular campaigner, and then failed to prevent the election of Sukarno's daughter Megawati to the chair of PDI. Feisal and Hartono, working through the local military commander for east Java, then sought to bar her from attending official party functions on the ground that her presence could lead to outbreaks of violence.

The Marsinah case reveals another side of ABRI's penetration of everyday life. Marsinah was one of twenty-four worker representatives who sought during a strike to present a list of twelve demands to the company P.T. Catur Putra Surya. One was for an increase in wages from 1700 to 2250 rupiahs a day (1800 rupiahs currently equals one Australian dollar). After a busy day of discussions and negotiations with the district military and the company and some social activity with friends in the early evening, she disappeared. Her mutilated body was found more than 100 kilometres from where she lived and worked. An already lengthy investigation is still proceeding, and it has not been established that she was killed by the military or even that her death was connected with the strike. But the publicity around the tragic incident has provided a revealing glimpse of the intricate political role the military plays in the nation's industrial relations.

Under what is called Pancasila Industrial Relations (Hubungan Industrial Pancasila—HIP), all worker demands are channelled through the All-Indonesian Workers' Union (Serikat Pekerja Seluruh Indonesia—SPSI), which is the sole and official union body. Only after SPSI has exhausted all other means in discussions with the employers and the government are the workers entitled to take strike action. Even then, the police and military have the authority to intervene and stop the strike. In the 1990s labour unrest grew and intervention by the police and military correspondingly increased.

The Indonesian Legal Aid Foundation, in a preliminary report on the Marsinah case in March 1994, lists the following forms of military intervention commonly used—spying, interrogation, arrest and detention, recommending dismissal, accusing workers of being the 'ghost' of the PKI, torture and physical terror. The military holds positions in the SPSI management, joins in negotiations, can enter factories at will, distributes black lists of workers to other companies, and in general is the active and co-ordinating body under HIP. Local units of the district or territory are normally used, but sometimes combat units are involved, such as cavalry, field artillery, anti-aircraft and the police mobile brigade.

For anyone who spends any time in Jakarta anecdotal evidence abounds of the intrusion of the military into civilian life. Many small to medium businesses have a military officer as partner, on the board or perhaps on salary, part-time so that they continue to work for ABRI. Lower-ranking officers usually don't stay in the same place for more than three years, so their opportunities are relatively menial. Their obvious tasks are protection, reassurance and intimidation. They have become specialists at collecting debts (like the Bataks, whose services are reputedly cheaper). Law firms also find it useful to hire a colonel or two, as a way of impressing rivals and opponents. A colonel who will sit in your waiting room for hours, day after day, is an unwelcome presence. As you ascend the scale of Indonesian business, the military presence becomes more impressive, if less visible. In the state-owned oil giant Pertamina it is, however, both impressive and visible. Oil has been an ABRI domain from the beginning. One of the old jokes in Jakarta is that if you want to explore for oil, join the army.

During the long years of the Cold War, the Indonesian military was seen, particularly in the United States and Australia, as a counter to the influence of the PKI. From this was drawn the conclusion, sometimes unavoidable in the abbreviations of journalism, that the army was 'pro-Western'. This was misleading. The Indonesian military was, and remains, strongly nationalistic. Its closeness to politics has made it something of an Indonesia in miniature.

In Asia (aside from communist countries, where the military has a clearly defined role as an arm of government), the army gained a strong political position in several countries—Burma, Indonesia, Pakistan, South Korea and Thailand. In India, Malaysia and the Philippines, countries with an established political continuity, it has not. It is worth noting that two of the countries with a strong military role are Muslim, two Buddhist and one Confucian, which challenges the picture, gained from the Middle East, that there is a special connection between Islam and military rule.

Originally, Indonesia's officer corps came from families which did not belong to traditional political groups such as landownership and commerce, nor were orthodox Muslim. Their background was middle class and Javanese, and the conventional prejudices you might expect were reinforced by discipline. They respected education and technology as aids to efficiency, and distrusted journalism and politics as temptations to licence. They spent much of their early careers putting down Muslim rebellions and were intensely nationalistic. Before the Japanese occupation, Indonesians had little chance of military service as a career. Soldiers, especially from Christian areas like Minahasa and Ambon, served with the Royal Netherlands Indies Army, but there were few Indonesian officers. A noted exception was the nation's premier soldier under Sukarno, Nasution, who was also exceptional in not being Javanese. Suharto received his first training from the Dutch, and his officer training from the Japanese.

By far the greatest number of senior officers who served in ABRI in its early years received their first training under the Japanese. The first army chief of staff, the late General Sudirman, and Major-General Achmad Yani (who was chief of staff when he was killed in the coup of 30 September 1965) served in Peta, the self-defence corps established by the Japanese in 1943, as did Suharto. By the end of 1944 there were 66 Peta battalions (about 500 men in each) in Java. The Japanese also recruited Indonesians to an auxiliary army and labour corps called Heiho.

A third group of officers came from the so-called *laskar* battalions (Laskar Rakyat or People's Army), independent guerrilla units which sprang up during the struggle for independence from 1945 to 1949. Armed sometimes only with spears, these groups roved throughout west and central Java, some of them hard to distinguish from Java's traditional armed bandits and marauders. They included political extremists of all kinds, and were the most difficult to bring under the single command of the official army, Indonesian National Army (Tentara Nasional Indonesia—TNI), when it was formed on 3 June 1947.

The army, in other words, did not appear on the scene, when the nation won its independence, as a unified and disciplined body. Guy J. Pauker made the point that had the army been well organized it might have intervened in public affairs 'only at crucial moments, decisively and purposefully'. Instead, riven by factions, it began a piecemeal involvement with politics, acquiring the habit of 'settling for small gains, individual rewards or, at best, tactical objectives'.

In 1948 Hatta began a rationalization programme for the armed forces which became a political time-bomb. The main instrument of the reorganization—and initially one of it victims—was Nasution, then a colonel, who had been to the Round Table Conference at The Hague in 1949 to assist in the final negotiations with the Dutch, and returned as army chief of staff and deputy chief of staff of the armed forces. Almost immediately he was attacked in parliament for urging Indonesia to enter the Korean War on the side of the United Nations. He was criticized both inside and outside the armed services for supporting the presence of a Dutch military mission in Indonesia, which he declared was necessary for expert military training of the rough and ready Indonesian forces. Also, he favoured dissolving the scores of roving armed bands. This latter issue, although presented as a military argument in favour of professionalism, was also an attempt to disarm the partisans, like Tan Malaka's army, who were politically leftist.

Moreover, the reorganization of the army under the new Defence Minister (the Sultan of Jogjakarta), the chief of staff of the armed forces, Major-General Simatupang, and Nasution affected the interests of many who had made a living out of the years of turmoil. There were, for a start, some 80 000 of the older men of the estimated army strength of 200 000 who were to be gradually retired, a prospect that did not appeal by this time, when the effects of the Korean War boom were wearing off. There were the regional warlords, local leaders who had been given high rank during the revolution to bring their units into the official army. Japanese-trained officers were placed at a disadvantage by the military techniques taught by Dutch experts. President Sukarno resented the decision to close down a military academy conducting a political indoctrination course at Bandung, where some of his friends, men of the Peta group, were in senior positions. A distant relative of the president's, Colonel Bambang Supeno, began to agitate for Nasution's removal.

The defence committee of the parliament, encouraged by party political rivalries, sought to publicize the grievances of some of the officers against the army high command. The high command, including Nasution, is believed to have seriously considered a *coup d'état* to break parliament's authority and establish either Sukarno or Hatta as the head of a military dictatorship. (It was then widely believed that the coup might have occurred had not Sukarno and Nasution disagreed over the list of left-wing politicians to be arrested).

On 17 October 1952 demonstrators numbering about 5000 and bearing slogans like 'Dissolve Parliament' and 'Parliament Isn't a Coffee Shop' broke into and damaged the parliament building in Jakarta. They then marched, swollen to some 30 000 to the president's palace, where they were supported by army tanks, armoured cars and cannon, which entered the grounds of the presidency with guns trained on the building. Sukarno came to the steps and in a masterly display of oratory, in which he both scolded and soothed them, dispersed the demonstrators. Immediately afterwards seventeen army officers, including Nasution, had an hour-and-a-half discussion with the president. They urged that parliament be dissolved, although there is still disagreement over the precise terms of the demand. In any event, the president refused, and although for a few days Jakarta was tense, with soldiers swarming the streets and the army command making several arrests, the expected army revolt did not take place.

The meaning of the 'October 17th affair' was difficult to isolate from the variety of intentions which brought it about. Some officers seem to have been prepared for Sukarno to take dictatorial power, while Nasution argued for—and Simatupang against—a military junta. Herbert Feith, in describing the incident in detail, writes of the 'independent initiative' of army elements in the affair. Most divisional commanders did not know the demonstration was to take place. 'Even at the palace there were contrasts in the behaviour of different members of officer group. Some were defiant, others had tears in their eyes as they spoke.'

The immediate effect, however, was that Nasution and several of his supporters were suspended and Colonel Bambang Sugeng, a former Peta officer, took Nasution's place. The official history notes that this 'solution of the October 17th affair' did not 'yield results'. To overcome the growing split in the army, 270 senior officers, including pro- and anti-October 17th factions, met in Jogjakarta in February 1955, and declared the army to be 'one and indivisible'—the 'Jogja charter'. They visited the grave of General Sudirman and read a statement: 'We are not yet able to offer you incense in the form of a free, secure, prosperous and calm Indonesia'. The conference also declared that the October 17th affair was 'wiped out' and it showed, in the wording of several resolutions, that it was determined to close army ranks against political interference.

A few months later the charter was successfully tested in the 'July 27th affair'. The cabinet decided to replace Bambang Sugeng, who had resigned, with Colonel Bambang Utojo, a junior and 'anti-October 17th' officer. The 'Jogja charter' committee urged that the appointment be made on the basis of seniority and ability, which pointed to the eligibility of Colonels Simbolon, Nasution, Gatot Subroto and Zulkifli Lubis. The boycott of the formal installation, organized by Lubis as acting chief of staff, was so effective that no military band could be found for the national anthem, and Bambang Utojo was sworn in to the strains of a fire brigade band. Pressure was brought on the Ali Sastroamidjojo cabinet in parliament, and the Minister for Defence, Iwa Kusumasumantri, resigned. But the army officers remained firm, and eventually the cabinet itself fell. The new government reappointed Nasution as chief of staff.

The 'July 27th affair' points to a refreshed appraisal by the army of its role of guardian of the republic. By 1955 disillusionment had set in and, if it had not been for the elections in that year, which promised, but in fact did not bring a solution, it seems likely that the army, or a section of it, would have acted to stop the succession of parliamentary governments by imposing a military regime. In that event, they would have anticipated Sukarno, who was equally dissatisfied with constitutional democracy, which he brought to an end in 1957 with 'guided democracy'. As it was, the army was itself moving toward greater disunity—the rebellion of 1955–61.

The colonels—Kawilarang, Simbolon, Husein, Warouw, Samual and Z. Lubis—who led the regionalist revolts in Sumatra and Sulawesi during those years were a mixed group, some Muslim, others Christian, with pro- and anti-'October 17th affair' factions both represented. Their competence and energy, coupled with sophistication in world affairs and military science, had marked them out as men of unusual capacity and likely attainment. At the beginning, their personal qualities were probably enough to gain them support. They were united in blaming 'Jakarta' for the nation's troubles, and later came to focus their political discontent on Sukarno's tolerance of communism, but their actions seemed born of frustration and desperation rather than practical political planning. Some were probably motivated by private ambitions, too, but they maintained an idealistic attitude. Their difficulty was that, although they had a clear emotional view of what they did not like about Indonesian politics, they were undecided as to what they wanted in its place. They stood against the 'Javanese-aristocratic' pole of Indonesian politics, but they were too much of a Muslim-Christian alliance to represent the other pole, 'Islamic-entrepreneurial'. 'Regional autonomy' was not the kind of rallying cry that would send men happily to meet their Maker, but it was, in the last analysis, all they had to offer. When they returned to 'the fold of the Republic' in 1961—in a remarkably peaceful ending to a costly civil war—they were acknowledging that their cause was not only lost, but essentially trivial.

The army proper gained from the rebellion, once Nasution and his senior officers had demonstrated their loyalty to the government and their superiority over the rebels in the field. In July 1959 Nasution entered the inner cabinet as minister for defence and security—the first military appointment to the post. He was able to arrange the amnesty terms for the rebels, which were an unexpected gain for army unity. Except for Warouw, who was killed in Sulawesi in 1960, the colonels returned to Java and, despite PKI and PNI protests that they were being treated too leniently, were detained as errants and not tried as traitors.

Using the war emergency regulations, the army reached into the administrative life of the country. It banned strikes, broke up demonstrations, controlled the use of slogans, closed down newspaper printing offices, ran the former Dutch estates. In July–August 1960 it moved against the PKI, banned the party newspaper *Harian Rakyat* and interrogated the leaders (Aidit for eight consecutive days) to the extent of 190 typed pages of questions and answers. It cancelled the PKI's sixth congress. When Aidit challenged Nasution, declaring the congress would go ahead as scheduled, President Sukarno intervened and the result was one of his compromises. The congress was not cancelled; it was postponed. When it was held, army stenographers, like police, sat in and took a record of the proceedings.

The army's use as an instrument of authoritarian government was not confined to action against the communists. It was generally tough on civil liberties during this period. In an effort to root out corruption it investigated thousands of charges, many trifling, without any noticeable result except that corruption appeared to spread to the army. With the responsibility of supervising import-export trade, rice supplies, government services, all forms of transport, to mention only some of its functions, the army began to develop as a duplicate administrative élite. An army signature was necessary in many daily transactions, and the citizenry began to complain about military interference. Foreign visitors were affected, being checked by the army on arrival and before leaving. In February 1959 two correspondents and I were trying to reach Bali from Jakarta in time to catch the Soviet Premier, Nikita Khrushchev, who was doing the usual grand tour for important guests. All planes were full. But we eventually got such a high army signature to our request that a capacity-load of tourists, block-booked from New York months before, was dislodged from an aircraft. We flew in lonely splendour to Denpasar airfield in Bali. Not only the PKI but the foreign ministry and the tourist agencies began to complain about the army.

With the end of the rebellion and especially after May 1963, when the emergency regulations were rescinded, the army's detailed supervision of Indonesian life receded. But its prestige and political authority increased. It grew in size (from 200 000 before 1958 to more than 300 000 in 1965) and became better trained and equipped. The armed forces reached a total of about 500 000 men (if the 100 000 police, of which a quarter were militarized, were included). With modern bombers (TU-16) and fighters (MIG-21), a cruiser, submarines and missiles, Indonesia was qualified, at least on paper, as a second-class military power. Her armed forces became, in fact, a status symbol of the ideological leadership which President Sukarno offered the world, or that 75 per cent of it which comprised his 'new emerging forces'. Nasution supported the president in projecting the image abroad of a powerful and dynamic nation, not afraid of military consequences; over Malaysia, it sometimes seemed that Nasution was leading the way.

The army gained in unity during this period. The officers' feuds seemed to have been exhausted by the rebellion, and the 'confrontation' campaigns over West Irian and Malaysia channelled loyalties and energy under Nasution's widely respected leadership. In addition, Nasution tackled the army's old problem of demobilization with vigour. His 'civic mission' was intended to absorb the army in building bridges, roads and schools as well as in production and distribution at village level. Nasution hoped, in effect, to prevent demobilization, allowing only for a wasting away of army personnel, mostly of older officers and poorly educated men. At the same time the army would be able to keep an eye on communist field work and establish links with (or also keep an eye on) provincial government. Communist infiltration of the army officer corps was checked. Nasution himself admitted to a figure of 10 per cent, with special concentrations in central Java, central Sulawesi and west Kalimantan, although some observers put the figure higher.

But the effect of the Indonesian military's symbiotic relationship with President Sukarno blunted whatever political drive may have come from its unity under Nasution's leadership. It lost reforming zeal, probably partly because of its experience of the difficulties of administering Indonesia, and more of its leaders, reaching middle-age, were prepared to settle for the small comforts that life as part of the Establishment brings. Like the PKI, it joined in the 'madness' to gain the 'spoils'. It certainly made no move to check the president in the critical years after 1963, apparently being content at that stage to build up its own strength, and keep that of the PKI at bay, for the post-Sukarno power struggle.

The outstanding figure in this period of ABRI's development, and the leader who for good or ill left his mark indelibly on Indonesia's armed forces was Nasution. Long retired, but still living in Jakarta, he has been at odds with the Suharto regime and its military cohorts for many years.

What kind of military leader was he? Again the labels are too neat—'anti-communist' and 'pro-Western' do not describe the values by which Nasution's actions appear to have been governed. As a Muslim, his devotion to Islam, though not fanatical, was serious and long-sustained; whether this disposed him for or against the Christian 'West' or for or against the communist 'East' is a matter for argument. He never gave any indication, in his various pronouncements on political affairs, that he believed in the private enterprise system of capitalism. He was more a socialist, in the Indonesian sense of believing that everything belongs to the nation and should be worked and distributed as communal property. In foreign affairs and defence, he followed a strongly nationalist line. He negotiated the Moscow arms deal in 1960 and has been belligerent on the Malaysia issue. In an interview he gave me in August 1963, Nasution argued strongly for the removal of British and American military authority from the region of South-

East Asia. While bases like Singapore and Clark Field (the American air base in the Philippines) remain under Western control, he said, Indonesia's security was threatened. Britain and the United States were major powers which Indonesia could not expect to control; it must therefore regard them—with the example of aid to the outer-island rebels in 1958–59 on record—as a danger.

Abdul Haris Nasution was born in Kotanopang, Tapanuli, north Sumatra, on 3 December 1918. His parents were Batak, educated but not rich. He went to a Dutch-operated secondary school in Sumatra and later to the Jogjakarta High School. For a year he was a school-teacher, but he was selected to attend the Royal Netherlands Military Academy in Bandung in 1940, and was commissioned as a subaltern in the Royal Netherlands Indies Army the following year. Captured by the Japanese in 1942 and imprisoned for a few months, he later worked for them, becoming leader of the Bandung division of the youth military organization Barisan Pelopor (Pioneer Legion), which the Japanese sponsored. Immediately the war ended, Nasution became involved in the struggle of the infant republic to survive. In 1945 he organized a security and defence force in Bandung, and as a major and later lieutenant colonel was chief of commando operations in the Bandung residency. A year later, at the age of twenty-eight, he was a major general and commander of the third (Siliwangi) division. His task was complicated militarily and politically—he had to fight the Dutch but at the same time watch the guerrilla bands. Some of the bit-terness of this confused period, shown in the official history of the armed forces, is reflected also in Nasution's later writings, when he complains that Indonesia's political leaders surrendered too easily in negotiations with the Dutch. Reduced to the rank of lieutenant colonel as a result of Hatta's reorganization of the army in 1948, Nasution was appointed deputy to the ailing commander in chief, General Sudirman.

Then came Madiun, when the communists seized power, an event that has probably remained more fixed in Nasution's memory, as a military man, than it has in the minds of the more ideological of the nationalist leaders. Nasution was chief of staff of operations at nearby Jogjakarta when Madiun was seized by troops of the fourth (Senopati) division, commanded by a communist sympathizer. Nasution acted immediately, sending a brigade of the Siliwangi division which, within twelve days, had recaptured Madiun. The back of the rebellion was broken and within three months it was over. But by then the second Dutch military action had begun. Sudirman was so ill that he had to be carried in a sedan chair to inspect his troops, and Nasution was made commander of all the forces in Java. His military reputation, which had already grown quickly, reached fresh heights at this time, when he led his troops in a famous 'long march' from east to west Java, executing a scorched earth policy behind the Dutch lines.

His career from the Round Table Conference in 1949 to the 'October 17th affair' of 1952 has already been noted. After his suspension, Nasution was for three years 'non-active', as the brief lines of his official biography put it. They were years of reflection, during which he helped to organize the League of Upholders of Indonesian Independence (IPKI) and write three books which have now become standard works of reference. The best-known, *Fundamentals of Guerrilla Warfare*, has been translated into several foreign languages, including English, and is required reading for foreign military experts on Indonesia.

This book reveals Nasution as a shrewd military strategist, with some knowledge of military history outside his own time and country. Compared with the communist classics on guerrilla warfare, like those of Mao Tse Tung or the Vietnamese general, Vo Nguyen Giap, Nasution's book lacks an explicit ideology, but there is no doubt of the importance he gives to ideology or of his position on the issue of the military in politics:

> The people adhere to certain ideas, nurture certain desires and needs and look forward to obtaining certain ideals. They will be able to discriminate which side can better provide these needs, and it is the side which can furnish them that will finally be supported . . . A guerrilla war is in principle merely an ideological war.

> The soldier . . . must not be isolated from politics. He must have both feet in the middle of politics. The education of an army must include that of political ideology as well as military technique. The awareness of a political ideology is his conscience and his strength.

Nasution's support of Sukarno followed logically his return from the wilderness. He had always spoken warmly of the 'spirit of 1945', partly to keep ahead of the PKI and the 'youth' or '1945 generation' in the competition for Sukarno's favours, but also because of a belief, which shows so clearly in his writings, that the noble, revolutionary spirit of that time had been spoiled by the politicians. He was also aware of the army's difficulties competing in a democracy with a popular movement like the PKI. In supporting Sukarno's return to the revolutionary spirit of 1945 and the enforcement of guided democracy, Nasution was in effect putting a stopper on the kind of constitutional democracy that may in the long run have given the PKI real political power, with the army forced to serve as its instrument. After entering the cabinet in 1959 he grew increasingly political. One close colleague and friend said: 'Nasution's weakness is that he will not think of himself as President', making the point that Nasution should devote himself to building Indonesia militarily and let the political future wait on events.

Nasution had been tested by events before 30 September, but he had retained, in his family life, a quiet harbour from the storms of politics. He lived unpretentiously with his Eurasian wife and two daughters in a suburban villa in Jakarta. They did not take part in the social round. After the death of his daughter—from bullets intended for him—and the murder of his colleagues, Nasution retired into grief and bitterness. Dismissed from the government by President Sukarno in February 1966, in a bold attempt to correct the trend of events since the coup, Nasution had the satisfaction of seeing the president forced to bring him back in the reorganization the following month. But it was the students, especially the Indonesian Students' Action Front (Kesatuan Aksi Mahasiswa Indonesia—Kami) which forced Sukarno's hand, rather than the unified strength of the armed forces or, for that matter, the army. Nasution's relations with Sukarno deteriorated sharply during these months.

Nasution aged under the pressure of his curiously muffled role in Indonesian politics. Lacking the flamboyance of Sukarno or the cunning of Suharto, he found it difficult in the hothouse atmosphere of Jakarta to project his ambitions, whatever they might have been. But he became over the years so entangled with politics that it was difficult for him to stand before Indonesians as a simple soldier, pledged only to safeguard the honour and dignity of the Indonesian state. His election in June 1966 as chairman of the MPR, which he retained until 1972, showed that Nasution was still drawn towards politics. He became increasingly dissatisfied with the New Order, however. He was a

member of the dissident Group of Fifty, which in 1981 issued a manifesto expressing concern about the nation's direction.

Chatting one evening in 1995 in the same house in which he had
given interviews thirty years before, Nasution talked about his failing
health and his disappointment at the lack of progress in democracy in
Indonesia. He defended his 'middle way' against the charge that it had
given Sukarno the green light to discard democracy, and repeated his
well-known public position against the interpretation of *dwifungsi* in
the New Order. All he had ever wanted for the military was the
umpire's role when politics failed—restore order, then hand power
back to the civilians—and 'in between crises' a civic role building
roads and bridges, assisting with transport and communications. He is
appalled at the 'blurring' of the military role now. It was hard enough
in his time to crack down on corruption; now it is hard to know what
corruption is.

He also talked about the night of 30 September 1965, the details of
which were still vivid to him. He pointed to the bullet holes. He noted
the organization—not just a few men but three platoons of soldiers
came that night. He spent two hours crouched by a tank over his
neighbour's fence, while they searched for him. He has no doubt that
Aidit organized the coup and that he was meant to be its main victim.
'Sukarno hated me.' I have met several times with Nasution over the
years and have always found him cheerful and open. Now frail, he is
not prepared to make specific accusations, but he clearly wants to leave
the impression that there is probably much more to the abortive coup
than meets the eye from official accounts. He notes that Suharto's
name was somehow not on the list. He notes that Suharto saw
Sukarno twice shortly before the coup, but accepts that Suharto's be-
havior at the time and since was decisive. A Batak Sumatran with a
direct manner and a winning smile, Nasution sometimes gives the
impression that Javanese politics is an unfathomable mystery.

No single military leader has emerged in the New Order with the
same political standing as Nasution had in his time, although both
Humardhani and Murtopo were influential for over a decade and
others were momentarily prominent. Opportunities for military
valour in the stable Suharto era have become scarce. Also, Suharto
himself, with his military background and his increasingly personal
style of leadership as president, has overshadowed all others. Try
Sutrisno is the most likely candidate from the military for political

leadership. Before becoming vice-president in 1993, he had served in the engineering corps and then moved steadily through the appropriate appointments after becoming an aide to President Suharto in 1974—army chief of staff in 1986, ABRI commander in 1988. Born in Surabaya in 1935, he is a conscientious Muslim and disguises a tough military record with a popular political style. Another soldier under close observation, for different reasons, is Brigadier General Prabowo Subianto, who is married to the president's youngest daughter and is the son of Dr Sumitro Djojohadikusomo, the talented and frustrated finance minister of the 1950s. Some regard Prabowo as talented and frustrated also. He has taken a special interest in East Timor, where he served three terms, and is currently head of the élite Special Forces regiment (Komando Pasukan Khussus—Kopassus).

But the soldier who succinctly sums up ABRI's role in the New Order is Benny Moerdani. Like Nasution he has been at the top of his profession and has also served as defence minister. No senior army officer has been more influential, first as the strong man of the regime, now as a determined king-maker. Like Nasution, he too has been in and out of favour, and understands without bitterness the temporary nature of power. Also like Nasution, he is a stubborn patriot, preferring substance to shadow play, and as a soldier was incorruptible.

Leonardus Benyamin Moerdani was born in Cepu, central Java, on 12 October 1932. His father was a civil servant with the railways. His mother, Rochmarie Jeane, was a Eurasian of part-German stock, a Catholic and his father's second wife. The first wife was Javanese and the four children from the first marriage were raised as Muslims. The nine children of the second marriage (Benny was the second child) were brought up as Catholics. (Many Indonesians at this time came from large families—Benny's wife-to-be was ninth in a family of twelve). From the age of four he lived an itinerant life, moving with his large family from town to town, always living near the railway. His clearest memory of childhood is the whistle of trains. He speaks now harshly of his father, who disappeared for a while, and adoringly of his mother, who managed her large brood without complaint during his father's absence. The family spoke Dutch at home and mixed with Europeans. They owned a piano and a refrigerator. When the Japanese came, however, they switched to Malay.

At the age of thirteen Benny joined the student army TRIP and for four years he fought the Dutch. A generation of Indonesian men has been affected by that experience—roaming the countryside in

teenage guerrilla gangs, heroes of the revolution before they could
properly read or write. Like many others, he took time to settle down
after independence. He gained some basic training and education at
the Centre for Education for Army Officers in Bandung and finally
completed high school in 1957. He became a lieutenant, training the
army's commando corps, then he took part in the campaign against the
rebels of PRRI and Permesta in Sumatra and Sulawesi. In 1961 he was
sent to the advance course for infantry officers at Fort Benning in the
United States. In 1964 he married Hartini, whom he had met when
she was a stewardess with Garuda airlines and whose family was
known to Sukarno. The president gave them a wedding party at
Bogor palace and tried to persuade the groom to join his personal
guard. Benny said he wanted to be a 'real soldier'.

When the New Order arrived, he was well situated to become
one, having been promoted to Lieutenant General at thirty-four. It is
surprising in retrospect that his next two appointments were abroad—
as defence attaché in the Indonesian embassy in Kuala Lumpur and
consul-general in Seoul. He had perhaps been judged close to
Sukarno. In any case, in 1974 he returned to Jakarta in a trusted political role—deputy head of intelligence and protégé of Ali Murtopo.
Until 1983, when he became commander of ABRI, he was the eyes
and ears of Indonesian intelligence and most of the stories about him
relate to that period. In 1975 he had a role in the East Timor military
invasion. His hand can be seen in the *petrus* incident—a series of unexplained, yet clearly official, killings in 1983—and the clash between
Muslims and the army in Tanjung Priok. He was minister for defence
from 1988 to 1993.

Moerdani now is a terse, reticent man who gives the impression
that, although retired, he is still watching over the fortunes of his
beloved Indonesia. He receives visitors in a spacious office in CSIS and
immediately gets down to business. He has three points to make. One
is that he does not understand the new breed of army officers. 'They
are more like businessmen or bureaucrats than soldiers', he grumbles.
He is like a disappointed teacher when he talks about the new generation of military leaders, or like an old soldier wanting a good stoush
to show the youth what's what. Another point he wants to make is
that the president should step down before it is too late, handing over
to the vice-president. He waves away the suggestion that he is out of

favour with Suharto because he raised the children's business activities with him. He does not contest the fact that he did, nor that the president may have been displeased, but he wants to treat the episode as minor when what is at stake is no less than the national interest. His argument for Suharto to stand down is motivated by patriotism, not revenge. His third point is that *dwifungsi* should stay. The world is a dangerous place and Indonesians should not be lulled into a false sense of security, simply because trade is at the top of the international agenda and the region was relatively stable. Trade wars were not unknown in history (a wry smile). Moreover, Indonesia is an extremely difficult place to govern. The problems of security are now, as they had been for some years, internal not external. The vast majority of the crises around the world that need 'peace-keeping' are created by the breakdown of internal law and order, not aggression across national borders. Indonesia is still a developing country and will be for a long while yet, so a strong military was needed to maintain internal stability while development took place.

Benny Moerdani is not a natural democrat. He is certainly not a liberal. His gruff and pragmatic manner, his connections with the CIA, his brutal decisions, have all built an aura around him of being a hard man, a hawk. Yet his Catholicism and his mother's German background have also influenced him. He shows sympathy for the marginal and underprivileged of Indonesia, the struggling little people. He has surprisingly good relations with Abdurrahman Wahid and Sukarno's daughter, Megawati. Wahid, who disagrees with Moerdani deeply about human rights in Indonesia, has written sensitively about the tension between him as an individual and as a group (military and national) leader. Beneath his gruff and taciturn manner, Wahid detects in Moerdani 'political integrity' of a high order and he draws attention to his protection of the Catholic community and other minorities.

To an outsider, Moerdani is a patriot still at work on the unfinished business of Indonesia's national development. His hardness is professional: his mind is strategic and duty an over-riding emotion. Everything he says and does now is devoted to managing the presidential succession. Everything he says and does now is consistent with the view that in order to get Suharto to reliquish power he must be reassured—reassured that the country is in good hands (which it is with Try Sutrisno), reassured that Suharto will not finish up (like

Marcos or the political leaders of South Korea) on trial for financial misdemeanors, reassured that the children's fortunes will not be in danger. Moerdani, more than anyone, knows where the bodies are buried. He has been as tough as any in enforcing the military regime of the New Order. Now he is managing the transition to another order from his chair in the CSIS building.

Benny Moerdani is part of the so-called Rainbow Coalition of senior ABRI officers and ex-officers, other leaders being Defence Minister Edie Sudrajat and Wismoyo Arismunandar, who in 1995 Suharto replaced as chief of staff of the army with Raden Hartono. He is reputed to be in almost daily contact with Try's office, watching like a hawk each move of Feisal and Habibie, Hartono, Prabowo and others. The Coalition strongly opposes a 'green' (Muslim) faction headed by Feisal Tanjung, and seems to regard Prabowo, perhaps mistakenly, as unimportant.

Official figures on defence expenditure show Indonesia today to be at the lower end among major countries, but the official figures may be misleading because of the blurring between civilian and military activity. Apart from the privateering of individual military officers, ABRI operated corporately a number of business enterprises, controlling several banks and industrial and commercial ventures. Still, military spending as normally understood has been kept at modest levels. Also, the armed forces have not increased markedly in size. In the early 1990s the total strength was 278 000 (army 212 000, navy 42 000 and airforce 24 000) plus a police force of about 180 000. This is less than it was thirty years ago, although the population of Indonesia has doubled. In the mid-1980s major reforms of the command structure were undertaken. Essentially these provided greater flexibility and mobility, but the motivation was also the need for economy. Also, ABRI has had to face the fact that Indonesia's relaxed foreign policy reflects a change of security priorities in the region.

Around the world, a range of strategies had been devised to disengage the armed forces from politics. In Venezuela, salaries were increased and terms and conditions (especially housing) improved. In Chile, the sweetener was that the former president, Augusto Pinochet, who as a general had led the *coup d'état* which put him in power, should remain as commander-in-chief. In South Korea and in the Philippines, the disengagement was gradual and peaceful; in Russia, it was replete with threats and discord. In Nigeria and Burma, there is a stand-off. In Algeria, the army has won the right to govern in a free election.

In Indonesia, the 'back to barracks' thesis has been raised (for example by the former Home Minister, Major General Rudini), and ABRI's 100 seats in parliament have been pruned to 75, but there has been no continuing debate, just a wary circling of adversaries. ABRI has become such an integral part of government that it is hard to imagine what kind of offer could be made which ABRI would consider seriously, or who would make the offer.

CHAPTER SIX

Economy

WHEN SUHARTO TOOK over the Indonesian presidency, the economy was a mess. Heinz Arndt, founder of the *Bulletin of Indonesian Economic Studies*, said in 1966, 'A decade of ever-increasing economic mismanagement in Indonesia has brought a degree of economic breakdown with few parallels in modern history'. His standards were high and there was an element of Western, Cold War judgement in much of the economic commentary at this time. Still, Indonesia was bankrupt. Its exports had fallen so badly that it could no longer service its foreign debts. Budget deficits had increased alarmingly, inflation was soaring.

The failures of the economy were handsomely recognized by the Sultan of Jogjakarta when he accepted responsibility for economic affairs in the government forced on Sukarno in March 1966. The president's 17 August speech in 1965 had been devoted to what he called the Year of Self-Reliance; in familiar language he had described Western aid as bribery and had proclaimed Indonesia's right to stand on its own feet. (An Indonesian acquaintance described this caustically as 'standing on our own foot'.) In a major policy statement in April, the sultan reversed the president's economic doctrine by stressing the need for foreign aid, for development of the private sector and for drastic cuts in government expenditure. Foreign debts then totalled US$2400 million. Exports had declined steadily since 1961 and in 1965 had fallen to US$450 million (excluding about US$200 million for oil). Servicing of foreign debts—the USSR being Indonesia's biggest creditor—would require in 1966 almost the entire export revenue. The modest deficits of the budgets of the 1950s—amounting to some 30 per cent of revenue—had risen to 100 per cent in the early 1960s and had leapt to 3000 per cent in 1965. General prices rose

500 per cent in 1965, with rice prices increasing 900 per cent. 'Our economic situation is very serious indeed', the sultan said.

The new direction taken under Suharto has brought about a general and consistent improvement in the economy and in living standards. Gross domestic product per head, which had been about US$100 under Sukarno, has climbed steadily to reach US$800 by 1995, the result of sustained growth at a rate of 6 per cent or more each year. The proportion of the population technically living in poverty, which had been as high as 70 per cent at the end of the Sukarno years, has dropped to 20 per cent. Rice yields improved so much that Indonesia became self-sufficient. A significant decline in the birthrate and a rapid growth in industry and services have held down unemployment and under-employment, although official figures are not available. Moreover, the economy is being transformed. The traditional dominance of agriculture has given way to industry, which by 1992 was 21.8 per cent of GDP compared with 19.5 per cent for agriculture. Most of the manufacturing was in clothes, textiles, footwear, plywood, and oil and natural gas processing, but new industries, such as electronics, steel, chemicals and automobile assembly, have appeared.

As in every other aspect of Indonesian life, there are elements of continuity as well as change in the story of the economy. The economic failure of the Old Order of Sukarno was mixed with some social success. The economic success of the New Order of Suharto is not a miracle of enlightened policy, but hard-won, spotty and, most important, incomplete.

Indonesia remains a poor country by international standards, at the bottom of the World Bank's 'lower middle income' group. It still depends on foreign aid to meet its development targets; its foreign debt, while not in the same category of danger as Mexico's, is uncomfortably large; double digit inflation seemed always to be threatening; interest rates are high; some unskilled labor sectors are becoming uncompetitive in the face of exports from China, India, Sri Lanka, Bangladesh and Vietnam. There is evidence of bottlenecks in plywood supply, which has lost exports to Malaysia and Papua New Guina. Exports of textiles and garments have declined. Also, although the dreaded Standard & Poor credit rating, important for foreign investment, has been upgraded, it is still BBB, below the A levels reached by neighbours Malaysia, Thailand and Singapore, not to mention Australia. Although foreign investors, especially Japanese, remain confident about Indonesia, the financial system presents an uncertain picture—bad loans have undermined the banks' reputation and the Jakarta stock exchange remains weak.

By the mid-1990s, in other words, the Indonesian economy was losing some of the momentum it had developed over twenty-five years of striving for greater efficiency. The economic reformers, such as Ali Wardhana, Sumarlin, Sadli and Widjoyo Nitisastro, have lost influence. Government control of the economy is increasingly an issue, because of the influence of the presidential family, preferential treatment of political allies in what was called 'crony capitalism', the economy's continued dependance on natural resources which the government controls, and the existence in any case of a vast array of state enterprises, dominated by the military. Tariffs remain high and cement, sugar, plywood and several other industries are controlled by politically well-connected monopolies.

Rhetoric and reality are increasingly at odds. In 1986, President Suharto called for deregulation of state enterprises. The finance ministry evaluated 188 of them and announced that 52 would become public companies, offered for sale on the Jakarta stock exchange. However, nothing happened. Instead, President Suharto further announced that 10 'strategic' state enterprises (armaments, steel, railway stock, telecommunications and electronics were among them) would be placed under the control of Dr B. J. Habibie, as minister for research and technology. Habibie's record as an innovator and even entrepreneur was commendable, but his record as a financial administrator was not impressive. The World Bank in 1993 reported critically on the concentration of government funds (about half) on Habibie projects and their lack of accountability. Also, despite the large government subsidies, or perhaps because of them, his big industrial operations showed low rates of return. In 1993 expert estimates were that of about 200 state enterprises, only one had been privatized and the vast majority were in ABRI's hands. These were used by the military as a supplement to ABRI's low budget and as a private source of income for high-ranking officers.

In 1990 Suharto summoned representatives of the 30 largest conglomerates (all but two being ethnic Chinese) to his cattle farm Tapos, outside Bogor, where he appealed to them to open up to the co-operative movement by offering equity, as a way of redistributing wealth. In the first public announcement, a figure of 25 per cent divestment was suggested. The business community was shaken. The co-operatives, although pleased, were confused. How was the proposal to be implemented? The divestment figure was later reduced to 5 per cent, and still later to 1 per cent. None of the figures were of signifiance, however, because nothing happened.

The size of the Suharto family's wealth became not surprisingly a subject of much speculation and disputed estimates. Four of the six children were active in business. A US Central Intelligence Agency estimate in 1989 of the family's personal wealth was about A$20 billion for Suharto himself and double that for the whole family, but some observers thought this was an exaggeration. In 1994, an Indonesian business magazine estimated the Suharto children had a combined worth of A$1.78 billion which, while considered low, ranked them third after the Sino-Indonesian families of Sudono Salim (aka Liem Sioe Liong) and Eka Tjipta Widjaya. An article in *The Australian* early in 1996 placed Liem among Asia's twenty wealthiest families, with a personal wealth of A$6 billion. In 1995, a table of Indonesia's 'Top 200' taxpayers, announced by the Minister for Finance, Mar'ie Muhammad, included seven members of the Suharto family.

There is little doubt that the Suharto family wealth is very large indeed, probably the biggest in Indonesia. As Suharto's simple background is well known, the speed with which the family has amassed its wealth is remarkable. Early in Suharto's presidency, his wife's business dealings were criticized, but they have now faded in comparison with the activity of the children. His second son, Bambang, was the first to go into business in 1982, followed by the eldest daughter, Tutut. In little more than a decade, they established powerful enterprises covering a diverse range of activity. The youngest son, Hutomo (Tommy), followed, with even more spectacular results. It was the mode of operation as much as the size of the Suharto family's wealth that created controvery. Exclusive contracts and licences, monopoly products and heavy state bank financing were features of the family's fortunes. Access to the president and the highest levels of decision-making through the family gave business partners an advantage over their competitors, bringing charges of 'crony capitalism'. In particular, several ethnic Chinese businessmen formed close commercial links with the presidential family—Liem the most important of them, but also Bob Hasan and Prajogo Pangestu.

A showdown on economic policy thus seems to be in prospect. On the one hand, the need remains to open up further the Indonesian economy along the path of the reforming years. On the other hand, control by the state—assisting the military, Habibie's strategic projects and the president's family and allies—is holding up reform. Economic growth has been the president's strength, enabling him to rule in a highly personal, authoritarian way. The signs are that this personal rule has become counter-productive for the economy and that he might have to choose between it and continued economic growth for Indonesia.

Suharto seems to be well aware of this. In 1994 he launched an ambitious three-year programme aimed at poor citizens. Around 20 000 of the nation's most backward villages were provided with 20 million rupiahs (about A$12 000) as capital for self-selected projects. The scheme was initially funded by the Indonesian government, but is now backed by Japan, the World Bank, the Asian Development Bank and the United Nations Development Programme. It has some interesting aspects—strict repayment conditions, strong local control. It has already shown—as have credit schemes in other developing countries —that poor people handle money carefully and pay back conscientiously. In short, they are a good risk. Whether the scheme will alleviate poverty remains to be seen, but it has already had a psychological effect. It helps to counter the impression that economic development in Indonesia is designed to benefit the Chinese conglomerates, the president's family and the military.

The Suharto government's first task was to stop inflation and stabilize the economy. It had achieved this by 1969, when the first Five Year Plan, Repelita I began (Rencana Pembangunan Lima Tahun—Five Year Development Plan). These plans, which are another element of continuity with the Old Order, have become a feature of the Indonesian economy. They begin on 1 April every five years, establish development priorities and set targets for sectoral growth. They are conceived as indicative rather than commanding, especially for the private sector, and are subject to annual review. Nevertheless, they provide a a ready reference of both problems and achievements for the Indonesian economy.

Repelita I (1969–74): The emphasis was on agricultural production and infrastructure, neglected under Sukarno. It encouraged foreign investors. Rice output rose by 25 per cent, although short of target (47 per cent). Fertiliser and cement production also fell short.

Repelita II (1974–79): This ran into trouble in mid-term, due to what became known as the Pertamina scandal. The international quadrupling of oil prices in 1974 seemed on the surface a bonus for

Indonesia, a major oil producer. However, the recession which followed in the industrial economies forced international banks to review their lines of credit, one of which was to Pertamina, the state-owned oil agency, which had generated debts of about US$10 billion—then representing about a third of the Indonesian economy. Pertamina had spread in reckless fashion under the direction of Ibnu Sotowo, a former military officer who had developed an interest in oil while posted in Sumatra. Expansion into steel, fertiliser, liquefied natural gas, insurance, hotels and other activities were not in themselves necessarily bad commercial risks, but the management of Pertamina's huge revenue was shown to be incompetent, corrupt and sometimes illegal. The Indonesian government was forced through its central banks to guarantee Pertamina's liabilities.

The rise in oil prices, while increasing government revenue, also increased the inflation rate. A priority of the plan was to improve standards of living and reduce unemployment, to both of which the financial crisis was a set back. However, some development projects were completed, agriculture grew at nearly 5 per cent each year of the plan and industry growth was nearly 13 per cent.

Repelita III (1979–84): The government's dependence on oil revenue was again shown when a decline in oil prices seriously affected Indonesia's balance of payments. Oil and gas accounted for about three-quarters of exports and two-thirds of government revenue. There was also rapid appreciation of the yen, in which about 40 per cent of Indonesia's debt was held. So there was a substantial rise in debt with a drop in revenue to service the debt. Policy during this period was at sixes-and-sevens, reflecting tension between conservatives who wished to continue the careful strategies of the two former plans and pressure from the new politically connected conglomerates. In the event, 47 projects worth US$21 billion were deferred, including some major public sector projects.

Repelita IV (1984–89): This period was notable for a serious attempt to grapple with the problems which had shown up in previous plans, especially dependance on oil. Reforms were made in customs, which were privatized in 1985, in modernizing the stock market and improving foreign investment guidelines and banking procedures. A large devaluation was undertaken and a series of measures to lower tariff and non-tariff barriers were introduced. On the basis of these reforms, manufactured exports rose rapidly. Most of the increase was in plywood, however, raising the question of whether Indonesia was replacing dependance on one natural resource by another. Finance from the private sector was sought for nearly half of the plan's investment funds, which proved ambitious, but an annual average growth rate of over 5 per cent was achieved.

Repelita V (1989–94): The main objective was to generate employment for a projected increase in the labour market of 12 million job seekers, for which a minimum growth rate of 5 per cent was required. Most of the investment (55 per cent) was private, with the rest coming from the government's budget (more than half of it from foreign aid). Expenditure was earmarked for (in descending order) communications and tourism, agriculture and irrigation, education and religion, mining and energy, regional development, housing, defence and security, health, manpower and transmigration, science, research and technology, manufacturing and development of business enterprise. Repelita V generally met its targets, but it also revealed some of the features of 'reform fatigue' which might become more apparent in Repelita VI (1994–99). The feature of all the plans, however, is that they have met growth rate targets. Indeed, in 1995 the government increased the projected growth rate for Repelita VI from 6.2 to 7.1 per cent and a greater share in GDP of manufacturing.

By the turn of the century, Indonesia intends to be classified as a 'newly industrializing country'. To do this it has targetted for development certain industries, some which meet pressing domestic demand, such as fertiliser and agricultural implements, food processing, cement and paper, and some which have an export market, such as petroleum products, plywood and textiles. Others to be given attention are the so-called strategic industries under Habibie's control, such as land, sea and air transport, steel and electronics, and a special category needed to stimulate economic activity outside Java, especially in east Indonesia.

The first five of the five-year plans have now been consolidated in what is called the First Long-Term Development Plan, PJPI (Pembangunan Jang-ka Panjang I). PJP2 will take Indonesia to the year 2019. Long-range planning has been a feature of the political administration of Indonesia's economy since the beginning. Sukarno started with five-year plans, which became grander as the economy deteriorated. The National Over-All Development Plan, otherwise known as the Eight-Year Plan, ushered in the 1960s. The plan was described enthusiastically by the president as 'rich in fantasy'. It was produced by twelve expert committees and three general committees (on population, national income and socialism) working 'day and night for almost a year' (as the process was officially described), with some 270 Indonesian experts making contributions. The chairman of the project was the late Professor Mohammed Yamin, an old revolutionary poet, historian and ideologue. The result, presented to the president on 13 August 1960, was a massive creation of 5100 pages, consisting of 17 volumes in 8 parts with 1945 paragraphs to symbolize the date of the Proclamation of Independence on 17 August 1945.

It was not the kind of plan that called on people to tighten their belts and knuckle down to work for later benefits, but as described officially, it was 'the first stage toward the ideal society'. In some respects, it foreshadowed today's plans, as it tried to push Indonesia into industrialization.

The Dutch left the Indonesians with a 'dual' economy, one part geared closely to the Netherlands and the great markets of the world and one part to the traditional requirements of peasant village life in Indonesia. It was obvious—Hatta seems to have been among the most clear-sighted of the early political leaders—that the economy would need to be drastically restructured. But, like the Russian general who didn't like war because it destroyed discipline in the army, Indonesia's political leaders tended to treat serious economic reform as if its purpose were to destroy the harmony of the people's poverty. The suffering of the Indonesian people and the utopian future to which their suffering entitled them were what mattered. From time to time, as the economic situation got out of hand or as immediate politics dictated, draconian measures were introduced—like those of August 1959, when almost half the currency in circulation was withdrawn by cutting the value of large denomination notes by 90 per cent and freezing bank accounts above a certain amount.

About one thing the Sukarno government was definite: no foreign capital investment. Loans and credits by all means, but not foreign capital, unless on the basis of 'production-sharing', a joint-enterprise scheme with which Indonesia had tried from the beginning without much success to attract foreign investment. Local private enterprise was welcome provided it recognized that its function was 'community prosperity' and not 'individual profit'.

Sukarno's Eight-Year Plan offered some idea of what Indonesian socialism meant, or was meant to mean. Socialism would be based on the 'Indonesian identity', which would by its nature ensure that social justice was done to 'the stupid and the handicapped, as well as to the clever and privileged, to the poor and the weak, as well as to the rich and the powerful'. The centuries of suffering by Indonesian people under colonialism required reparation. The Indonesian revolution carried out this Mandate of the People's Suffering and Indonesian socialism was the offered balm. 'Close, warm human relations' were ranked highly in the plan's scale of values.

Indonesian socialism was strongly nationalist rather than internationalist. It offered a helping hand to struggling humanity and certainly to those still under colonialism, but it was not internationalist, like capitalism and communism. It was based on the family system, as a training ground for combining the 'two ideas of serving a group and, at the same time, of exercising authority as an equal member of that group'. It was based also on *kerakjatan*, a democratic principle which 'stresses the ideal of the entire people in action in society, rather than the mechanism of the ballot box'. Decisions were reached through *musjawarah* (deliberation) and *mufakat* (unanimity). *Gotong royong* (mutual co-operation) was also frequently described as basic to Indonesian socialism. More precisely, 'only those enterprises which do not affect the lives of most people may be in the hands of individuals'. The rights of private enterprise were not derived from natural law, but were defined by the Indonesian government. Ownership of home and land was permitted, but the 'earth and water and natural riches contained therein' (such as minerals and oil, for example) were the state's property and should be used 'for the greatest possible prosperity for the people'.

Indonesian socialism was not a ready-made system, which could be introduced or imposed, it was said, but a guide to action. Using the constitution and the *Pancasila* as a 'fundamental rule', the Indonesian people were expected to create Indonesian socialism as they went along. As President Sukarno had said, 'each day must give birth to inspiration; every day must produce concepts; every day must give birth to ideas that are better than yesterday's as a continuation of the result of yesterday's work'.

In 1945, when Sukarno enunciated the *Pancasila*, he spoke emotionally of one of the principles, Social Justice. 'Do we want an independent Indonesia whose capitalists do their unscrupulous will, or where the entire people prosper, where every man has enough to eat, enough to wear, lives in comfort, feels cherished by his Motherland which gives him sufficient *sandang pangan*, the basic necessities?'

Sandang pangan was for Indonesians older than capitalism. It is a traditional central Javanese expression, meaning a time of economic welfare, a peculiar economic category which Javanese call *tjukupan*, to 'have enough'. For most Indonesians Sukarno's words had the same connotation as the 'decent living' promised by Western politicians during the Depression to do away with the indignities of the employment queues and the dole. In his Independence Day speech of 17 August 1963 Sukarno apologized for not keeping his promise. 'Go ahead, be angry with me; go ahead, point your finger at me; go ahead, pour your wrath upon me—and I will accept it all with a calm heart . . . I say: Be patient a while longer, be patient.'

In some respects, the lot of ordinary Indonesians improved under Sukarno. In 1958 Selosoemardjan, a native of Jogjakarta, told how he stood on the side of a road near a village outside the city at 7 a.m. and counted 170 bicycles in five minutes going toward the city. The bicycle was to the Javanese peasant as the small car is to the average Australian family. It increased his mobility, enabling him to bring his goods more quickly to market and to commute daily to town during off-seasons for an additional job. Selosoemardjan pointed out that the cow and the buffalo were no longer status symbols for the peasant; a bicycle and education for his children were taking their place. The peasant or farmer is better off than pre-World War II, Selosoemardjan argued:

> The average peasant of 1938 had a bamboo house, usually no more than one suit of clothing, no furniture in his home except his bamboo bed, and almost no cash in hand. In 1958, in part because of his growing awareness of his human dignity and his dignity as a citizen of the state and also because of the means that he has at his disposal, more and more brick houses are replacing the old bamboo shacks, while thatched roofs are rapidly giving way to earthen roof tiles. Chairs, tables, and other pieces of furniture are now to be found in many village homes. In general, both men and women have three suits of clothing. They no longer need to wait naked when their clothes are being dried in the sun after washing.

On the other hand, greater mobility, education, newspaper reading and so on had raised the level of most Indonesians' material requirements and expectations. Not only rice and fish were now demanded, but bicycles, pens and propelling pencils, cameras and radios, even automobiles. Also, the social structure was changing. If the peasants' rice income was not much affected by inflation between 1938 and 1958, Selosoemardjan estimated that the wage labourer's had dropped by one-half and the civil servant's was one-thirtieth of its pre-war value. He noted also that the average government official could live for only eighteen days on his monthly salary, which opened up excellent prospects for corruption. The social gains were gradually being undermined by mismanagement and a kind of romantic defiance by Sukarno of the 'bottom line'.

When a Western diplomat called on President Sukarno early in 1963, he found him preoccupied with economic problems. 'Everyone tells me there's inflation and something must be done about it. I don't think there's too much inflation, do you?' he asked.

Inflation, in fact, was rampant. But behind the president's naive observation was the confidence of experience. The collapse of the economy had seemed imminent for years, and Sukarno had had fun with the predictions of the Western experts. Of course, the collapse might already have taken place, if it were defined in terms stock-holders would understand. Production was down, exports were down, per capita income was down, foreign exchange in the sense of reserves was non-existent, depending as it did on foreign aid and the state of trading month by month. But somehow the economy went on, with sufficient ramshackle strength to maintain a population then of 100 million. For Sukarno, population was a vital statistic, attesting to the strength of the Indonesian nation. 'We are a nation of 100 million people, the fifth largest nation in the world', he said in a speech to the National Front in Jakarta in February 1963. 'When I recall my aunt, who has 23 children of her own, I am sure that before long our Indonesian nation will number 250 million people.'

One factor in Sukarno's optimism, as it is still in some Indonesians' view of economic issues, was nature's abundance. The Indonesian islands are rich in food and, although Java needed then to import rice, which carried its own insult to the ingenuity of the originators of the marvellously reticulated paddy fields, the land is generous. Water is available and fruit is never far from hand. When, in an exceptionally dry period toward the end of 1961, famine occurred in Lombok Island and some parts of Java and people were reported to have died of star-vation, the surprise expressed showed the essential difference between the traditions of the tropics and the arid regions of the world. In the Indian subcontinent, China and the Middle East, famine has traditionally taken its toll almost as a matter of course. In Indonesia, food is taken for granted and clothing, in a tropical climate, is not demanding. About 70 per cent of the Indonesian economy in Sukarno's time was rural subsistence. When things were bad, as measured by foreign exchange reserves, exports-imports and other indices of the monetary system, the people retreated, as they do in Western countries in a minor way under emergency rationing such as in wartime, into the old, well-trodden ways of the barter economy.

Another factor was foreign aid. Indonesia was courted by all sides in the Cold War. The total aid given to Indonesia from independence until the end of 1963 was in the region of US$3000 million—an average of about US$200 million a year, which was just about what Indonesia needed each year to service its debts. In 1963 this amount was estimated to be US$225 million, with the Soviet Union (US$80 million) the largest creditor.

In other words, it was a mixed picture thirty years ago, and, in some respects, it still is. The economy is much stronger now and about five times as big as it was then. But foreign aid is still crucial, foreign debt is high, and the unbounded optimism and ambition of political leaders still troubles the bottom line. Also, economic success, just as it did thirty years ago, breeds its own discontents.

Politics in economically developing countries does not have the same fine sense of principle separating left from right that it has in the democracies of the industrialized societies. In Indonesia, despite a strong private sector, much money-making and considerable effort since 1965 to create an efficient economy to compete in the global marketplace, a kind of co-operative and communal ethos pervades popular thinking about economic development. It owes something to the underdog spirit that accumulated under colonialism. Indonesians have always seen themselves as having had to fight for their independence, which gives them a more nationalistic and emotional approach to politics than you find in countries which gained independence through pragmatic diplomacy. In South-East Asia, they share this nationalism with the Vietnamese, a communist country. It owes something to the yearning for a better life that is present among the ordinary people of all societies, especially in very poor countries, and something to communitarian values.

With the destruction of the PKI, capped off by the end of the Cold War, it might have been expected that Indonesia would swing whole-heartedly into the camp of capitalist true believers, and some observers believe it has. But capitalism is, just as much as socialism, a many-splendoured thing, a multi-coloured pie chart in which the Indonesians have their own, rather indistinct, slice. They have shown themselves, from Sukarno to Suharto, to be reluctant to embrace the philosophical rigours of capitalism. They enjoy making money, but the cut-throat competition of private enterprise in its more heroic forms is unattractive to most Indonesians.

President Suharto has written that *Pancasila* 'may be considered as a teaching with a tendency towards socialism' but he further defines this teaching as 'socialistic religious' (not 'religious-socialistic', which he rejects). He says he once asked Sukarno for guidance. 'Is (*Pancasila* society) socialistic, religious or is it a capitalistic-liberal society?' Sukarno replied: 'No, it is none of these things on its own. It is socialistic-religious. *Pancasila* society is a socialistic-religious society.' Suharto explains: 'Being socialistic alone does not necessarily indicate that one has faith in God. Communists do not believe in God. On the other hand, religious people may be capitalists and do not find socialism significant.' He goes on to argue that the philosophy of *Pancasila* reflects humankind's dual nature of individual and social needs, which is God's creation. But, 'If we go deeper in our contemplation of life, we come to the realization that a great deal of our lives depends on others. Therefore, it is community life which really is more established, more stable, although individuality should not be set aside or abolished.'

Indonesia, like many countries, is caught between the demands of economic development and political reform. It is trying to find its own answer to the question which in one way or another, governments and people all over the world are asking: 'What is the best political way to manage a market economy?' The end of the Cold War, the lowering of trade barriers, the transnational development of communications, investment and finance, the growth of regional trade and economic co-operation—these are just some of the challenges which could transform the Indonesian economy, if the political system would allow.

For a while it did, because the economy had collapsed and Indonesian politics had dramatically changed, But now the weakness of the political system is again showing in its inability to define and direct the economy. There are expert minds available, as shown in the early period of the National Development Planning Agency (Badan Perencanaan Pembangunan Nasional—Bappenas) and there are competent economists as analysts and teachers. But the politicians must make the decisions when a Bappenas-inspired reform runs into social welfare criticism, especially in the rural community.

Even in a country as politically safe for courageous leaders as Indonesia, economic reform is intractable. Either the reforms themselves are too difficult or the status-quo too attractive for those who would wish to join in the spoils. There is a persistent reaching back into Indonesian culture to give a perspective to economic decision-making, but nothing comes of it. Often it seems no more than an exercise directed at the ethnic Chinese, who continue to have a dominant role in the economy, as they did under the Dutch. Traditional concepts exist, but they are not implemented. No Indonesian ideas for economic management have emerged comparable with, say, Singapore's on enforced savings, Australia's on an accord between government and trade unions, Japan's on producing rather than consuming. The co-operative movement in Indonesia has a substantial history, but there is no scheme of worker participation, and no Indonesian Tony Blair talking about a shareholders' society.

Yet reform has not stalled completely and Indonesia's record of the last thirty years shows sustainable gains. Targets in the distant future may well be a way of lulling the public into a false sense of economic security, but the fact is that the most important of the targets, growth, continues to be met. Public accounts are more accurate and credible. The government, while understandably trying to juggle economic efficiency and social justice, has been in the last resort more practical about the economy than political. Also, there is a world outside Indonesia. As Indonesia moves from agriculture to manufacturing, some countries are moving from manufacturing to service industries, and Indonesia has to gauge where it best fits into the world and the region and over what length of time. Suharto's leadership ambitions have given him a leading role in APEC, which has put pressure on Indonesian tariffs. The World Bank and some of Indonesia's foreign aid donors have been critical of the way the five-year plans are financed, suggesting that private capital rather than foreign aid would be less expensive and more efficient. Income tax has been introduced—representing the search for revenue in a more competitive world and a recognition that many Indonesians now have incomes that are taxable. The region and the world keep forcing Indonesia's hand.

CHAPTER SEVEN

Culture

WHEN THIS BOOK was first published, more than 100 million people lived in Indonesia, making it the fifth most populous country in the world. Indonesia's population has since doubled and, since the break up of the Soviet Union, it has become the world's fourth most populous country, behind China, India and the United States of America.

The land these people live in comprises 13 000 islands—and many more too small to be counted—stretching some 5000 kilometres from the western tip of Sumatra to the border of West Irian and Papua New Guinea. This land is an astonishing natural phenomenon, rich in resources and in beauty. Its region is one of the most volcanic in the world. The surface of the earth seems still to be in formation and the Seismographic Institute of Jakarta usually registers two or three earthquakes a day. Whether you fly into Jakarta westward along Java or from Singapore or Bangkok over southern Sumatra and the Sunda Straits, you will see the great cones through the clouds. On Java alone there are forty-four volcanic cones between 2000 and 3000 metres, and fourteen even higher. Mount Agung, on Bali, just off the eastern tip of Java, erupted in 1963 with great loss of life and property. Like the explosion of Krakatoa, in the Sunda Straits, in 1883, it was a reminder of the natural dangers in whose shadows the Indonesians live. The speeches of President Sukarno used to be studded with references to the active Javanese volcano, Merapi, whose fiery outbursts from the depths of apparent slumber were symbolic, he claimed, of the spirit of Indonesian nationalism, and a warning to nations who take her peaceful appearance for granted. On Java the volcanic soil is so rich, and land so thickly populated, that the farmers press close to the treacherous crater. Their fields and houses are often destroyed, but they return with a prayer on their lips and a wooden hoe and mattock in their hands.

It is not hard to imagine that this sporadic violence has been an incentive to the animist belief in the spirits of earth, air and water which was the earliest Indonesian religion. Bogor, in west Java, has more thunderstorms than any other place in the world. Parts of Sumatra, Kalimantan and West Irian have over 5000 millimetres of rain a year. Padang Tingi botanical gardens, a few kilometres east of Padang, has perhaps the heaviest rainfall in the world—up to 10 000 millimetres annually. The mountains, jungles and rushing rivers on the larger islands, which separated the early people, allowing the development of distinctive cultures, are also an impressive reminder of natural forces.

Most Indonesians believe in spirits. Clifford Geertz, the American sociologist, records in *The Religion of Java* the matter-of-fact presence of spirits in people's lives. 'I don't know how it is in America', he was told, 'but here they are always upsetting one'. People mentioned the danger of 'bumping into' spirits when out walking. Beneath the formal religious observances, whether they are Muslim, Christian or Hindu-Buddhist, there is in Indonesia an awareness of things that go bump in the night. Among the educated younger generation there is less of this 'spiritualism', but there is not in modern education the great counter to the folk beliefs that there was in Western education during the hey-day of rationalism. Science, having opened the atom and found that the mystery continues, is less likely to scoff at the idea of 'spirits' in stones and trees than it was when mechanical explanations seemed enough. Also, love of nature has been pushed to the forefront of global consciousness by conservationists, who see it being destroyed by the rational processes of industry and commerce.

The chief counter to mysticism in Indonesia are the established religions. Islam is a rational faith, in the sense that it invokes conscience and moral responsibility for one's actions, but Geertz's book shows how much even the *santris* (devout Muslims) are affected by traditional, local beliefs. This is not surprising. In any country where tradition is strong and elaborate, the invading religion, whatever it is, will seem 'foreign'. It may be accepted, because it is backed by power, because to belong to it confers prestige or facilitates wealth, or even because it is rationally convincing, but the local customs, with their racial or tribal memories, do not easily release their hold on the imagination. In Indonesia, this hold remains strong. There is an Indonesian saying common in Sumatra and Borneo: 'Religion [*agama*] comes in from the sea, but custom [*adat*] comes down from the mountains'.

Adat has been a powerful unifying factor. The pattern of *adat* is similar throughout the islands in its approach to the essentials of life, especially social stability. It became so entrenched that none of the many changes of rules and kingdoms altered it significantly. Perhaps the long Dutch rule might have done so, but except for an unsuccessful period of 'unified law' between 1904 and 1927, Holland generally accepted *adat* as the separate law of the Inlanders or 'natives'.

Adat was based on the needs of the village community and, especially in areas such as Java, Bali and parts of Sumatra, where paddy or *sawah* (wet rice) was grown, the demands of planting, irrigating and harvesting made mutual co-operation, or *gotong royong*, a necessity. Originally all the land belonged to the whole group, but gradually limited ownership developed into full ownership, or all land became the property of the hereditary ruler of the region. (The Dutch disturbed this by choosing to regard village land as communally owned, to facilitate their 'culture system' of forced cultivation.) The village chiefs were not elected, but were chosen through the mutual agreement of the villagers, and were considered not so much leaders as 'first among equals' who decided important questions through mutual discussion or *musjawarah*, resulting in a consensus, or unanimous agreement, *mufakat*. The principle of election by vote was first introduced to Indonesia by the Japanese during their wartime occupation of the islands, and to most Indonesians the idea of '50 per cent plus one' does not seem at all democratic, as it does not take into consideration the disagreeing 49 per cent. The 'tyranny of the majority' as argued in Western democracies would be understood instantly by *adat*-oriented villagers; President Sukarno, when he introduced 'guided democracy' was exchanging a Western for an Indonesian concept of democracy, as he stated on numerous occasions, for instance in a speech at Hasanuddin University in Makassar on 31 October 1958:

How was democracy of former times in Indonesia? It still is practised in the villages in Java, Minangkabau, Sulawesi, Lombok, Bali and other places . . . But do they in these village meetings apply the practice of voting? Of free-fight liberalism where half plus one is always right? No, my friends . . . Everybody says something different until at one time a compromise is achieved out of all these different opinions, without voting . . . There is no dictatorship in *musjawarah* and *mufakat*. That is why democracy with leadership is a true, original Indonesian democracy . . . not American democracy, Dutch, French, British, German, or Soviet or anybody else's democracy.

There is a Javanese word, *tjotjog*, which means to agree or to fit as, according to Geertz, 'a key in a lock, good medicine does a disease, a solution does an arithmetic problem, a man does with his wife (if not, they get divorced)', and the successful use of *musjawarah* results in a harmonious *tjotjog* of various elements, leading to *mufakat*. This idea was expressed to Geertz by a *dalang* or puppeteer of the ancient and highly popular *wayang kulit*, or shadow plays, which usually tell stories from the Indian epics the *Ramayana* and *Mahabharata*, or of the Indonesian kingdoms of Mataram and Majapahit. He said that the *wayang* has meaning for today too. 'The thing one has to do is talk and talk; and slowly the people come to agree (*tjotjog*) and then there is peace. Otherwise, if the talk breaks off, there is war.' It is interesting in this connection that the traditional five senses, to the Javanese, are seeing, hearing, feeling, smelling and talking.

Gotong royong, or mutual help, is based on the ideal concept of a family, extending to a community, in which the leader, or father, is expected to lead his people or family through their love and affection for him, supporting him by freely stating their opinions to help him make up his mind, and sharing in the group's goals of happiness and prosperity. In village *gotong royong*, people co-operate as families, not as individuals, and in village councils only the heads of families have the right to express their opinions, in line with the traditional view that the family is the smallest village unit. This concept is so firmly fixed that often when they are married, both bride and groom drop their former names and take on a new name to show that they are now a 'family' with a new social position and role. *Gotong royong*, which was a mainstay of village life, had not existed as a national concept under Dutch rule or during the Japanese occupation. But after independence was proclaimed it became an administrative ideal in many parts of Indonesia, with the administrative head being referred to as the *bapak*, or father.

Under this system, which came to be known as *Bapakism*, superiors no longer issued orders until the question at issue had been discussed with their subordinates and their agreement in principle obtained. The enthusiasm of Indonesians for the official approval of such an extended *gotong royong* system, which was taken from the administration into the republic's guerrilla units during the post-war fighting against the Dutch, sometimes resulted in loyalty to the *bapak* which superseded loyalty to the higher command, and in the administrative system made it very difficult for the government to transfer a *bapak* to another post. President Sukarno, though he was also known as *bung*, or brother, was the nation's ultimate *bapak*. President Suharto has taken the concept even further, because he is fatherly in manner. The Australian prime minister addressed him as '*bapak*' during their several meetings in 1995.

With the development of a money economy came the custom of a financial gift to your host at a party or feast to help cover his costs in food, the amounts and methods of presentation being fixed by a well-known *adat*. But *adat* principles still affect Indonesian life in a more direct way. The women of a village help each other with the transplanting of each family's rice seedlings, men join together to build a neighbour's house, and in many communities there are group collections of the plates, cups and other things which are needed to give a party or the traditional religious feasts at such times as childbirth, circumcision or marriage. In the post-war period, financial co-operatives were sometimes organized to buy these festive necessities, which were then shared around the group as they were needed.

Another unifying force in Indonesia is nationalism. The variety of people and the scattered geography give real meaning to the national motto 'Unity in Diversity' ('*Bhinneka Tunggal Ika*'). It is not unusual for a nation to have to weld together peoples of different and competitive histories—the United Kingdom is a union of Scots, Welsh, Irish and English which has seemed unlikely at times; Russia ranges from Europe to Asia. At this early stage of her history as a nation, Indonesia's diversity is a potent fact, regarded with both fear and pride.

Regionalism, as was shown in the 1950 revolt in south Maluku, the 1953 rebellion in Aceh and the 1958–61 rebellion in Sumatra and Sulawesi, is a threat to national unity. On the other hand, the diversity of peoples was a useful argument against the view that West Irian was ethnically separate from the rest of the archipelago; what was more 'different' about the Papuans than the wandering negrito-type tribes of Sumatra or the primitive inland Dyaks of Kalimantan? Compared with the Javanese aristocrat, they were all like people from another world. The backwardness of the Papuans, or anyone else, is also in itself a contributor to nationalism, for it was the Dutch who made them that way, as it was the also the Portuguese who kept the people of

Timor in a state of colonial torpor. President Sukarno gave the order that 400 000 (or nearly half) of the Papuans—those living in the jungle without outside contact—were to be drawn from the wilds ('at bayonet point if necessary', the then ambassador to Malaya, Lieutenant-General Djatikusomo, is reported to have suggested enthusiastically), and their level of life raised to that of 'us all' in five years. In October 1962 Dr Subandrio made an emotional address to a group of West Irianese visiting Jakarta, in which he told them he had wept in New York when he had seen the film *The Sky Above and the Mud Below*. He felt ashamed that his 'own brothers' were being 'put on show to the whole world as though they were half animals and half humans'. (After seeing the film, he resolved 'willy-nilly to liberate West Irian'.)

Many times during the long West Irian crisis, Indonesians privately expressed the view that the Papuans were their 'brothers' and that whether or not Indonesia could afford to look after them as well as the Dutch, the Australians, or some international agency might do, it was 'better' for the Papuans to be part of their own family. The same sentiments were later expressed, although less confidently, about the people of northern Borneo (Sarawak and Sabah) who had joined Malaysia. Provided the view was taken that Malaysia was 'neo-colonialist' and therefore not part of the family, the Dyaks, Dusuns and others were artificially separated from their Indonesian 'brothers'. This was not the official view, at least as it was publicly expressed, but at the emotional level at which the Indonesian people necessarily consider their relationship with others, it was easy to define 'diversity' very loosely and 'unity' very broadly, so that the concept of the Indonesian 'family' and its moral, indefinable ties became a force for nationalism.

During the Cold War, Indonesian nationalism was kept alive by non-alignment, or neutrality, in the ideological conflict between East and West. In the 1990s, when one might have expected that nationalism would fade, it was revived by the spectacle of failing states and disintegrating societies, as the resources of the Cold War were withdrawn and redistributed. The collapse of the former Yugoslavia was a dramatic lesson to Indonesians. As the conflict between Serbia, Croatia and Bosnia intensified, Indonesian forces were sent as part of the unsuccessful United Nations bid to keep the peace. The memory of their own regional and religious diversity was never far from the minds of those responsible for Indonesia's security.

For the sake of statistics, Indonesia is regarded as 90 per cent Muslim. Islam is also regarded as a useful link with countries of Africa and the Middle East, and Pakistan. It is sometimes called upon to justify the 'brotherhood' of Indonesians and Malaysians, although the argument of common racial stock, which then includes the Christian Philippines, is more widely used. However, while culturally the Javanese remain dominant in Indonesia, Islam in that country, like Indonesian Hinduism, Buddhism and Christianity, is a pliable plant.

The Javanese have a genealogy of the creation in which Nabi (Prophet) Adam married Babu Kawa (Eve) and had two sons, Nabi Sis and Sajang Sis (the *wayang* clown figure Semar). Nabi Sis gave birth to all the Prophets, such as Nabi Ibrahim (Abraham), Nabi Nure (Noah), Nabi Muhammad and Nabi Isa (Jesus). The various Western peoples descended from their Nabis (the Arabs from Muhammad, the Dutch from Jesus, etc.) and Sajang Sis, or Semar, gave birth to the Hindus and the Javanese. Thus, all people and all religions are the same.

One day, in the middle of the Muslim fasting month in the 1960s, I had a lunch appointment with a minister of the Indonesian government. As food is prohibited between sunrise and sunset (or between the times when you can tell the difference between a black and a white cotton thread held at arm's length), I wondered what my host would eat while his guest enjoyed—I hoped—a good assortment of satay sticks, curry and other Javanese delicacies. In fact, we ate at a Chinese restaurant and my host consumed as much as I did. So did two of his officials, who shared the meal. After three hours of food and talk, when we were all amiably at the point of collapsing into sleep, I managed to ask one of the officials, out of the minister's hearing, whether this was the normal behaviour for Indonesian government officials during the Muslim fasting month. 'It depends', he replied, 'on the guest'. This was not meant to reflect on the appetite of Australian visitors, although in the best Javanese circles hearty eating is associated with a thick head and rapid physical decay. It was a simple example of the flexibility of Indonesian standards.

Many Westerners feel they cannot 'trust' Indonesians. What an Indonesian may regard as flexibility and common sense, or a proper deference, a Westerner may find dishonest or indefinite. The Indonesian will almost certainly say the Westerner's principles are harsh and arrogant. 'Westerners are too nervy', an Indonesian told me. 'You need to relax more, remove some of the tension.' Apparent lack of tension in Indonesia, which should not be confused with an absence of violence, is not only a matter of climate. It is supported by a complex philosophical system, developed on Java by the upper classes in their courtly societies, which has now seeped down to the people and is 'good form' at all respectable levels of Indonesian life. Javanese life, which sets the pattern in Indonesia, especially in official circles, is disciplined by a set of ideals and stylized behaviour patterns which are as sophisticated as any of the great aristocratic fashions of Western civilization.

As developed over centuries, the central aim of the upper class, known as *priyayi* (a Javanese word meaning 'official'), was absolute self-control, leading to spiritual enlightenment. Only when the two forms of self-control—the ordering of one's inner nature and of one's relationships with others—were perfected, could one achieve the mystic understanding which resolves earthly ambiguity. External self-control was the first aim, as it was easier to achieve than internal control, and its perfection was meant to lead to a state of calm in one's relationships which, in avoiding emotional extremes, such as feelings of being startled or disappointed, left one free to concentrate on creating internal control. The ideal emotional state, a kind of unshakeable evenness of feeling, is expressed in the negative maxim, 'happy now, unhappy later'; one tries to get beyond happiness and unhappiness, as other mystics attempt to escape good and evil.

This approach to life has resulted in the two concepts, *alus* and *kasar*. *Alus* is the desired external attributes, including what is pure, refined, polished, polite, exquisite, ethereal, subtle, civilized and smooth, while *kasar* is the disapproved opposites, which include such things as 'badly-played music, a stupid joke or a cheap piece of cloth', to quote Clifford Geertz. Passion is fit only for children, animals, peasants and foreigners, and the *alus* attitudes which lead to a placid stability have been codified into patterns of behaviour which, although quite logical when viewed in context, may be irritatingly illogical when seen through Western eyes. It is, for instance, not only regarded as usual, but as a positive virtue, not to say what one really means, or to express one's true feelings. This is partly a matter of *priyayi* etiquette, as it is good manners to hide one's own wishes in deference to the other person—a perpetual and subtle 'after you, Alphonse; no, after you, Gaston'. It is also because negative feelings toward another must never be shown, and positive ones only in situations of intimacy—strong feelings which upset another person will rebound, and one's own emotional equilibrium will be disturbed.

The result is that Javanese expect to have to read between the lines of other people's speech and attitudes, and have themselves come almost automatically not to say what they mean, with an instinctive dissimulation called *etok-etok*. 'Bluntness is simply not a virtue, and by the time one comes to the point in a well-modelled *priyayi* conversation, everyone should know what is going to be said, and often it is not necessary to come to the point at all—a great relief to everyone', writes Clifford Geertz. He describes a village politician saying in an election speech, 'I too never say what I really think, and you can't tell how I feel about things by what I say'. In the same vein, one must never directly refuse to do something which a person requests, as this is both impolite and likely to lead to unpleasant feelings. Rather, one agrees, and then uses various *etok-etok* excuses until the person realizes one wasn't serious in the first place. A common style of praise for someone is 'one can never tell how he feels inside by how he behaves outside'.

There are also certain stylized forms of politeness according to rank, which were so nicely observed that quite separate Javanese languages have evolved for speaking to your inferior, your equal and your superior (in addition to an ancient poetic language, a classical Javanese, and special vocabularies for the royal court and for the gods). One reason that is given for the colonial Dutch insistence on the mutual use of Malay as a lingua franca is that officials, used to dealing with Javanese royalty, knew only the forms of language used for equals or superiors, but would not allow Javanese to use these forms. (They would not allow Indonesians to address them in Dutch, because this also implied an unacceptable equality.) Another rule of etiquette is that it is impolite to have one's head higher than another's, especially when the other person is of higher rank. Geertz describes as impossible manners, to a Javanese, the typical American action of clapping someone on the back while towering above them and saying 'Let's go into town'—it is too direct, too intimate, and implies superiority. This overall control is expressed in language in another way also—'the higher social level of dialect one uses in Javanese, the more slowly, softly, and evenly in rhythm and pitch one speaks'.

Many Westerners have noticed a tendency for Indonesians to laugh and behave with studied nonchalance. The hero figure is a casual, elegant stylist, with an unfurrowed brow and an air of confidence. A report in the press during one of many foreign crises in 1963 pictured the foreign correspondents—Australian, British, American, Malaysian, Filipino and others—in a state of confusion, trying to establish what was going on inside the conference room. They turned to an Indonesian reporter named Charlie. 'Come on, tell us what your Indonesian officials are really out to do, huh? . . . Come on . . .' Soft-spoken Charlie just smiled. Whether Charlie knew about *priyayi* ethics or not, his behaviour was splendidly in the tradition. The concept of outward and inner calm as an ideal state has been adopted by Javanese who are not of the *priyayi* class. So, an animist talking of spirits explained to Clifford Geertz that 'if a person is startled, confused, mixed up, and doesn't know where he is, he becomes empty and the *djinn* can enter him easily'. People who talk loudly, are aggressive, lack manners, dress sloppily and blurt out whatever they're thinking are considered un-Javanese, and like children, or wild animals. Most Javanese drink very little intoxicating spirits, not only because liquor is expensive, but because they intensely dislike the feeling of lack of control that drinking produces.

(It will have occurred to discerning readers that the problems in all of this for Indonesia's neighbour, Australia, which has a reputation even among Western nations for direct speech and child-like behaviour, are considerable. An attempt to deal with them is made in Chapter 10.)

The traditional art forms, which include the *wayang* (theatre), the making of *batik* (patterned cloth), and classical music, dance and poetry, are all included within the framework of *priyayi* philosophy, although they were until recently—and in many places still are—the favourite arts and entertainments of the whole population. Thus, the famous *wayang* stories of ancient Indian and Indonesian kingdoms, wars and religious struggles, are to the village people both an entertainment and a protection against the spirits (a *wayang* performance often lasts all night, from 9 p.m. until 6 a.m., and while one is in attendance the spirits cannot cause harm). But to the *priyayi* they symbolize, in an elaborate interpretation, the conflict between *alus* and *kasar* feelings, the struggle between people's refined and base impulses, which, when successfully resolved, brings the ultimate mystic understanding, the merging of feeling and meaning, which is called *rasa*. In some views, the puppeteer or *dalang* is symbolic of god, the light which projects the puppets' shadows on to the screen represents eternal life, and the shadows themselves are people's souls, while the puppets are their bodies.

The making of *batik* was considered a spiritual discipline because of the months of 'great inward concentration' which it took to design and dye a piece, and a mystic experience is still described as 'drawing a design on the heart'. Certain patterns could only be made by *priyayi*, and in the pre-war period, some wives supported themselves and their families by making and selling *batiks*, their husbands seldom earning enough money through the prestige work of administration in the sultans' *kratons* (palace cities).

Much of the aloof social distinctiveness of the *priyayi* ethic disappeared after the war, especially in the Jogjakarta area, where the sultan led the way in introducing democratic standards, and it is now possible to be considered a *priyayi* because of one's education, work or position. This has itself created difficulties, particularly in the new education. The 'white-collar' attraction is strong, buttressed by centuries of extremely formalized Dutch education habits. The struggle that science and technology had in Western countries to be recognized as equal in status with the humanities is reflected in modern Indonesian education. It has been especially difficult to turn the genuine enthusiasm for learning, such as in removing illiteracy, toward practical benefits for an essentially agricultural community. Applied biology and chemistry are as useful to Indonesia at this stage of its development as the prestigious international studies of law and languages on the one hand, or nuclear physics on the other. Nor are the *priyayi* virtues good for business, although young Indonesians have been as fashionable as young Asians generally in pursuit of postgraduate degrees in business administration.

The *priyayi* influence in modern Indonesia should not, therefore, be over-stated. Obviously, the rules of etiquette are no longer formally followed as they were behind the walls of the king's *kraton*. But they remain, as a core of formality, in the attitudes and behaviour of some élites and official Indonesia, which is probably at least as bureaucratic as the old Javanese states. As the seat of government, Java's influence is paramount, and under both Sukarno and Suharto this influence has been given full rein.

There is already a tradition, among writers in particular, to work at the world they see and feel for themselves, rather than the shadow world of the puppets. In 1922 what is considered Indonesia's first 'modern novel' was published, *Siti Nurbaja (Miss Nurbaja)*, by Marah Rusli, which described the conflict of a Minangkabau girl caught between *adat* demands that she marry someone of her parents' choice and her love for a young 'modernist'. It was written partly in the old, stylized Malay poetic form (*pantun*), but partly in modern Malay, which as Bahasa Indonesia was adopted by Indonesian nationalists as the national language at the All-Indonesian Youth Congress in 1928. Between 1922 and 1933 several other sociological novels were written, almost all of them, like the first, by young writers from Minangkabau, one of whom, Selasih, was Indonesia's first woman novelist. The preponderance of Minangkabaus among twentieth-century Indonesian writers is partly explained by the fact that their language is very similar to the Malay that comprises Bahasa Indonesia, and it was easier for them than for other Indonesian peoples to obtain a rapid fluency in the national language. But the Minangkabau excel in many fields and some observers believe that as monotheistic, mountain people they are tougher and more independently creative than the more verbal, stylized Javanese.

The most influential of the groups of Indonesian writers that arose during the 1920s and 1930s was Pudjangga Baru or The New Writer, an organization which began to publish a magazine in 1933 dedicated to 'the new dynamic spirit' and the creation of 'the new Indonesian culture—the culture of unity in Indonesia'. One member, Takdir Alisjahbana, a Sumatran who became a lawyer, wrote a popular novel called *Lajar Terkembang* (*Unfurled Sails*) which argued for the emancipation of women, and was the first novel to insist that national progress could not be achieved unless women studied and worked along with men. He strongly opposed the work of another of the New Writers, Sanusi Pane, because his verse and drama concentrated on the Hindu-Javanese period (in, for instance, a play called *The Twilight of Majapahit*) which Alisjahbana called 'pre-Indonesian'. Pudjangga Baru was suppressed during the Japanese occupation, but the man regarded as the greatest poet of the young Indonesian republic, Chairil Anwar, born in Medan in 1922 of Minangkabau parents, began to write during this time, although most of his work was not published until after the war. Another who began his work during the occupation was the short-story writer Idrus, a Minangkabau born in 1921 whose style has become a model of succinct vividness.

In 1946 Anwar and other writers and painters founded an association called The Arena (Gelanggang), which published two magazines and held art exhibits. It opposed the resurrected New Writer (which was dissolved as a group in 1954) as stereotyped and out of date and, in its manifesto, declared itself the heirs of 'world culture', refusing to define Indonesian culture except as all the manifestations of the people's creative impulses. Its younger generation opponents, who included the poet Sobron Aidit, younger brother of the PKI leader, formed the People's Cultural Institute (Lembaga Kebudayaan Rakyat —Lekra) whose aim was 'critical realism' and 'romantic revolutionism' and who renounced Gelanggang as interested in individuals rather than the social good.

Chairil Anwar died of typhus in 1949 at the age of twenty-seven, after a riotous life which reminds one of the romantic European poets of the nineteenth century. He is being rediscovered now in Indonesia by a new generation of poets, and praised for his rebel spirit and his celebration of the senses. 'His was the first and last insolence', writes Goenawan Mohamad, lamenting the effect of censorship on the vitality of Indonesian writing. One of Chairil Anwar's more conventional poems, dealing with the guerrilla struggle against the Dutch, became an Indonesian classic.

> *We who lie between Krawang and Bekasi*
> *We are not able to shout 'Merdeka!' and take aim again.*
>
> *But who will not hear our coming?*
> *As a vision, we charge with beating hearts.*
> *We speak to you in the quiet of the night*
> *When the bosom is empty of feeling*
> *And the clock is clicking on the wall.*
>
> *We die young. What is left is only dusty bone.*
> *Remember, do remember us.*
>
> *We have already tried what we can*
> *But work is not over yet—far from it.*
>
> *We have already given our lives*
> *But work is not over yet, meaning has*
> *not yet been given to four or five thousand lives.*
>
> *We are only scattered bones*
> *But they are yours*
> *You have to decide the value of those scattered bones.*
>
> *Whether we lost our lives for the sake*
> *of Freedom, Victory and the Future*
> *or just in vain,*

We don't understand, we are not able to speak.
You have to speak now.

We speak to you in the quiet of the night
When the bosom is empty of feeling
And the clock is clicking on the wall.

Remember, do remember us
Continue, do continue our spirit.
Guard Bung Karno
Guard Bung Hatta
Guard Bung Sjahrir.

We are now dead corpses
Do give meaning to us
Do guard the border line between reality and dream.

Remember, do remember us
We who are only dusty bones,
Thousands—we lie between Krawang and Bekasi.

In the 1960s there were attacks in the press on 'intellectualism and cosmopolitanism' in Indonesian literature, condemning Chairil Anwar, Takdir Alisjahbana, Idrus and others. The life of the creative intellectual in nationalist Indonesia, when the Great Leader set the standards and monopolized the symbols, was frustrating. The breakthrough came in March 1966 when the students brought the Sukarno regime to its knees. The so-called 1966 Generation—with Mochtar Lubis, released from gaol, as its hero—became the symbol-bearers of Indonesian culture in the New Order.

The New Order has been notable for economic development, however, not for creativity in the arts. Censorship has cast a pall over poetry, novel-writing and theatre. The local film industry has almost disappeared, swamped by cheap imports. A woman novelist N. H. Dini was admired in the 1970s and another woman writer Marga T wrote popular romances. A Catholic priest and radical architect wrote a celebrated novel in the 1980s, *Burung-Burung Manya* (*The Weaverbirds*). Indonesia's greatest contemporary novelist is Pramoedya Ananta Toer, whose major historical work (beginning with *Bumi Manusia—This Earth of Mankind*) covers the half-century before Indonesia's independence. Pramoedya was imprisoned as a communist sympathiser after the 1965 abortive coup and sale of his work is still illegal in

Indonesia. Sales outside Indonesia have been considerable. In 1995 he was awarded the Magsaysay Prize for literature, creating controversy in Indonesia, where in the media he is treated as a non-person and because Mochtar Lubis, an earlier recipient, handed back his award.

The sudden death in 1989 of Soedjatmoko was a loss to Indonesian culture. His voice as journalist, diplomat or scholar, always hopeful and constructive, had been heard for so long on all the big issues linking Indonesia with the world that it seemed to represent an abiding Indonesian quality which governments had lost.

But culture is not just the expressive arts, nor the contemporary media, but also what is in the minds of people as they perform their daily rituals and live out the details of ordinary lives. Indonesians have been swamped with the modern world, it would seem, and sometimes, when you walk through an arcade of shops in central Jakarta, the goods on display and the style of the shoppers is indistinguishable from those in any large city in the world. There is little of national culture to be seen, and one might be led to assume from this snapshot that Indonesians, and especially young Indonesians, are becoming part of a global culture which owes nothing to Indonesia's own history. While true for a few, this cannot be said of most Indonesians. Even among urban, educated youth, there is less simple imitation of the Western world than there was thirty years ago. The Asia-Pacific countries, including Indonesia, have become more economically and culturally confident.

One incident in Indonesia's contemporary history continues to haunt the memory of thoughtful Indonesians. The mass killings which followed the coup of 30 September 1965, and which have become an indelible aspect of the transition to the New Order of Suharto's presidency, have been wiped from the official record, which concentrates instead on the unpatriotic infamy of the communists who were under the influence of outside ideas and political powers. Luang Buaya (Crocodile Hole), the waterless well at Halim where the bodies of the slain generals were dumped, has become a shrine and a tourist attraction. Busloads of schoolchildren arrive to file on the viewing platform erected at the opening to the well. The six martyrs form a monumental statue overlooking the site. Two huts nearby are presented in *son-et-lumière* style as the command headquarters of the coup leaders, where the generals were tortured and killed. A short walk away is a modern museum presenting the history of the PKI's traitorous struggle against the Indonesian state.

But beneath the official surface, disquiet remains. Why did it happen? How did it happen? For a variety of reasons, the disquiet was much stronger in 1995 than I had expected. Because of the half-century celebrations, history, and especially Sukarno's part in it, was in people's minds. Also, the question of the presidential succession, and how it will be managed, was uppermost in political calculations. In addition, the thirty year anniversary of the coup jogged memories, alerting some to the likely release of official documents in those countries, such as the United States, Britain and Australia, which had a political interest in the effects of the coup and its aftermath.

There is still uncertainty about the statistics of the killings, which range credibly from some hundreds of thousands to a million, but the actual figure is not as important as the way the killings occurred. At a certain point, debate about the scale of mass killing becomes a distraction, like argument about whether the victims of the Holocaust were less than six million or whether Pol Pot was per capita a greater murderer than Stalin. What troubles some Indonesians is the nature of their own killings, what they reveal about Indonesian culture and whether they can happen again.

The killings were both contrived and spontaneous, subject to both national and local factors. If we accept as plausible that the 30 September coup was a clever manoeuvre which failed dismally, the key responses afterwards are not difficult to understand. The bodies of the six generals and Nasution's aide were exhumed and prominently displayed in the print media. A lurid account was circulated that women from the communist organization Gerwani had stripped and performed a *tarian harum bunga* ('dance of the fragrant flowers') before an audience of PKI cadres, culminating in sexual mutilation of the officers, living and dead, before their bodies were dumped in the well at Halim. In a society where treatment of the body after death is subject to careful ritual, such rumors were heard with horror. The term 'Gestapu' was coined (Gerakan September Tiga Puluh—Movement of September 30) inferring an evil comparable with the Nazi Gestapo. These steps and many others in the days and weeks after the failed coup were part of a transparent campaign of fear and loathing intended to demonize the PKI.

But the feature of the killings that followed was that they swamped parts of the country—Java and Bali—like a giant tidal wave. Initiated by army leaders, they were carried out spontaneously, like a vast pogrom, with a complete absence of constraint by the police and other civil authorities. This was not a massacre, in the sense that unarmed civilians were killed as deliberate policy by armed servants of the state. It was not amok-running, if that description characterizes a frenzied form of defence which usually results in the death of the amok-runners. The term could have been more aptly applied to the communists, if they had tried to escape in this fashion, but in fact they went quietly, often passively, to their deaths. The killings did not in any way resemble, therefore, the inevitable loss of life of a civil war. They were the result of mass violence, directed by the new national masters in Jakarta and carried out indiscriminately at local level sometimes by the army itself, sometimes by vigilante groups, often by a combination of both, and sometimes as a result of local religious antagonisms, business rivalry, family feuds and artistic prejudices.

One recurrent theme in the killings is the tension, especially in east and central Java, between the *abangan* and *santri* streams of Indonesian Muslims. In west Java, the mass violence was considerably less, due it is thought to the fact that this was the home of fundamentalist Darul Islam, which had been subdued by the army and was not trusted now to be unleashed. Nominally Muslim, *abangan* Javanese followed pre-Islamic, Hindu-Buddhist beliefs, mixed with animism and mysticism, while *santris* were more orthodox and avowedly Muslim. The PKI's following was almost entirely *abangan*, while traditional Muslims turned more to Masjumi, Mohammadijah or Nahdatul Ulama. The main killers apart from the army itself were drawn from the orthodox Muslim streams, especially the youth group Ansor, associated with Nahdatul Ulama. From all accounts, the high politics of the communists did not worry traditional village Muslims as much as their irreligion and 'black magic' practices. But it is also likely that the very practical issue of land reform was part of the tension. In some areas the mosques were considerable landowners, and the PKI had nailed land reform to its mast.

The communists' passive acceptance of their fate is a feature of accounts of the killings. Some undressed, some paraded in white funeral clothes for their execution. Did they face death calmly because they were convinced of the historical inevitability of their cause? Was their serenity part of their belief-system, an acceptance of fate? Or were they humbled by guilt? Or lost and confused, abandoned by their leaders? Because such a blanket of silence has been thrown over the traumatic events of 1965–66, except for the official version, accounts of the killings are spare and lack the kind of imaginative sympathy that creates an understanding of human tragedy. Much of the above detail is drawn from *The Indonesian Killings 1965–1966*, edited by Robert Cribb and published by Monash University.

Indonesians today worry over this piece of their history partly because it has been suppressed and partly because they fear that it demonstrates something about the tensions within their society which, in the event of another power struggle over the succession in Jakarta, could trigger again mass violence in the countryside.

In 1983 a series of unexplained killings took place which became known as the *petrus* killings (*penembakan misterius*—mysterious shootings). They began in Jogjakarta and spead widely, eventually running into thousands. The victims were usually known criminals or escaped prisoners whose names were on a blacklist, and the killers were usually squads of military personnel. The killings, although unexplained, were widely publicized and were clearly part of some official campaign. As in 1965–66, the forces of civil law and order observed what was happening with their hands firmly behind their backs. In his autobiography, President Suharto accepts responsibility, with only a murmur of concern. There was nothing mysterious about the killings. These were criminals, who were murdering, robbing and raping innocent people.

Of course we had to take drastic action and give these people treatment commensurate with their conduct. But how drastic? Well, we had to use force. But this did not mean that we just shot them, bang, bang and were finished with it. No! Those who resisted, yes, they were shot. There was no other choice, because they resisted.

Some of the bodies were just left where they had been shot. This was meant as shock therapy so that people would realise that loathsome acts would meet with strong action . . . And so these despicable crimes came to an end.

For most Indonesians, history and memory are not two separate streams of the past—one with dates, events and interpretations, the other personal and microscopic. They are entangled in the one thread. The killings, justified by the state, have become part of Indonesian culture, to the concern of Indonesians who prized its elegance and its restraint.

CHAPTER EIGHT

Land

'FROM SABANG TO Merauke', the geographical catch-cry of Indonesian nationalism, defines the nation by its territorial limits. The 13 000 islands between the nation's western extremity, Sabang, an island off the tip of Sumatra, and its eastern limit, Merauke, a town almost on the border with Papua New Guinea, are so varied, however, in both land and people, that this chapter is no more than a simple guide to one of the most complex countries in the world.

In the far west, closest to the Malaysian peninsula, is Sumatra, or Sumatera as it is spelled in Indonesia. When Marco Polo came there in 1292, he called it 'Java the less', but Sumatra (460 square kilometres) is in fact three times as large as Java (or twice the size of Victoria). Marco Polo's derogatory comparison has echoed down the centuries, with rebellious consequences that persist today. Sumatra is similar in climate to the Malayan peninsula, and the narrow, shallow Strait of Malacca has been a point of contact between the two land areas rather than a factor of separation. More important as a barrier have been the swamps and marshes on the east coast, which contrast with the mountains of the west. Some of the most spectacular scenery in all Indonesia—which is saying a great deal—is found along the parallel chains of western mountains, punctuated with volcanic peaks, and the valleys lying between them, flooded with lakes. Lake Toba, the biggest, is 75 kilometres long, surrounded by cliffs up to 70 metres high, themselves split by deep gorges and watched over by dormant cones. The world's largest bloom, the *Rafflesia*, whose flowers may be as much as a metre in diameter, luxuriates on the west coast. Much of central Sumatra is a jungle plain crossed by rivers and inhabited by elephants and tigers (and, until recently, by a few remaining orang-utans). It was in this region that the rebel colonels and economists of PRRI fought their losing battle in 1958.

The most extensive cultivation is in the north, adjoining the Strait of Malacca. Here the Dutch established an elaborate plantation system in a region known as the East Coast Residency, now run by the Indonesian government, producing rubber (no longer Sumatra's most important crop, although still strong in the area of Jambi), tobacco, tea, palm oil and fibres. Palm oil has become the major crop. Medan, in this area, is Sumatra's largest city and a cultural melting pot as a result of labour imported mainly from Java and other islands to work the Dutch estates. A significant mineral resource is oil, and Palembang in the south is one of Indonesia's refinery cities. Aceh in the north also has oil and natural gas, as well as a long-held attitude toward Jakarta of independence, even defiance. Sumatra has more mining enterprises than any other Indonesian island, especially in coal which has become a major export. The tin-producing islands of Bangka and Billiton lie off the east coast. Although tin as an industry has lost much of its significance, one way of knowing you are in Sumatra rather than Java is the change from terracotta to tin roofs. The bauxite islands of the Riau archipelago, some of which can be seen from Singapore's harbour, are also off the east coast.

Sumatra is the second most populous island in the archipelago. Its 36.5 million people (growth rate 2.7 per cent) are mainly smallholders cultivating commercial produce and some dry food crops (such as corn, cassava and dry rice). They live in strongly differentiated societies, whose patterns of *adat* and religion have been so strict that since the end of the last century successive younger generation intellectuals and traders have escaped to the relativism of Java, where they are noticeable for a direct outlook, open faces and energy. Sumatrans have stood in disproportionate numbers among the forgers of the Indonesian Republic, as political leaders like Hatta, Sjahrir, Nasution, Adam Malik, Natsir and Agus Salim, and as writers, among them Marah Rusli, Alisjahbana, the Pane brothers, Chairil Anwar, Idrus and Sitor Situmorang.

The Acehenese, in the far north-west of Sumatra, were the first to welcome Islam and among the last to succumb to the Dutch. The people are known for their martial spirit and sense of freedom, and during the police actions of 1947 and 1948 the Dutch significantly left them alone. Aceh has been washed for centuries by the flow of peoples over the Indian Ocean and it has ancient associations with Arabia. In the sixteenth century many Indian craftsmen, including slaves, lived there. The Acehenese represent the strictest, or most fanatical, Muslim variant in Indonesia. Aceh has the status of a 'special area' (like Jogjakarta—and as some East Timorese have demanded).

The Batak peoples live in the mountains around Lake Toba and part of the east coast. Batak was originally a derogatory Malay term, meaning 'robber' or 'blackmailer', and the tribes were traditionally repressed, squeezed as they are between the Acehenese and the Minangkabau. About half of the Batak people are Muslim, having been almost isolated until the middle of the nineteenth century, when Dutch Protestant missionaries arrived. Now about half the Toba Batak are Christian. A few of the other Batak tribes are still animist. Batak clans warred with other clan-villages; the rivalry between the Toba and Karo Batak is still a factor of local politics. Rigid kinship ties and communal authority over land may have been a factor in extensive Batak migration to other islands during this century, and Christian Toba Batak are prominent in the army, education and commerce.

The Minangkabau, to the south-west of the Batak, live like them in the interior highland valleys centred around the town of Bukittingi and in coastal Padang. Their language is closely related to Malay and in their border areas they merge with the surrounding coastal Malays. The Minangkabau people have been Muslim for three centuries, but have retained their matrilineal family structure, in which descent and inheritance are determined through the mother, not the father, with a woman's brother, rather than her husband, ruling the family group. Their elaborately decorated houses, with roofs curved like buffalo horns (*minang kabau* means 'our buffalo has won', which folk-stories say is how, in a challenge-fight with the buffalo of another people, the Minangkabau founded their homeland), testify to a high standard of culture and skill. When the Dutch stopped the system of forced coffee growing in 1910, cash-crop farming of copra, coffee, rubber and coconuts became a primary interest, and the Minangkabau's commercial shrewdness enabled them to exclude Chinese middlemen, which few other Indonesian peoples were able to do. Interest in education has always been high, and this, in combination with the tradition of a trip outside the region by almost all young bachelors, to give them standing in the female-oriented society, has resulted in a migration of Minangkabau traders and intellectuals throughout the archipelago and into high positions in the government and civil service.

South Sumatra is now administratively a separate province. In the area of the Lampung people, it has a sizeable population of Javanese immigrant rice-farmers, as well as former plantation labourers from central and west Java. Small-holder coffee plantations are now common, and pepper is exported.

Moving in a clockwise direction, Kalimantan (Borneo) lies east of Sumatra. It is the third largest island in the world, and about three-quarters of its 720 000 square kilometres is Indonesian, an area slightly less than New South Wales. The island of Borneo has an active history, centred on Brunei, now a small, oil-rich sultanate and independent nation, but once a maritime kingdom embracing most of the island. Han dynasty (first century) ceramics have been discovered in east Borneo, as have the oldest inscriptions in Indonesia, which are in Sanscrit and date from the beginning of the fifth century. During the seventh century China traded with Borneo, primarily for pearls, and birds' nests for soup. But with Brunei's waning power and the division last century into British and Dutch Borneo, the island became known primarily for its natural resources, especially primary rainforest which is quickened by an average rainfall of nearly 4000 millimetres a year. Ironwood used to be exported, as were tobacco, pepper and ivory, but now the main export is plywood. Of Indonesia's 114 plywood factories, 65 are in Kalimantan, which has the worst rate of deforestation in Indonesia. Experts estimate that approximately 60 per cent of Kalimantan is still forested, and the forest exists in large continuous blocks, unlike Sumatra where it is found in fragmented pockets. Gold, diamonds and coal are mined and oil is produced on the east coast near the town of Balikpapan (Indonesia's main refining centre) and on the east coast island of Tarakan. There are no active volcanoes in Kalimantan. In the forest, the boiling rivers and south-coast marshes and mangrove swamps, wild life flourishes, including the vanishing orangutans, proboscis monkeys, gibbons, wild oxen (used on the republic's crest to symbolize the people's sovereignty), crocodiles, honey bears and leopards. There are more than 600 varieties of birds, and ferns, orchids and pitcher plants deck ground and trees.

The 9 million people (growth rate 3 per cent) who live in Kalimantan are fairly sharply divided between the coastal people—Malays, Bandjars in the area around the south estuary city of Bandjarmasin (the largest in Kalimantan), and Chinese, most of whom live on the west coast nearest to Singapore and in the major town of Pontianak—and inland tribes. The coastal peoples are mostly Muslim and engage in commerce and smallholder cultivation of rubber, coconuts and pepper. The peoples of the interior include Dyak, Kajan, Dusun and Murut. They are primarily animist, although some have become Muslim and Christian, and tend to live nomadic lives, dependent for their rice, maize, cassava and vegetables on the slash-and-burn method of *ladang* cultivation, clearing new areas of farmland every year. This system has resulted in serious soil exhaustion and erosion in several areas. Like Kalimantan itself, most of its people's resources have not yet been tapped. An Australian coal company is working in east Kalimantan and there have been discoveries of oil and natural gas.

Sulawesi (Celebes), lying west of Kalimantan across the Makassar Strait, is surely one of the most curiously shaped islands in the world. It has four tentacular arms, and was called 'the' Celebes by the sixteenth-century Portuguese, who thought that the arms were separate islands. The fourth in size of Indonesia's 'big five' islands (155 000 square kilometres, or somewhat smaller than Victoria), it is, like Kalimantan, extremely mountainous, with volcanic activity in the northeast. Because of its rugged terrain, there has never been an important estate agriculture. The interior peoples practise shifting cultivation, which in some areas has led to serious erosion; they grow dry rice, maize and coconuts. Some irrigated rice is grown in Toraja. In south Sulawesi, both *sawah* and *ladang* rice is grown. The major export, especially in the north, is copra, which is Indonesia's second most important small-holding crop. Coffee, nutmeg, rubber and kapok are no longer exported, nor are the horns and hides of the cattle raised on the rich pastureland of the interior plateau. (In fact, these are now in short supply and have to be imported). But cocoa, produced in the south, has become a major Indonesian export and about 40 per cent of the cloves Indonesians need for their distinctive *kretek* cigarettes is produced in north Sulawesi. Nickel is well developed, but iron, gold, copper and lead are mined now only in small quantities in the south. The adjoining island of Buton produces asphalt. Sulawesi is poor in animal species compared with the rest of Indonesia, but some unique varieties are native, including the black-crested baboon, the dwarf buffalo and a pig called the pig-deer because of its long slender legs and curved, hornlike tusks.

There are 12.5 million people (growth rate 1.9 per cent) on Sulawesi. The north-east and south-west are the most densely populated, with peoples who, except for the Manadonese in the north-east, have made their names known throughout the world for their seafaring activities. The Buginese and Makassarese, both ardently Muslim, live in south-west Sulawesi, the most fertile part of the island, which in parts has a population twenty times more dense than the rest of the island, and during the fourteenth to eighteenth centuries was divided into many coastal kingdoms. The Buginese, whose name is still almost synonymous with 'pirates' in South-East Asia, were among the world's most intrepid ocean-going warriors, and their square-sailed, high-prowed ships still anchor in picturesque clusters in harbours throughout the region. Their principal kingdom was Bone (the Gulf of Bone between Sulawesi's two southern arms bears testimony to its fame) from which they warred with Makassar over the centuries, and they maintained colonies in the Rhio Islands, Borneo and elsewhere in the archipelago. Because of this and their extreme mobility, Buginese are now to be found in many parts of coastal Indonesia.

The Makassarese are centred around Makassar, which is Sulawesi's largest city, capital, and chief port and trading centre. From their kingdom of Gowa they used to sail and trade as far as China. Before the Dutch 'pacification' of 1905 they had large numbers of slaves, and an exclusive aristocracy. The Makassarese are a proud and competitive people, and their society is one of elaborate personal and political rivalry, with almost unlimited possibilities for individual achievement.

In the rugged mountains of central Sulawesi are the Toraja, who before 1905 were one of the fiercest and most isolated peoples in Indonesia. They lived in small, walled fortress-villages, each atop a hill, like the castles of medieval Europe, and warred almost constantly with each other for heads and slaves. Headhunting was a political, religious and social requirement; taking the head of an enemy robbed his village of vital supernatural powers, and enemy heads were a necessary offering to ancestral spirits at burials and temple consecrations, ensuring the village's welfare and its agricultural and human fertility. Convicted sorcerers were sold to other villages where they were beheaded. Only women and transvestite men could become witch-doctors, but the villages were governed by family headmen under one chief. People were buried at death, and then again several years later, when their bones were cleaned and their spirits transformed from devils to guardians. Each village owned the jungle around it, where slash-and-burn agriculture was practised. After 1901 the Dutch moved the villages down into the valleys, built connecting roads, instituted individual money taxes, and forbade headhunting, bone-cleaning and witch-executing. Most Toraja are now Christian.

The Minahasans and Manadonese live in Sulawesi's north-east, close to the Moluccas Islands. Because of their early and extensive contact with the spice islands' traders, they are racially mixed. The Dutch East India Company gained control of north-east Sulawesi in the seventeenth century and the Minahasans and Manadonese became Protestants. Throughout Holland's rule they supplied mercenaries for the Dutch army. Many emigrated to other islands and entered the colonial civil service, particularly on Java. The major city of the area is Manado, which is the second largest on Sulawesi.

The Moluccas, called Maluku in Indonesian, lie between Sulawesi and West Irian. Its population is 1.8 million (growth rate 2.7 per cent). The chain of volcanoes which runs through Sumatra and Java continues, but Maluku also contains some flat and swampy islands. The total land area is about 87 500 square kilometres, and the main islands are Halmahera, Obi, Sula, Seram, Buru, Ambon, Ternate, Tidor, and the Banda, Kai, Aru, Tanimbar and Wetar island groups. There are not many varieties of animal, but birds, including the bird of paradise and, on Seram, cassowaries flourish, as do shellfish, including trepang, or sea-cucumber, with a trade in mother-of-pearl. The main exports are, of course, spices, primarily cloves and nutmeg, but include sago and copra.

The islands' agricultural riches, which made them an early focal point of world trade, and attracted the Dutch to Indonesia, brought economic and social impoverishment to the people. From the fourteenth century on they were dominated in turn by Muslim Ternate, Catholic Portugal and Calvinist Holland. Christianity remains strong in the Moluccas. As a result of intense Dutch missionary activity, the level of education on Ambon was among the highest in Indonesia, and many Ambonese worked in the colonial administration and were an important and privileged segment of the Dutch army. After the revolution, some Ambonese chose Dutch citizenship and went to Holland. Amboina on the island of Ambon is the largest city and was the islands' administrative centre under the Dutch. The Ambonese language no longer exists, having been replaced by Malay and Dutch during the colonial period.

West Irian (Irian Jaya), the easternmost part of Indonesia, comprises the west half of New Guinea, the second largest island in the world (Greenland is the largest, if we exclude Australia, an island-continent). West Irian's 330 000 square kilometres is 22 per cent of Indonesia's total land area. It is about 80 per cent rainforest, and its interior is largely unexplored, ranging from steamy swamps to snow-capped mountains as high as 4800 metres. Rainfall is more than 6000 millimetres a year in places. Generally, soil is poor, and commercial agriculture was traditionally limited to coconut plantations for copra, mostly in the hands of Chinese in the Radja Ampat group of islands off the west coast, followed by crocodile skins and copal. Oil was produced in 1948 near Sorong, and the following year nickel was discovered near the capital (then called Hollandia, renamed Sukanopura and again renamed Jaya Pura). Pigs are an important livestock, and wallabies are hunted. Sweet potatoes and sago provide the staple diet.

The population is 1.6 million (growth rate 3.4 per cent), primarily Papuan, a people of stone-age culture, and Melanesian (in the coastal towns), with a baffling variety of tribes and language. No one language is intelligible to more than 150 000 people. Most of the West Irianese are animist, with some Muslim and Christian influences.

Irian Jaya has been a troubled province from the beginning. A guerrilla movement wanting secession (Organisasi Papua Merdeka—OPM) has survived since the 1960s. It has been active in resisting the American mining giant Freeport-McMoRan which has been digging for copper and gold since 1967. A spine of mineral wealth runs through the island (and into Papua New Guinea) of such potential that Freeport has teamed up with the British miner RTZ Corporation to exploit it. In 1988 a rich lode was discovered at Grasberg, 4000 metres up in the central mountain chain, and new sites at Etna Bay and Wabu are being explored.

Bali is one of the islands of the Lesser Sundas, which have a total population of 10 million (growth rate 1.8 per cent) and stretch from the western tip of Java eastward to Timor, making up Indonesia's southern boundary. It is separated from Java only by a narrow strait, and is similar to Java in climate, flora and fauna, and in its configuration of west to east volcanic chain, which includes Mount Agung. Like Java, Bali is intensively cultivated and *sawah* rice is a staple. Coconuts, sugar cane, tobacco, cocoa, indigo and peanuts are cultivated and some coffee is grown for export, although Bali has never had an export agriculture or exploited mineral resources. But the 2.7 million Balinese (growth rate 1.8 per cent), some of whom live on the

western end of the adjoining island of Lombok, are not like the
Javanese, nor like any other Indonesian people. The inheritors of a
unique blend of Hindu, Buddhist and local animist religions, untouched by Islam as a result of their ancestors' fierce protection of their
island from all invaders (including, until 1910, the Dutch), the
Balinese remain creative in their ritual society, building new temples,
inventing new music and dances and designing new sculptures and
paintings in honour of their many gods and spirits as well as maintaining the customary purification rites, processions, offerings and cre-
mations which fill their lives. Despite the twentieth century influx of
tourists and a recent growth of commercial activity (conducted largely
by the old nobility), Balinese society remains tightly knit, and few
people migrate to other islands. There is a patrilineal kinship system,
but family groups tend to overlap into the hundreds of temple associations, agricultural societies, and hamlet councils which interlock
throughout the countryside. All land is privately owned. There is little trace of the old Hindu castes, although the Brahmin priests are the
highest social class and there are still some marriage restrictions
according to rank. Marriage is by consent or by pre-arranged 'elope-
ment', and the young couple usually go to live with the groom's parents, unless the bride is the only daughter in the family. The capital of
Bali is Singaradia on the north coast, and the largest town is Denpasar,
in the south.

Bali has suffered two shocks since the first edition of this book was
published. One was the killings which followed the attempted coup of
1965, which were on a scale even greater than Java's. Another was,
and is, the tourist trade, which has grown from a trickle of visitors
drawn by the natural beauty and unique culture of the island to a flood
of packaged tourists seeking rest and recreation.

The other islands of the Lesser Sundas (called Nusa Tenggara,
'South-eastern Islands' in Indonesian) are influenced by the presence
of the Australian continent. Timor has such Australian flora as the
eucalypts, while Lombok has prickly pears and cockatoos. The people
of the Lesser Sundas are very mixed, including Malay, Papuan, Polynesian and indigenous groups. The islands are largely agricultural,
noted earlier for the production of sandalwood and horses. An attempt
has been made to develop new industries and commercial crops, but
the development of Timor in particular has been overshadowed by the
contentious political issue of the incorporation of the Portuguese half

of the island by Indonesia, which has not been recognized by the United Nations. The Timor Gap treaty between Indonesia and Australia (1988), a compromise agreement to set boundaries for oil exploration within the Timor Sea, was taken unsuccessfully by Portugal to the International Court of Justice. The major islands in addition to Bali and Timor are, from west to east, Lombok, on which is one of the highest volcanoes in the archipelago, Sumbawa, Sumba and Flores. The small island of Komodo is the home of the dragon lizards, oldest living genus of lizard—about 60 million years—which can reach a length of three metres.

The islands of Sulawesi, the Nusa Tenggaras, Maluku and Irian Jaya are sometimes grouped together and called Eastern Indonesia, defined by being east of the Wallace Line. This was drawn by the English naturalist Alfred Russel Wallace to separate what he considered South-East Asian flora and fauna in the west from that of Papua New Guinea and Australia to the east. The Suharto government took the unusual step of designating Eastern Indonesia as a region requiring attention in development, which ran against the long-held nationalist theme of 'unity in diversity'. However, the figures show that Eastern Indonesia has lagged behind the economic transformation of the rest of the country. Industry and infrastructure are relatively undeveloped. It contains the poorest parts in all of Indonesia. Gross domestic product per cepita is three times higher in Kalimantan, for example, and 70 per cent higher in Java and Bali.

Java (Jawa), separated from Sumatra by the narrow Sunda Strait and lying south of Kalimantan across the Java Sea, is radically different in appearance from the other major Indonesian islands because of its heavy population and almost total cultivation. It is one of the most densely populated places in the world. In a territory of 127 000 square kilometres, or about a fourteenth of Indonesia's total land area (almost twice the size of Tasmania, or about the same area as England and Wales combined), and with Madura, the smaller island just north of its eastern tip which is usually included in its statistics, it has a population of 108 million (growth rate 1.6 per cent) or nearly 820 people per square kilometre. Java is also by far the most urbanized of the islands.

Over 100 volcanoes, 17 of which are still grumbling, animate the mountain chain which runs from west to east close to Java's south coast, as a continuation of Sumatra's mountains, dividing the island into a narrow coastal strip on the Indian Ocean and a fertile plain which stretches north to the Java Sea. The climate is hot and wet, with some surprising variations—on the Dieng Plateau in central Java, the top of a 2000 metre filled volcanic crater, the temperature may fall below freezing, and rainfall ranges from 4150 millimetres at Bogor near Java's western tip to 875 millimetres at Asembagus in east Java, where the pronounced wet and dry seasons are caused largely by the nearness of the Australian continent. A quarter of Java's land area is given over to *sawah* or wet-rice cultivation, in irrigated fields and stepping up the terraced hillsides, where food fish are also raised (only 1 per cent of the land outside Java and Bali is *sawah* cultivated). Very little dry rice is grown; in the drier areas of eastern Java, cassava and maize supplant rice. Sweet potatoes, peanuts and soya beans are also important crops, and the government-run estates, which were second only to Sumatra's in extent but have declined in importance, produce tea, coffee, rubber, cinchona, cocoa, sugar and tobacco. But these export crops are not much help to the overcrowded peasant population, whose farming is almost entirely for subsistence, rather than the cash-crop small farming done on the other islands. The government land reform programmes are based on two hectares of land as a minimum holding for individual farmers, but in 1957 some 78 per cent of Javanese *sawah*-owners had less than half a hectare and 90 per cent less than one hectare—and today the figure is even lower. Farmers with such small holdings cannot make ends meet. In any case, there is not enough land in Java to give all of its landholders the 'minimum' two hectares and, unless the government is more successful than it has been in persuading Javanese to migrate to the land-rich outer islands, the standard of living will become an even more serious problem than it is now. Another difficulty due to over-population is the over-clearing of land, which has reduced Java's forests to about 3 per cent of the land area, resulting in extensive erosion during the monsoon seasons.

In the 1960s, 61 per cent of Java's population was categorized as very poor. In the 1990s, the figure is about 10 per cent. (Outside Java, the earlier figure was 52 per cent and in the 1990s about 7 per cent). Many Javanese are employed in the island's various industries, which range from cottage crafts like batik making and rattan weaving, to factories producing a growing range of goods, including cigarettes, textiles, soap, cement and paper, with some high-technology industry in Bandung. The most important mineral resource is probably still oil, which is found near Tjepu, on the border of east and central Java, and at Wonokromo, close to Surabaya, which is Indonesia's second largest city and the capital of the province of East Java. No oil has yet been discovered, however, in the Java Sea. Manganese, sulphur, gold and silver are mined, and there are extensive salt-works on Madura.

Despite the relative scarcity of forested land, a few one-horned rhinoceroses, and wild oxen, tigers, leopards and apes still exist on the island, as well as some 400 species of birds, including peacocks and edible-nest producing swifts, and more than 100 varieties of snakes, among them the great python. Some 70 per cent of all Indonesian cattle and water buffalo are concentrated in Java and Madura, where they are used as work animals. Teak, bamboo, casuarina and many varieties of fruit trees grow prolifically.

The Javanese peoples are not as distinctively separate as those in most parts of the archipelago. The reasons are population pressures, the large number of towns and roads, the steady influx over the last centuries of peoples from other islands, and the Arabic, South Indian and Chinese traders and settlers which the spice trade of the fourteenth to eighteenth centuries brought to the many coastal kingdoms which rose and fell in west and north Java during that period. In fact the residents of Jakarta, the largest city in Indonesia, are so mixed that they have developed a Malay dialect of their own, and the Dutch considered them a separate people whom they called the 'Batavians'. The Sundanese have retained much of their identity. They live in the mountainous areas of west Java, except for the western tip of the island around the town of Banten, where the Bantenese maintain some cultural distinctions of their own. The Sundanese language is still spoken, especially around Bogor, which was the capital of the twelfth-to-sixteenth-century kingdom Pajajaran. The people's historic rivalry with the central Javanese kingdoms and their intense dedication to Islam helped to make west Java a centre of the separatist activities of the Darul Islam ('Islamic State') which waged a rebellion from 1949 to 1962. Many Madurese, who are also strict Muslims, live in east Java as farmers and fishermen.

Central Java is the home of the Javanese proper. Although its capital is Semarang, the cities of Jogjakarta (whose area, under the governorship of Sultan Hamengkubuono, has the status of a special area) and Solo (formerly Surakarta) are the emotional and cultural centres, having both been capitals of former Javanese kingdoms, and frequently rivals. Although Javanese culture is the source of much of the communitarian ethos that has Indonesia's official imprimatur, the Javanese have an individualistic kinship system—which centres on the small family unit, with descent traced through both mother and father, and inheritance the same for daughters and sons. They have few organized communal features in their villages, such as landholding or ritual groups, and religion is a private affair. The divorce rate is high. As the bearers of one of the oldest civilizations in the world, Javanese claim the right to be exceptional, even in respect of their own rules.

CHAPTER NINE

People

1996

A. IS SMALL, QUICK-MOVING and thinking, equipped with a mobile phone, carelessly dressed as if his mind is on other things. He has a calm countenance which might be the result of contemplation. He is active in Nahdlatul Ulama, lives quietly in an outer suburb of Jakarta with his wife and three daughters, reads voraciously magazines and newspapers in both Bahasa and English. When he picks me up in his car, there is an open book turned over on the seat. In some way which I have not asked about, he has a small, family income. He is busy with various causes, such as legal aid and including NU, without receiving a regular salary, but his wife works in the library of one of the embassies. He admires Abdurrahman Wahid (using his affectionate nickname Gus Dur—Gus from *Bagus*, a complimentary Javanese word, and Dur from Ab*dur*rahman).

I joined NU after Gus Dur took over. Before then I had always thought of it as too religious and too conservative for me. Anyway it seemed irrelevant. When I was growing up Indonesia was run by army generals and economic technocrats and you didn't take Islam seriously as a guide to running the country. Also, NU was part of PPP, which was just a blur to me. But when it withdrew from PPP and Abdurrahman Wahid became chairman in 1984 it acknowledged what had been worrying me for some time.

Indonesia had become a corporate bureaucracy under Suharto's New Order. Not a police state, not a dictatorship, but something we hadn't seen before. The control of ABRI, both political and economic, the influence of the big commercial corporations run either by Chinese families or the president's family (or a combination of both) and the highly personal rule of the president himself—all this meant that ethical questions were being brushed aside. Islam as a force in the life of ordinary Indonesians was being stifled.

I know that whenever serious Muslims like me talk about the life force of Islam, people like you take fright. Most Australians, like most Westerners, would like Indonesia to be irreligious, I suspect . . . just a nice, big consumer society shopping happily in nice new supermarkets containing the world's goods and kept nice and orderly by an army that isn't so brutal that it creates headlines or pictures for the television news but is brutal enough to keep everyone in their place. Right? In fact, Suharto's New Order! The ideal neighbour! But, you see, you are up against the nature of human beings. They *want* to be religious. They *want* to understand what they are doing on this earth. Suharto is right at least in that. Indonesians are essentially a religious, or if you like spiritual, people and no amount of consumerism or bureaucracy will remove that. It's a quality that's been nourished for centuries. It's down there at the village level, in the lives of ordinary people, and that's where NU has its members.

One reason I didn't join earlier was that many people of my generation in NU were those who took part in the massacre of the communists. I am a devout Muslim and have no time for communism, but I hate political violence. It's not just that I don't like violence—it's politically dangerous in Indonesia because we are still working out our political and constitutional procedures. We don't want to have a situation where dissent and democratic reform is effectively suppressed until it breaks out in mass violence. We don't want a situation where political change is only possible when one side of politics physically wipes out another side. That is the danger of this personalized, bureaucratized form of consensus government that we have evolved. It controls peaceful change and reform so tightly that it encourages the belief that violence is necessary to break the mould.

What NU wants is more democracy, as part of the peaceful evolution of Indonesian society. That is why in the wake of the *Monitor* affair, Gus Dur helped to set up Democracy Forum. That is why we are active in helping workers to organize themselves to get better wages. The big step in Muslim thinking in Indonesia which NU now represents is in *itjihad*, or interpretation of the Koran. We accept that one authoritative interpretation is impossible. It flies in the face of modern scholarship and common sense. We think that an analytical approach to scripture is both ethical and useful in today's society, while a dogmatic approach breeds conflict and authoritarianism. This leads us to support the separation of church and state and to work for a genuinely plural political society. We are right behind the president on *Pancasila*—but we say, not just lip service, make it work.

I am pleased that we have established good relations with the PDI. We both have strong followings in east Java and Gus Dur and Megawati make a good pair. Their credentials are strong. Our opponents spread stories, but they are not believed. For example, in the Samudra Beach hotel at Pelabuhan Ratu, on Java's south coast, room 13 is reserved for the Sea Goddess and is never let to visitors (although the actual number is not on the door). When Gus Dur and Mega visited, they were taken to room 13. Mega had no trouble asking the Sea Goddess for her blessing, but Gus Dur had to be careful. When he was asked later, he said he had gone to room 13 and he had sought the Sea Goddess' blessing, but he had also recited verses from the Koran. 'Ah, but to whom did you recite the verses?' 'To Allah,' he said. He's quick. You need to be alert to be a religious leader these days! Gus Dur had the same problem when he made a visit to Israel. Politically, of course, the Sea Goddess is a very positive symbol in that part of Indonesia. Most Javanese believe in some kind of mysticism. The Sea Goddess is part of the Hindu tradition in Java of many gods (before Islam brought belief in one God) and the people of the south coast make offerings to her regularly. She is supposed to rule not just in Java but in its southern seas. You should watch out in Australia!

We in NU emphasize the cultural and social approach to democracy in Indonesia, rather than the political approach. We are not interested in coming in at the top, as it were, and manipulating the system like everyone else seems to want to do. Frankly I'm sick of politics. I can't speak for Gus Dur. He always has a political glint in his eye, and I have a sneaking suspicion that he enjoys politics.

NU is interested in building Indonesia from the bottom up, not from the top down. Democracy has to be nurtured, like a garden. Or, as someone has said, we need to pump up a few flat tyres.

Education is important to us. So are human rights. Justice and equality before the law, for example, are important principles of Islam. The dignity of labour is also important to us. You can imagine that we are not as popular with the authorities as we would like!

B. IS A HARVARD-EDUCATED lawyer in her thirties. She also spent two years in Paris, which seems to have influenced her more than her time in Cambridge. She has a Parisian dress style and a passionate manner of argument which reflects her contact with some of the radical elements of Islam who have made France their home. She is a member of ICMI, writes occasionally for *Republika*, works for the government on social and economic research.

It's our turn now. The army has had the reins of government in their hands for thirty years, longer if you want to be historically precise. It's time we were in the driver's seat.

I started to think like this after the Malari Affair, 1974. I was only a teenager at the time, but it left an impression on me. I was on the fringe of some student activity at the time. We used the visit of the Japanese prime minister to protest against generals like Murtopo and Humardhani, who were using foreign investment for their own political patronage. We called for the end of *Super-semar* and *Dwifungsi*. Pretty rash, but, well, that's the way we felt. Then there were the riots at Tanjung Priok ten years later. I wasn't in Indonesia and I learned only in dribs and drabs what had happened, but it was clear that the army had behaved in a brutal fashion, shooting people, breaking into the mosque. The combination of economic factors—unemployment was high in Tanjung Priok—and religion brought home to me how the ordinary people of Indonesia have suffered under military rule. When I came back to live in Indonesia and ICMI was formed in 1990, I had no hesitation in joining.

Yes, I know some people say ICMI is full of opportunists. We're all supposed to have jumped on the bandwagon, burning with ambition. Well, look at it this way. What can you do— actually do, not just talk about doing—in Indonesia if you are interested in politics? Everything is so tightly controlled that you're either part of the government or, if you're independent of government, you are seen as a rival or a threat, and you can't do

anything. You just become a dissident. Who wants to be a dissident! (Toss of the head). The great advantage of ICMI is that
you're part of government, yet able to think and work with a
good degree of freedom.

My time in France taught me how to choose perfume, certainly, but it also taught me how to work within the system. In the
United States, the state is weak and society is strong, the opposite
of France, which is much closer to the situation in Indonesia. You
are not opposed to the state in France. You do not retreat into society as you do in America and belittle and demean government,
trying to make it weak and ineffective. Rather, you exercise your
right as a citizen to turn the state to your advantage. You join the
state and fight your battles within it.

In any case, ICMI—and CIDES, its think-tank—are only
doing now what CSIS has done for years on behalf of the government and the armed forces. CSIS was established as an anti-
communist brains trust for the Cold War, based on presidential
approval, political support from the military, funds from Chinese
Catholics and the co-operation of American intelligence. Well,
the Cold War is over and the influence of CSIS with it. ICMI has
presidential approval and political support from several Cabinet
ministers, including B. J. Habibie who is no Muslim fundamentalist but the most technocratic, successful, non-military figure in the
Cabinet. Funds? We're not as flush as CSIS with private funds, so
most comes from the government. Nothing from abroad. But
there's enough.

I don't know why ICMI was established. Some people think it
was a move by the president to counter the influence of Benny
Moerdani, who is a Catholic and closely connected with CSIS.
Some think it was a move by the president and Habibie to counter
the influence of the NU, which had been revived under Abdurrahman Wahid. Some see it as a move by Muslims who are disil-
lusioned with PPP and the military's control of the political process
to get into government. And don't forget, this is Indonesia, where
reality takes many forms, so some see it as a device by the president
to head off the Muslims! It could be any one of these and is probably a combination of them all. From my point of view, ICMI was
a personal opportunity. The timing was right. As I said, it's our
turn. Not just a matter of army then, Islam now. It's generational.

When I was in Paris I met some radical Muslims, including some Algerians. I admire them. I don't share their view of Islam, but I like their activist political style. I'm against Javanese mysticism. People say Islam is fatalistic, but I think the Hindu-Buddhist-animist thing is so convoluted and murky it leads, if not to a fatalistic philosophy, at least to passivity, inaction. I like the clean, austere approach of Islam. I think Islamic art is the most beautiful in the world and if I weren't attracted to Islam for political reasons I would be attracted to it for aesthetic reasons. The colours and shapes are just stunning. There's also something about the moral harshness of Islam that appeals to me. Perhaps it is because Indonesia is so corrupt. You feel something sharp and unyielding is needed to cut through the complexity and hypocrisy of Indonesian society.

I am not in favour of an Islamic state for Indonesia and I do not know anyone in ICMI who is. I know it is put about that ICMI is not happy with the religious pluralism of the Pancasila because we want an Islamic state, but there's no evidence. It's a rumour put about by certain groups who want to discredit us. Indonesia is far too diverse a country to be run as a theocracy. It is just not an issue. What ICMI is concerned about are economic and social issues. We focus on the people of Indonesia, its human resources, and how they, rather than the business community, the bureaucracy and the military, can benefit from development. We are concerned about population growth, poverty, sustainable development, human rights, not whether state and religion should be separate or unified. We want a modern, Muslim Indonesia which can cope with the twenty-first century.

My personal view is that we have to move away from authoritarian political leadership in Indonesia. My ideal would be a political system in which the president had ceased to matter—because there would be political leaders, including incidentally some women, at several levels and throughout the entire country, thrown up by the system. Obviously the president is important, but the system is more important. I'm not much of a *bapakiste!* The fact of the matter is that the presidential office grows more powerful year by year, while the system becomes weaker.

The army needs to get out of politics. By all means let army leaders seek political office, because some of them have considerable skill and experience, but let them choose to do so, choose *between* the army and politics, not be in politics *because* they are in the military. Our parliament must have real authority. At the moment it has none. Our political groups need to be democratised, so that members of parliament have a connection with their electorate and therefore some direct responsibility for their constituents. Golkar needs to be a real political party and stop masquerading as a functional group. The whole system is designed so that Golkar will win elections. Golkar should be put on the same footing as PPP and PDI.

I am probably not a deeply religious person, in the sense that I am not concerned with intellectual and theoretical debate about the real nature of Islam and those kinds of things. However I am a believer and I take my religious beliefs seriously. I pray five times a day and I send my children to Muslim schools. I am quite conservative in my personal and social life. I would never dream of having a sexual relationship outside my marriage. I have never smoked and I rarely take alcohol, even though I have lived in the West for long periods. I like bacon rashers for breakfast, but beef, not pork. Most people would think I am very modern. I dress in Western style and have never worn the *jilbab*. I am concerned to keep fit, keep my figure. I have a whole room in my house with equipment which I use regularly. I am also very independent about my career. I have left my children with my husband or some member of the family for long periods—as long as a year—while I studied or worked abroad. There are many like me in Indonesia. We are the rule rather than the exception.

We don't want Indonesia to be just like every other country, and especially we don't want it to be just like a Western country. It's not that we are anti-Western. On the contrary, we like the West. We like to visit. It's exciting. It's a kind of modern frontier, where things happen that could never happen in Indonesia. The West is like the cinema—but when we come back from the cinema and enter our own house, we know that real life is different from what you see in the movies.

We need the West. But our feelings about Indonesia are different. Indonesia is family. Indonesia is home.

C. IS A BIG, DOLEFUL man, who sits through the conversation with his shoulders hunched, as if he finds it painful, or at least uncomfortable. He speaks slowly, making sure that what he is saying is what he wants to say. He radiates a mixture of sadness and hope, resignation and determination, acceptance and defiance. He is not, however, self-absorbed. He is courteous and cheerful, greeting with a handshake, offering a plate of biscuits. We meet at a mutual friend's house in semi-secrecy, because he was for many years a political prisoner. The friend did not want trouble (he was careful to see the size of the gathering was less than the legal limit of five).

I always thought Sukarno would walk away from us. He embraced us when he needed us, then left us when it suited him. He didn't understand the dialectic. He didn't have . . . what do you call it? . . . backbone. He was flexible. Very flexible. I'm not bitter. He was a great teacher and, until this happened, a great leader. He was the one who gave us *Pancasila*. Indonesians will return to his message one day. I don't blame him. I blame our own leaders in the PKI.

The first I knew about the coup was when I heard the announcements on the radio. I said to a friend, 'It can't be true.' There had been no preparation. The masses were not ready. The party line was that the masses should be armed—with weapons and, if that was not possible, then at least with information. There had been talk about a council of generals for weeks, so we were wondering. 'Is something going on?' We were waiting to be told what to expect, what to do. But nothing was said. Then suddenly comes this Colonel Untung and the announcements. All those names. What were we supposed to make of it? And where was Sukarno? I said to my friend, 'It's just a game someone in the palace is playing.'

I didn't even change my plans. I was going from Jakarta to visit family in my village near Semarang. I went. No-one on the bus knew anything. No-one seemed to care much, either. They were all talking about the cost of living. If I remember, kerosene had just gone up again, or was in short supply. When I got there I heard that something had happened in the army in Semarang or in Magelang, led by another colonel. I still couldn't believe it had anything to do with the PKI. I thought it must be an internal army affair. The colonels who want to be generals. It's part of the dialectic. My faith in the party was strong. I had learned how to understand politics while I was in the party and I trusted the leaders. They knew what was going on, not just in Indonesia but in the world.

But when I got back to Jakarta, it was obvious that something had gone wrong. The party had supported Untung's revolutionary council, but there was no leadership from Sukarno. Suharto was against Untung and seemed to be taking over. Then, after a few days, the bodies were discovered in the well at Halim air base. The party newspapers were closed down and we began to hear stories of army units visiting houses in Jakarta and making arrests. There was huge publicity for the funeral of the generals. Also, Nasution's little daughter died. Sukarno had a meeting in the Bogor palace with all political leaders, including some from the PKI (Lukman, but not Aidit, who seemed to have disappeared). Sukarno called for calm and Lukman said the PKI had nothing to do with the coup. It was an internal army matter. But the army and anti-communist groups went on the rampage as if the president didn't exist. There were rallies and slogans all over Jakarta. Muslim youths attacked the PKI headquarters building and set it on fire. Nobody tried to stop them. We heard there was trouble in Aceh and in villages in Java.

I was arrested at the beginning of November. I knew I would be arrested. I was a member of the PKI, just a rank-and-file member, nothing special, but they were arresting not just members but non-party activists, so I expected they would get to me eventually. People in my street knew I was a PKI member. I hadn't tried to hide it. I was proud of it. We were the only party that was really concerned with the welfare of the ordinary people. It's ironic, but the fact is that many of these ordinary people turned away from me and my family after I was arrested, even before. Not just the ones you would expect, who never liked the PKI, but others you thought were sympathetic. Supporters of the PNI for example. Well, they were scared, I suppose. These army units were all over Jakarta. They had a list of names and addresses on a piece of paper. They came to the door and, if you were in, they took you away. If you weren't they left instructions for you to report to some army address. Not to the local police station.

I didn't have a trial. Some of the coup leaders and important PKI and other political figures did, but we were just asked a lot of questions. The questions weren't legal or technical. The fact that you were at home, hadn't done anything and were as surprised as everyone else by the coup and the killing of the generals made no difference. The PKI was guilty. As a member of the PKI you were guilty with it. On this basis, thousands of us were dealt with quickly. I never went back to my house. My family brought me food and clothes. First, I was kept in a detention centre in Jakarta. Then in 1966 I was sent to Buru.

I was twelve years at Buru detention camp. Buru is an island off the Maluku coast, between Sulawesi and West Irian. You are on your own, miles from anywhere. You don't have many visitors, it's too far away. I used to have visitors about twice a year. You became part of a community at Buru and you learned a lot about human nature. One thing I learned was that sometimes the worst gaolers were ex-PKI. They joined the gaol staff to get a good deal for themselves. They were the ones who beat you most. They were anxious to show their new bosses that they weren't still sympathetic. The food was simple, but quite good, lots of fish. I was fit. I've put on weight since I came back to Jakarta, eating too much fried food. We had lots of serious discussions. They didn't mind you talking among yourselves. Well, they couldn't stop you, really. I wasn't in the same section as Pramoedya, the writer, but we used to hear about him, how he was writing his novels in his head at night and telling the stories the next day, so they would be recorded.

I thought a lot about the dialectic, how it explains history and determines social and political progress. The dialectic was my guiding spirit in prison. It helped me to hold on. It is still in my heart. The situation at the moment is dark, but I am still confident that Indonesia will move forward to a new stage of human development eventually. It has to. You can't keep people in poverty and fear forever.

My life now is still restricted, although I have been out of prison for seventeen years. Each month I have to report to the local authorities and sign a register. My identity card carries the letters E.T., which means Ex-Tapol (Tahanan Politik—Political Prisoner). I haven't had a job since I returned. If you employ someone from Buru, you are under suspicion yourself. I have heard that some ex-Buru people have jobs, but they are unusual. They are the ones with professional skills who have been given work by non-government organizations, such as legal aid. Many PKI members were teachers and they have not been able to find employment. I was a clerk in the civil service, so that was the end of that. I rely on my family and doing odd jobs. But we have banded together and help one another. We try to meet socially. We have to be careful. But we find ways. We have no organization or anything like that but we manage to keep in touch. The dialectic is still at work.

Thank you for coming all the way from Australia to hear my story. It's been a long time. No-one wanted to know anything about what happened in those years. They accepted what the government said and went on with their lives. I wonder if people are becoming interested again.

D. IS A RETIRED BUREAUCRAT, tall, languid, *priyayi*. He has even developed the arisocratic habit of not completing his sentences, as if the complexity he has been asked to speak about is beyond normal comprehension. He has travelled a lot, lived abroad, done many things, seen everything, and now it is hard to know what he believes. So it is a shock to realize that he remains, in the midst of all his cynicism, intensely patriotic. He is suspicious not only of liberal-minded Westerners, but also of religious zealots, businessmen, professional women, non-government organizations—and the president. He thinks Suharto has become captive to the outrageous demands of his children and their cronies.

Suharto has lost his nerve. Not his cunning. Just his nerve.

Everything he does now is directed at his own security or his family's security, not that of his country. This is not good for Indonesia . . . Eh? One can understand it in him, because of his upbringing, but it has become an obsession which . . . It is affecting the country. It used to be the Marcos example that worried him. Now it's South Korea. He's got to pull himself together. If you're a leader, you've got to lead. Otherwise no-one knows what . . . to do.

He has manipulated the system so carefully for so long that now he personally controls everything. So you have someone who is in control of everything, but doesn't know what to do. Eh? Not good. People think the army is in control of Indonesia. The army is the cement that binds the bricks together. But Suharto designs the building, decides the budget, how many rooms you can have . . . eh?—and almost certainly someone in his family makes the bricks! Probably the cement too! (If you think this is an allusion to the possibility that the president or someone in his family is thinking of getting control of the army as well, you would have read my thoughts quite accurately).

A little bird told me that the president wants to be sure that the country is secure. Well, it is. There are no threats on the horizon— no 'adverse challenges' if I might use the words of the security agreement we have signed with your . . . illustrious government. What about the sinister forces at work under the surface? The formless organizations? You may smile, but they exist. They have always existed in Indonesia. Eurythmics, aerobics . . . don't believe it. They're all study groups, plotting to overthrow the government. But we know how to take care of them in Indonesia. We have been trained by the Dutch. And the Japanese. And the CIA . . . Eh? Nothing to worry about. The army will take care of them. And Try Sutrisno has shown that he is quite capable of acting decisively in the national interest. Do not forget that he was in charge of the operation at Tanjung Priok. In fact, I would say that he is even more decisive in these matters than the president. The president was decisive thirty years ago and we all recognize his great contribution to Indonesia's national integrity at that time. But lately his mind has begun to wander.He is trying to do too much, trying to be everything to everyone.

If we go on like this for another five-year period, the country will be in danger, not from adverse challenges . . . eh? but because the bureaucrats will be so confused they won't know what to do. A bureaucrat must know what to do, or the whole place . . . shudders . . . to a halt.

These . . . NGOs. What are they? They behave as if they have an existence in spite of government, even that they are *better* informed than government, are better than government. What nonsense is this! Who do they think they are? They're never satisfied. No matter what the government does, they want more . . . or less . . . more forests, less pollution . . . they'll never be happy. It's always more or less. Never just right. Better to lock them up! Send them to Buru. Makes life easier for everyone.

What's important in life? Peace and quiet—and your country held in decent regard by the rest of the world. That's about it. I travelled abroad for years with ministers on official visits. I could chart for you the way Indonesia's reputation has gone up and down by the reception we got on those visits. It's been up for years. Suharto has done it, no doubt about it. But he's dropped the baton lately. You've got to have leadership. East Timor? What is it? Nothing, not even a pebble in our shoe. A small pimple perhaps. What I'm saying is this: we musn't be stopped in our tracks by all these quibbles. Everyone's got them, look at America, Europe . . . Australia!

Nobody's perfect . . . Eh?

E. IS AN ALERT, thrice-married woman in her forties. Her first husband was a communist who disappeared in 1966. Her second husband was a soldier who did not return from a posting. Her third husband is self-employed. She has a round face with a high colour and darting eyes. She is a servant in the household of a Bandung businessman, but she regards herself not as a servant but as a relative of the man's family and a businesswoman herself.

You can get on in Indonesia if you are prepared to work. There's plenty of opportunities to make money if you keep your mind on it. The trouble with most people is that they expect someone to hand it to them. Someone up there—or the government down here. They just wait around, with their hand out. They become lazy. If you're lazy, you get left behind. Then you complain even more. So it goes.

I started with nothing. I had worse than nothing, really, because I had a baby to feed as well. Now I have a house of my own. Not as big as the house I work in, but it's solid brick. It has tiled floors and a carved wooden front door. It has two bedrooms. And the telephone. I need the telephone for my business. The baby is now an engineer. Just imagine. He's just graduated, but I 'm sure he will get a good job. Technology—that's the future for Indonesia.

For years I worked just for my wages. I was paid well and given food, but that was that. I could save nothing. Then people started saying what a good cook I was. Guests would come to the house and I'd have to turn on a feast for them. I used to make a special yellow rice dish that everyone liked. So, I thought, why don't I sell it. I made a few and took them to the market, where a friend had a stall. They sold like . . . *es cendol*, that coconut and palm sugar drink Indonesians love. That's how it started. Now I make about forty a day, less on Saturday, more on Sunday. They are twice the price of other rice dishes, but they go off quickly just the same. That's another mistake people make. They think ordinary Indonesian people are so poor that they won't pay a little more for quality. That's not true. People will pay a bit more for the extra taste—it gives them a lift. Anyway, they pay a little bit more for mine. I've bought a house from the profits and I don't have to go to the market anymore. I sell from the house. People come there. I have an assistant who looks after things when I'm away.

I still go to the big house every day except Sunday. They let me use their rice for my dishes. They pay me less than I earn from my rice dish, but I don't consider myself an employee now. I look after them as if they were my own family and they help me as if I am part of their family. They helped me with money for my son's education. I look after them when they're sick. Now their children are growing up and getting married I look after their children sometimes the way I did when they were little. You need a lot of energy to keep all this going, but my health is good. I don't have time to be sick!

I married when I was fifteen. My first husband was a good man, but he disappeared after the trouble. I suppose he was one of those who were killed. I just don't know what happened to him. He's the father of the engineer. Anyway, I married again—a soldier. He didn't come home every night. I found out that he had taken a second wife. She came to me when he started meeting another woman. We became friends. She helped me with the rice dishes. Then she left, ran away. When my husband was posted, I didn't go with him. After our divorce, I married again. I like to have a man around the place, although I'm too busy to look after him properly. This one is sort of in business, too. He repairs radios and television sets. He picks them up from people's houses and brings them home. I'm sure the house attracted him, but I've kept it in my name.

I'm glad my son is an engineer, because he can get a job in one of those big firms, but I personally think Indonesia will be a better place to live in if ordinary people are helped to run their own businesses and get a start in life. There's too many soldiers and other kinds of officials in Indonesia telling people what to do. I think the Marsinah case is scary. She was just standing up for her rights.

1966

F. IS IN HIS FORTIES. He lives with his wife and family in a suburban street in Jakarta. It is a pleasant house, its porch covered with bougainvillea and separated from the front fence by a small green lawn. The family car, a Volkswagen, is big enough, as they have only two children, a boy and a girl. They profess no religion. They are Western in habits as well as in dress. The meals they serve are, except for the lack of meat in them, the thick Java coffee and red chillis, not substantially different from simple food in a middle-class Australian family. The study is full of books, in English, Dutch, French, German and Bahasa Indonesia. They subscribe to European and American magazines, popular and seriously intellectual. He is a lawyer but his professional employment has been restricted, since he belongs to a party out of favour with the government. He is loyal to his country, but he is not fanatic about anything, including nationalism. He dislikes the trend under Sukarno with the deep instincts of a rational man, but he has accepted it as a—he hopes not fatal—stage in the country's evolution. I enjoy asking him the 'big' questions about Indonesia.

Do you think Indonesia is becoming expansionist?

Not if by expansionist is meant the intention to expand. I think some of the leaders may be *historically*-minded, i.e., they remember the Indonesian, especially Javanese-based glorious empires of the past, and being intense nationalists may believe, in an emotional way, that it might happen again. But they don't think about it in a practical way, I'm sure. They somehow expect the rest of the world to fall down and recognize Indonesia's greatness, to accord her rights based on her past greatness, her sufferings under colonialism and her potential for the future: they don't plan it, however. They don't *plan* anything—that's my complaint.

But if you are thinking that expansionism, of necessity, may follow the course our leaders are at present following you may be wise to think so. It is the duty of any country near Indonesia to pay attention to this. The fact is the Sukarno government has failed dismally to provide the Indonesian people with a reasonable minimum of economic welfare. While there is such potential unrest, fanned all the time by nationalistic slogan-shouting, you can never be sure what will happen, what the government will commit the country to abroad and then have to justify. It may not be territorial aggression as such; but it could be. It might well be the expansion of Indonesian *authority* in the South-East Asia region. They would have no trouble justifying this. There are many Indonesians who, in the state we are in, welcome the chance to do something definite, such as fight an enemy.

Would you say the Indonesian people are becoming militaristic?

No. There are deep currents of violence in the Indonesian make-up, but the people are not military minded. The trouble is that a nation has to *do* something. Even in settled countries, like Australia or the United States, there must be a *raison d'être* for the nation, which the government must claim, on behalf of the people, to pursue. At the very least, the government must convince the people that it can provide them with the security to go on living their private lives as they want. But, as the election of Kennedy in the US showed, even this is not enough; people want to feel that their nation is playing a significant role in world affairs in some capacity or another. In Indonesia this desire is tremendously strong because the nation is still a matter of wonder and pride to the people.

The removal of colonial rule has released the pent-up spirit of the people. Static for so long, they are now in a state of dynamism. They have a feeling of *power*, a feeling of being able to manage, manipulate, even to create their lives for the first time. They want to *do* something, to use this new sense of power. This is where the leadership becomes important. You cannot stop this urge, this dynamic movement of people. But you can channel it. You can turn it into productive channels. In Malaya, I think nationalism has been channelled into getting a high living standard. This is the way of the new Japan. In Indonesia nationalism has been directed *against* things, rather than *for* things. We are against subversion, rebellion, colonialism, capitalism, etc., etc. What are we *for*? The new emerging forces? Change everywhere, wherever or whatever it is? The president keeps talking about transforming the world, but what about transforming Indonesia? Nothing has been done here that a wind wouldn't blow over. The 'revolution' in Indonesia is just a farce. The communists are quite right in their criticism that no *structural* reforms of significance have been introduced in Indonesia. Sukarno wants to change the world, because if he starts to change Indonesia, there will be trouble.

Do you think Sukarno has the makings of a military dictator, whether or not the people want it?

Good gracious, no. The Bung is no more a military dictator than I am. He wants to live in luxury, above reproach or criticism, mediating between God and his people (though, not, I suspect, between his people and God), loved by all. He has no stomach for the harsh realities of dictatorship. He is an artist, creating his own reality. Unfortunately, we are landed with him—and it.

Do you see Sukarno as a real danger to the development of the kind of Indonesia you want?

I am beginning to think so, although I did not think so some time ago. In many ways, I have sympathy with Sukarno, although I do not want to go back to the Indonesian roots he keeps talking about. I can see that, at this period of nation-building, he has been a unifying force. Indonesian nationalism is necessarily anti-West, because it is from Western colonialism that we have struggled free. We are in the Western 'sphere of influence'—like Cuba is, which is one reason why there is so much sympathy here with Cuba. So our revolutionary *spirit* is naturally anti-West, while our *situation* is Western, in terms of trade, military logistics and so on. By going back to the pre-colonial Indonesia, to the traditions of village and family life as they have been practised here for centuries, Sukarno has avoided a split, which would have been disastrous. It may still come, but it will be less likely the longer Sukarno stays.

What worries me, rather, is that there is no structure of restraint. Take the US president, for example, perhaps the most powerful single political leader in the world. He is surrounded by a framework of critical restraint—press, pulpit, opposition parties, and a whole public philosophy to which his critics and advisers can refer in restraining or urging him. Even in communist countries, where power is more naked, there is a significant structure of restraint in Marxism-Leninism, which can be refined and revised, but only through persuasive argument, and by the party, which has its own long-term interests. Here, in Indonesia, we have no such restraints by which the satisfaction of power can be controlled. Everything—education, law, even religion—can be used in Indonesia to sanctify power. The restraints on Sukarno are negative and usually bad. For example, he cannot get rid of some of the incompetents in his cabinet because immediately the communists would clamour for admission. There is no general framework which can be used, publicly, to define his authority and his tasks. All this ideology which he and the government propaganda machine produces—what does it *mean*? No one can say, 'But Sukarno, that is contrary to *Pancasila*, or *Manipol-Usdek* [an acronym for the five points of a political manifesto], etc.', because these are only what the state and the government, at any given time, say they are. A while ago, the OK word was 'retooling'. Now it's 'new emerging forces' or 'self-sustaining growth' or some other nonsense. Nobody knows what these words are supposed to mean as a guide to action. Who and what is to be 'retooled'? Who are 'the new emerging forces' and what are they supposed to do? How do we develop 'self-sustaining growth'?

But is this fantasy of meaningless symbols as you describe it, dangerous? Doesn't it keep people interested—make them believe something is happening? Indonesians keep telling me that the shadow is more important than the reality in Java, a legacy of the wayang.

I don't believe this. It is mysticism. I don't believe that the Indonesian 'identity', whatever it is, can cope with the real forces at work in today's world. It is only child's play, nursery oratory, sentimental bed-time tales that a child must forget when it grows up and goes into the world or it faces destruction. The Indonesian's 'identity' is just a joke to the rest of the world. We need to consolidate what we have gained—our independence as a nation. We need to strengthen our country, so that it can take its place in the world community. Sukarno is old-fashioned, wanting to revolutionize the world. Most people, in the east and west, as well as in the 'non-aligned' countries, want peace and stability, in order to build and grow. Sukarno is never satisfied. He is always on the lookout for a fresh 'concept', like a fresh ankle. As a revolutionary poet, perhaps, he could be properly honoured. But as a leader he is dangerous.

What is dangerous is that Sukarno's rule is sanctifying the use of power without limits. At the moment this power is limited by his appreciation of the dramatic balance of forces under him, by his instinctive caution and by the inertia of our economic mess. But if any of these influences are removed, the danger increases that the power will run wild. Then it will have to be limited from the outside, which could mean war.

G. IS A PROTESTANT Christian from the Minahasa region of north-east Sulawesi. Aged thirty, recently married, he has the look of a young warrior. His long, unruly hair frames an open, rough face, with a slow grin. He rides a motor scooter and, as his pillion passenger several times, I can vouch for his high spirits. He is, I suppose, a religious man, although I have no direct experience of his sincerity as a Christian. We usually talk politics. He was disturbed by the rebellions in Sumatra and Sulawesi and at that time his loyalty to the central government was strained. His parents and close relatives now live in Java, but they maintain a regional loyalty. Younger and married to a Javanese, B. has adapted himself more easily. High spirits have helped him, turning his troubles into a wry joke. It was he who first told me the classic joke on Indonesian politics: 'If you understand the situation, you are obviously badly informed'. He works for Garuda Indonesia Airways, the national air-line, and is a spare-time teacher.

What attitude does the average Christian in Indonesia have to the present government?

We are quite satisfied. What we fear most is a Muslim theocratic state, as they have in Malaya. While President Sukarno stands by the *Pancasila*, which underwrites belief in God, without saying what kind of God, we support him. We have two Christians in the cabinet.

Where do Christians stand generally on political issues?

> I would say in the middle, with the nationalists. The Muslims tend to be on the right and the communists on the left. The Catholics are perhaps more with the Muslims on political issues. On the issue of the secular state, however, Christians and communists were on the same side.

Do you think Christians in Indonesia feel free to live according to their beliefs?

> Oh yes, there's no doubt about it. We don't feel restricted. One example, our newspaper *Sinar Harapan* [*Hopeful Beam*]. It was founded only a couple of years ago by a non-profit-making organization of some thirty Protestant groups. It has already reached a circulation of 25 000 and can't expect any more because of the newsprint rationing. The government does not discriminate against Christians. When West Irian was taken over, the government allowed missionary activity to continue. The Christians are responding to this by trying to adapt their activities to the basic feelings of the national revolution. For example, the Toraja people in central Sulawesi have very strong local customs, *adat* and so on. The Christians are now trying not to displace this culture, but to use it as a base for Christian beliefs. This produces some interesting problems. The traditional Torajas follow ancestor worship, so we have to adapt this to the Christian worship of God. The government is pleased with this approach.

Isn't this the famous syncretic approach to religion that you outer-islanders are always attributing to the Javanese?

> It's not deliberately so. We—I mean Christians rather than Minahasans—don't favour relativism. You never know what the Javanese are thinking. Our beliefs are clear and in this case we decide, as a matter of policy, to do it this way. But perhaps in the long run it will amount to a syncretic religion of its own—Christian ancestor worship!

What do you think is the basis of religious tolerance in Indonesia? It is
not common in the rest of the world.

A lot has depended on President Sukarno, who is not religious.
Certainly he is not a religious fanatic, and has been able to hold the
predominantly Muslim element at bay. And syncretism does come
into it. So much has been taken in by the people of Indonesia—
Hinduism, Buddhism, Islam, Christianity—that, although there
has been some fierce fighting in our history, people now believe
that we in Indonesia can absorb any new idea. This applies to
communism. All these religions, including communism, have
travelled a long way by the time they reach us in Indonesia. They
are a long way from their original source and are probably weaker
—so our basic culture has been able to withstand them.

I've often wondered what you Protestants, with the puritan strain of the
Calvinists and Dutch Reformed Church in you, think of the oriental
splendour of President Sukarno's court?

As you know, most Protestant Christians in Indonesia are middle
class. We tend to come from the better educated groups in society,
and we are interested in the professional skills and disciplines. We
tend to discourage spendthrift finance, lax morals and a display of
worldly things. President Sukarno has an artistic temperament,
which does seem to please most of the people. We recognize that
we are in a small minority, perhaps 5 million Protestants (and
about 2 million Catholics) in a population of 100 million. Sukarno
works very hard for the country and he is not a ruthless dictator.
Personally, I would rather have Sukarno's kind of government
than a Catholic dictator like Ngo Dinh Diem, or Synghman Rhee
and Chiang Kai-shek, who are Methodists.

H. IS A SENIOR bureaucrat, an official of the foreign ministry. He has
the deceptive appearance of many Indonesian men, and is probably a
good deal older than his boyish face suggests. He lives in a small new
house in Kebajoran, a swanky Jakarta suburb, with his wife and three
young children. They have lived abroad and have acquired an
American car, about 1957 model. He is ambitious, and his wife is interested in his promotion. They are friendly to foreigners and I have

been, as their guest, the only stranger at small social gatherings of his
friends and their wives. Although most of his colleagues are Javanese,
C. is from Sumatra; a Muslim, though not a strict one. Years of living
in Jakarta and his professional concern with national policies in the
international setting have weakened any regional loyalties he may have
had. Dark-skinned, with short thick black hair and an athletic figure,
he has a military demeanour, but in fact he has a subtle mind and a
rather easy-going disposition, which make him an ideal companion.
He cooks, which is an unusual skill in a land of servants and domesti-
cated wives, but prefers, when entertaining, to go to a Chinese restaurant, where he orders a special kind of hot-sour Szechuan soup
which has become identified in my mind with Indonesia. We have
met in several places—at the United Nations in New York, in Bali for
a moonlit walk on a beach, in Jogjakarta for a conference, in Manila,
Tokyo and Singapore also for various conferences and, of course, in
Jakarta. We were together once in Hollandia, as it was becoming Kota
Baru, when the Indonesians took over the administration of West
Irian. He went to look at a Dutch political detention camp and became very emotional. He has one grave fault: he takes foreign observers like myself far too seriously.

*Do you think that the government is losing its authority in the country be-
cause of the economic position?*

> You may as well ask me if I think the Indonesian ocean—the one
> you call the Indian ocean—is going to dry up. Of course not.
> Economic hardship has been with the people for centuries. They
> will bear it; now they can feel they have a reason for bearing it.

What reason?

> A national identity. You laugh when we talk about national iden-
> tity as if it really means something. It does mean something to us.
> You will never understand what it means for us to be able to stand
> up in public and say, 'as an Indonesian, I feel . . .' You take your
> nationality for granted. But for us it is still a thrilling experience to
> be able to use those words. The *meaning* of it—if you want con-
> crete reasons, à la Marx or Freud or the balance sheet—isn't easy
> to explain. Indonesians have always 'belonged' somewhere, to
> family or tribe. We do not need an 'identity' to provide emotional

security, as you might say. We've always had custom or religion there, to explain things. But we were never able to achieve things for ourselves; there has always been someone in power over us, telling us what to do, telling the world what we were like, what we wanted, what we should be allowed to do. Now there is no-one over us. Our leaders have power, but it is our power. In the world, we are an equal with everyone else—no-one can order us about. That's why the foreign ministry is so important in every-one's eyes—it is the prestige service because when we are abroad we are in fact representing the whole nation.

Is it obligatory to wear the black cap abroad, to establish your Indonesian identity?

No, a matter of choice. So are sun glasses! But it isn't a matter of choice to know Manipol-Usdek and to understand what is im-plied in the return to the revolutionary 1945 constitution. And it is not a matter of choice to do everything we can, all the time, to advance Indonesia's interests. Your diplomats probably think of diplomacy as a career for themselves: what is in it for them. For us, it is not just personal satisfaction. We are entrusted with the sacred rights of the Indonesian people.

Other nations have rights, too, and other diplomats take them seriously. Why do Indonesians so often give the impression that they are not aware of this?

We are aware of it! Very much so. But it is our duty to look to our own. We do not believe that, having won independence, it is all over. We know we will have to defend this independence at every point. We are not so naive as to think that Indonesia's struggle to survive over all these centuries is now over.

Who is going to take your independence from you?

Many would like to, especially the powerful Western countries. They want capitalism to flourish in South-East Asia. They want anti-communism to flourish. Indonesia is non-aligned and so-cialist, so the Western countries do not want her to succeed. Our environment is hostile, so we have to prepare to defend ourselves.

But don't you think the West has given up anti-communism? Socialist, non-aligned countries are now accepted happily. Surely, all the aid that has come from Western countries to Indonesia is proof that the failure of Indonesia is not wanted.

Frankly, I think the aid is for the West's own benefit. I think it is hoped that aid will mean that Indonesia will open its doors to foreign capital—to capitalism in other words—that it will 'buy Western' and so on. It is self-interest.

And aid from the communist bloc is disinterested?

No. But one thing we do know. Economic aid from communist countries is a lot easier to accept. The terms are good and there are no pressures to conform afterwards. And there is not so much song and dance about it! Western countries, especially the United States, are forever talking about foreign aid. There are arguments in parliaments, the press takes it up: 'Is this country good enough to receive our aid?' In communist countries, they give you the aid and shut up about it. Ever since we became independent the West, especially the press, which is hopelessly misinformed generally on Indonesian politics, has been sitting in judgement on us. The insults to us, as a nation, and to President Sukarno, who is our head of state, have been really unpleasant. We are not insulted by the communists. Why is this so? We are not communists and never will be. There are communists here. Why not? Is this sufficient reason for the West to insult us? No, it is something more, and deeply we suspect that while the communist countries want us to succeed, as we are, the West does not.

Perhaps it depends on what you mean by 'succeed'. If you mean succeed in stirring up trouble around you, it's not surprising the West is critical and the communist bloc is not. If Indonesia were in the communist 'sphere of influence' Moscow would roast you, as they did—and Peking still does—Yugoslavia, for trying to be independent.

It's not geography. It's that three-quarters of the world is at present in the midst of changes, growing and developing out of backwardness and exploitation. One-quarter is facing a decline from its peak of power. We are part of the three-quarters and so are the

communists. The West is the one-quarter. This is what we mean
by the new emerging forces and the old established powers.

*What does this division mean? It is not a racial division, nor economic,
nor political, nor religious, nor strategic. You put certain nations into one
group and others into another, but this is like solving a problem by
definition. 'New' and 'emerging' are not absolute references. Why is the
Soviet Union, for example, a new, emerging nation? It has never been
under colonialism. A revolution occurred in 1917, which replaced one
form of government with another, but the nation did not emerge then, and
if it had, it's getting on for half a century ago. Is that new?*

The USSR is included, as all communist countries are, because
they are in favour of revolution and change, because they are part
of the three-quarters.

*You are deluding yourself to think so. The communist countries are in
favour of change only at someone else's expense. Any change directed
against them is counter-revolution. Try it and see.*

We do not want trouble with the communist countries. They
helped us over West Irian. The Western countries did not.

*It was an American, Mr Ellsworth Bunker, whose proposals brought the
negotiations to a point where agreement on a treaty became possible.*

But it was our policy on confrontation, backed by arms which the
Soviet Union gave us, which made the Dutch agree to look at
Mr. Bunker's proposals.

And so you go on 'confronting' for ever?

The president has said that our revolution is endless. We in the
foreign ministry try to nail things down a little more. I would
guess you won't find us settling down for, say, the rest of this
century.

I. IS A GREY-HAIRED, laughing Sundanese. He has a large, growing
family, all intent on serious education, which keeps him poor. We met
at a friend's home and D. spent the entire evening talking of his

children's education. Not that he was boring; he is a lively, charming
conversationalist who expects you to contribute your share. But he is
obsessed with the idea that Indonesia is going to pieces, morally and
economically, and that the only chance for his children is to stay out of
politics, learn as much as they can, and wait for the catastrophe to pass.
He is cheerful about it and even a little excited at the prospect of a
cataclysmic change. But he is basically a serious man, with a great love
of his family and a strong code of honour and self-respect. Being
Sundanese, he is suspicious of the Javanese, and he has a contempt for
President Sukarno that is so insulting that it is almost familiar. He
works as a clerk in a bank and has rigid views about money. The
following monologue was discreetly jotted down in the back seat of a
borrowed car while he drove me one morning for a visit to Punjak,
the mountain resort outside Jakarta. One of his sons, who sat in the
front seat with him, remained quiet throughout the journey. I managed only to murmur non-committal encouragements. He began by
reading a slogan.

Hajo Pertinggi Produski! Come On, Let Us Increase Production!
What is the use of increasing production if the leaders take all the
money? They drive around in big cars, take wives left, right and
centre, eat in expensive restaurants, and tell us we are lazy. The
Indonesian people lazy! This is against my heart. The leaders are
rich by privilege, not by work, rich by corruption.

At least my children know their father is earning his living
properly. We don't live well, but we are honest.

I'd give them production! I'd give them the guillotine, like the
French kings. But we have no power because we have no guns. It
is as simple as that. If we had guns we would rise up against them
and shoot them.

They made lots of promises, but now they have good positions they have forgotten their promises. They say the people are
looking fatter than under the Dutch. I tell you, my friend, it is
beri-beri, from lack of vitamin B, eating too much cassava and not
enough rice. Even *tjing tjao* [a green drink made from leaves] is
going up in price. The leaves are still the same price, I suppose, but
the man says he can't afford rice to eat.

The President says we must sacrifice. What? Our lives, then
we will be heroes. Heroes of the Revolution, so he can talk about

us on Heroes' Day. Revolution! Now we've had our national revolution, we need a social revolution to get rid of our leaders.

Oh, it's terrible, this country. Really terrible. The leaders are all going mad. Maybe Jakarta is too hot.

Celebrations! They come to the kampong asking for donations for the August 17th celebrations. I told them, 'The people are sick of celebrations'. Let us have no more celebrations, but cheap school books instead. The students at the Bandung University booed the president when he said they were always complaining about the high cost of books. When he was a student he had to sleep on a rattan bed on the floor without cushions and read by an oil lamp—so he said. That was forty years ago, under the Dutch! Are we no better off now?

Economic reform! Since they announced the economic reforms, the price of sugar has gone up four times. One kilogram of second-class rice is twice the price, and going up. But the leaders go abroad and buy their wives jewellery and clothes in Hong Kong.

Malaysia! We will confront the neo-colonialists! We will kill ourselves doing it. We should mind our business and confront our leaders. The president is a colonialist—he dominates us! His police guard is full of Javanese. He wouldn't trust anyone else to guard him!

I was better off under the Dutch. So were most people in the cities.

My friends said to me: Tell the Australian journalist what you think. Maybe it will get into the foreign newspapers. It is the only way to stop the madness. So that I am doing. I hope you are not an intelligence agent.'

J. IS A PRETTY Minangkabau girl in her early, twenties, working as a receptionist in Jakarta. She always wears Western dress. One of her ambitions is to meet a Hollywood film star. Failing that, she might be content to marry an ordinary American, Australian or Englishman. She does not like Asian men, especially Indonesians, because they are too short, too poor and because she wants to travel. She occupies her leisure in going to the cinema—only to American or European films; she never goes to Indonesian, Chinese or Indian films—in sailing, and in trying to meet Western men. Her family lives in Jakarta and are a lively and interesting group. Her mother and father, who is in business, encourage the children to have independent views and they are not strict Muslims. Her brother is studying to be an engineer.

I understand this Russian film is well worth seeing.

But if you're staying at the Hotel Indonesia, you can get tickets for the Tony Curtis film. Otherwise, I'll never see it. I don't like Russian films. They're communistic.

Aren't Hollywood film capitalistic?

Oh, they're just about people. They don't have propaganda in them.

Do you think the twist is out of step with the revolutionary rhythm, as President Sukarno says?

Oh, the president's old-fashioned, like my parents. I like the twist. We do it here at parties and nobody cares. *We* used to do the cha-cha, too, when that was banned.

Why did they ban the film Never on Sunday, *do you think?*

Because it's sexy. They don't like sexy things.

But they don't seem to mind sex in practice. I've always thought that Indonesian men and women treat the subject pretty calmly, and your president is noted for his mature interest.

People like to talk about having babies and that kind of thing, but they don't like sex in the movies because it's exciting, snappy. And they don't like looking at kissing.

Do you think Western morals are decadent?

I don't know what all this about decadent means. I think it's just another way people have of trying to stop you from having a good time.

But surely you can have a good time 'à la Indonesie'?

> Where do you go in Jakarta to have a good time? No nightclubs.
> No shows or anything like that at the restaurants. The shops have
> nothing in them in the way of clothes. The young men are either
> trying to get on in the government, or are in some mad business.
> They're not sophisticated. When they look at you, they're either
> solemn and stupid-looking or they show off and whistle and that
> sort of thing. They're not sensible and dignified with you, like
> Western men are.

*Maybe the Western men you've met and those on the screen are not the
average. You'd find in their own countries they show off and whistle, too,
and the girls think they're stupid.*

> But I'd be different, as a visitor. People say you can have a
> marvellous time.

*What do you think about the youth groups that take part in demon-
strations outside embassies and so on?*

> They're maniacs. It's just communist politics.

Is your brother interested in this kind of politics?

> He's not interested in anything except studying. He's mad on
> building things.

*Does he feel sure that when he's finished his studies, there'll be work for
him to do?*

> My father says there'll be a lot of building to do in Indonesia for
> the next hundred years.

*What do you think of the government? I know you don't care for politics,
but would you rather have this kind of government or some other kind?*

> What other kind?

Any kind. Just a change.

> Oh, the government's all right. But there are things all the time—
> one after another. There's always a crisis and yet things go on the
> same. I want to get away and see some of the world.

K. IS A MEMBER of the Indonesian Women's Congress (Kongres
Wanita Indonesia). She has a large grown-up family. She is a doctor,
although she has not fully practised for some years. I suppose she
would be considered a feminist, but she remains intensely feminine,
always wearing the traditional combination of *kebaya*, a filmy, tight-
fitting, long-sleeved blouse, and sarong, usually of bright *batik*. Indonesian women are organization-conscious, due, they claim, to their
adat background of participation in communal activity. The Women's
Congress has many activities, ranging from child-care and health centres to marriage bureaux and adult education for women labourers. Its
fundamental interest, however, is in removing discrimination against
women which, in a Muslim country where men are technically permitted four wives, is even more of a task than in the West.

**Women in Indonesia seem more active and independent than in other
Muslim countries?**

> Perhaps so. It is true that we have no Madam Pandit [Indian pol-
> itician and diplomat, sister of the Prime Minister, Jawaharlal
> Nehru], but we have never had purdah either. We have women
> in the government and in the diplomatic services. We have twenty
> women judges, two public prosecutors. Seven per cent of the civil
> service is women. You'll find women in many municipal councils.
> On the whole, Indonesian women are politically equal with the
> men. Most discrimination is at the social and economic level.
>
> Since there's a surplus labour force, it's hard for women to
> claim their rights, even when they've got guarantees written into
> legislation. In some industries—batik, tea processing, cigarette,
> cocoa and chocolate factories, for example—about 60 per cent
> of the workers are women, but they're piece-workers without
> guaranteed rights.
>
> What we want more, though, is Article Sixteen of the United
> Nations' Declaration of Human Rights, which gives social equal-

ity, especially in marriage and divorce. When I tell you that the divorce rate in Java is as high as 50 per cent and that it is extremely difficult for a wife to get a divorce unless it's written into her marriage contract, you can see what a high time the men are having!

Does your adat act as a counter in marriage and divorce to the male-favouring Islamic law?

Yes, but mainly indirectly through the inheritance laws. *Adat* does not stop child marriages and it permits polygamy. The penal code, which is a combination of both customary and Islamic laws, is biased against women. For example, adultery committed by a husband with an unmarried woman is only punishable if his marriage law is based on monogamy, as it is if he's a Christian. So a Muslim husband committing adultery with an unmarried woman cannot be punished, while all married women committing adultery are liable to punishment, as are their accomplices. We would like an age limit for marriage—fifteen for women, eighteen for men— and the consent of both parties as a stipulation.

We also want to do away with polygamy. Why should one man equal four women? Islamic law requires that all wives be treated equally! As if this were possible emotionally—and in any case, there is no punishment for non-fulfilment!

Do you think you have a chance of getting through such a law?

Why don't you add, 'while Sukarno is president?' That's what most visitors say. Actually, the president does set a bad example as far as we are concerned. He talks about women being the glory of God's creation, like a beautiful flower, etc., but he isn't prepared to deprive himself of his right to pluck the flower when he feels like it. When he married Hartini, some of us refused to acknowledge her socially. If second wives are made to feel ashamed, fewer girls will be willing to marry a man who already has a wife. Also, some of our people on the Family Planning Associations have something to say about *Bapak* Sukarno! But the president isn't the only one to blame. Many of his ministers are just as bad.

Are you against Sukarno's kind of government?

That's a complicated question, as they say. It seems to me that women were better represented in some of the earlier governments, like the Sjahrir and Sjarifuddin cabinets in 1946–48. Women are particularly hard hit by inflation, too, which has increased tremendously since Sukarno introduced 'guided democracy'. Also I think we should benefit from regular elections. The right of franchise is given to all Indonesian citizens, male or female, over the age of eighteen, and there are more women than men. Undoubtedly most women would vote the way their men voted, as my friends tell me they do in Australia, but we—I mean the Congress—would have a chance to act as a pressure group for reform. As it is we are represented in the various bodies headed by Sukarno but we don't get far with matters that the men are united about—even if they won't openly admit it. They shake their heads and say, 'Yes, yes, but the economic situation is difficult, as you know, and we are very busy at the moment.'

Where do you think the best chances of improvement for Indonesian women lie?

Compulsory education is one field. Even before World War II we had some women medical doctors and lawyers. Now we have women engineers and technicians and women economists. Women with an independent livelihood and standing in the community can force through changes. Kartini, who is considered the pioneer for the emancipation of women in Indonesia, began in the field of education, but in her days only upper-class girls could go to school. Until compulsory education is a fact—for probably a generation—we can't expect too much, I suppose; I'm told that Australia is still a man's country although the women have had their educational rights for years. But that doesn't stop us from trying.

L. IS A SMALL, gentle Javanese who, with the changes of government in March and July 1966, became one of the most influential men out of the public eye in Jakarta. His wisdom has long been available to his friends; it is now at the service of his government. He is caught in a flurry of activity but his old composure remains. He sits smiling in his garden, his grey hair ruffled by a breeze. We drink tea and he offers delicate cheese biscuits. Under guided democracy he lived somewhat precariously, teaching and translating; his sympathies were with the men who stood opposed to Sukarnoism and who feared the growing strength of the PKI, but he was not himself active. Today, as always, he tries to answer my questions precisely. Even when he gets started on one of his favourite subjects he is courteously sensitive to one's response. His eyes search and play and his soft voice can always be stopped. I have been trying to explain to him the shock outside Indonesia at the mass killings of communists after 30 September 1965.

Yes, of course, I'm not surprised. It was not, however, such a shock to us, although even now we do not know for sure the magnitude of it. The murder and mutilation of the generals brought an army reaction, understandably you might say, and for those who remembered Madiun the reflex was sustained by a political determination to get rid of the communists once and for all —not perhaps realistic, but again understandable. The people joined in for many reasons, some quite personal and local, some political and religious. But the charge that gave this thing its dimension of horror—and meant that many innocent people were chopped up—was fear, fear that the government had lost control and it was 'them or us'.

It was not pleasant. But I hope now that it is over, and I don't think I have to apologize to you for it, any more than I would expect a Frenchman to apologize to me for the Terror or an Indian or Pakistani for the race riots after partition or a Chinese for the elimination of the landlords. It happened. It was understandable. I could not prevent it. It has given some of us the opportunity to see that nothing like it happens again.

Would you agree, however, that something can be done about the political prisoners? It seems there are perhaps as many as 200 000. The gaols are full, make-shift detention quarters overflowing. Would not your government demonstrate its strength and its resolution that things will be different now by seeing that these prisoners are treated justly?

It is more possible to be humane than just in these circumstances. Some will be charged with involvement in the 30 September plot. They will be tried—that is justice—but they are few. Many thousands will be sent home; they are innocent victims of a rampage. Many more, the majority, will be re-educated, indoctrinated if you like, shown the error of their ways and then allowed to return to society. But many will have to remain in detention. They cannot be tried for anything. It was not illegal for them to be communists. But it would be madness to release them, to allow them to begin subverting and sabotaging, infiltrating and threatening. You might be impressed outside with such a demonstration of our strength, but Indonesians themselves would be astonished at such an indication of weakness. It is safe for them to stay inside—probably safer for themselves at the moment as well as for the government.

And I'm not sure that outside Indonesia a legal gesture would mean much, except among my Western friends. Even in the West, some nations which offer encouragement to Indonesia now say it would be dangerous to let the communists out. They are relieved, in fact, that the communists have been cornered. Our neutralist friends are not concerned, many of them have been locking up communists and others for years. Mr. Lee Kuan Yew and Tunku Abdul Rahman, who are our neighbours, understand the necessity of detaining communists without trial for security reasons. Even the Soviet Union seems to understand our predicament. It seems to think that we have two kinds of communists and it appreciates that Indonesia's security requires that the pro-Peking group at least should be kept under observation. So perhaps the only country which would be quite happy if we were to release all the political detainees is the Chinese People's Republic and our relations with Peking at the moment are not such that we should jeopardize our security in order to try to strengthen them.

I accept your ironic tribute to the complexity of foreign relations. But I had thought when you spoke about wanting to 'rejoin the international community' that you might have had in mind accepting some of its standards and aspirations.

Who is to say what these are? No, we want to 'rejoin' in that we want to get back into the United Nations, stop this nonsense over Malaysia and get international assistance for our economy. In other words, our reasons are practical. I don't think the feeling here is that we have done wrong, that we should apologize and

promise to behave better in the future. No nation admits that, unless it is hopelessly beaten in a war, and even then—as in Japan's
renunciation of her military ambitions—it is unusual. We feel we
can make the corrections ourselves. Not all of what has happened
in Indonesia under Sukarno's guided democracy has been bad. It
is part of our history, part of our suffering.

How do you think Sukarno will accept these corrections?

It will not be so difficult for him as you might think. I am, of
course, one of those who think that Sukarno should stay. He gives
us continuity, which is important during a time of crisis. He is
important for internal security and for our relations with some
nations.

At the moment, he is difficult for us to handle, but as time goes
on and he gets used to the idea that he isn't the executive authority any more we are hoping that he will spend more time writing
and, perhaps, speaking. After all, he has complained a good deal in
the past about being over-worked. In his old age we are hoping
that he will settle down and become, really, a father figure and
stop trying to be a revolutionary, an *enfant terrible*. It is probably
unlikely that he will be able to give us positive leadership any
more because the programme of the new government doesn't in-
spire him. We believe that everything now depends on getting the
economy to work and then on restructuring it. The president is
suspicious of economic reform partly because, like most artists, he
thinks it is humdrum and partly because he suspects that it will
provide an opening for the *necolim* [neo-colonialism].

Will it?

Ah! Are you thinking of fiendish instruments of international
capitalism like Naspro? There must be some symbolism in that—
the only Australian investment in Indonesia is a company which
thrives on our headaches! I think you'll find that we will be fairly
careful about foreign investment. But the president is right in one
respect: it is true that if we are going to concentrate on the economy we will not be able to take up strong attitudes abroad.
Frankly, I think that's good.

Do you think you are wise to commit yourself so fully to economic issues?

Some of our own people ask the same question. 'Perhaps the Bung was right—nothing can be done about the economy', they say, after a first look at the economic mess. But I don't think the Indonesian economy is nearly as mysterious as some think. The mismanagement has been really monumental. We need about three years to stabilize inflation and get the economy working again. I think the Indonesian people will give us that time.

That isn't to say that the economic problems aren't immense, especially as we are faced by annual increases of population which eat up what little gain is made. There's not much enthusiasm for birth control, apart from the fact that the president would almost certainly consider a reversal of his own policy on that matter to be the unkindest cut of all.

But I think that we will be able to mobilize national action on the economy, as the nation was mobilized by Sukarno in the past on other issues. This is our big test because, in a sense, the basic Indonesian problem is action. You have in the West an active tradition—Christianity, material progress. You have conscience, which arouses you, and you understand and can use power, which defines what you can do. The communists also have a philosophy of action. But our tradition teaches us how to accept, how to blend. Sukarno had a true insight into this difficulty. He tried to lift the people, stir them into action as a nation. He chose issues which suited his temperament and his skills. We think the economy is an issue which suits the temperament and the skills of this new government. We're a humdrum lot! But we are at one with Sukarno in believing that you can only mobilize the Indonesian people, especially the Javanese, in ways which they can relate to their traditions. We don't propose to modernize Indonesia on either a Western or a communist model.

Is that what some Indonesians mean when they say now to Westerners: 'Look, we've accomplished here in a few months what you're trying to do in Vietnam the hard way?' In other words, leave us alone and you'll find we're on your side?

Not quite, or shall I say, only for the moment. We would like you to think that, but we do not really think it ourselves. If you were to say it to us, we would react. There is a parallel with Vietnam to the extent that I think Indonesia can say to the West, which means particularly the United States and Australia: 'If you push us, only the communists will benefit.' Indonesians do not want to join any 'Western bloc'. This applies to military arrangements—we can defend ourselves, provided we are friendly with our neighbours. It also applies to economic aid: we don't want to become dependent on any one nation or one bloc. We want room to manoeuvre in our own interest. But I would agree that these interests coincide with yours now much more than they do with those of any communist nation. For example, in education. Our textbooks, especially in politics, economics, sociology and related subjects, are pathetic—Sukarnoism run riot. Our brains need to be refreshed with some real thinking. The administrators can hold the present situation, one hopes, but Indonesia's future will depend on creative and confident work in education, especially in our universities, in the next ten years. You can help us much more here than the communists can. We don't propose to exchange one hotch-potch of propaganda for another.

Do you think the Indonesian communists will make a come-back in, say, five years or so?

No. It depends, of course, what you mean by a come-back. They will obviously exist. They may even reorganize. Our job will be to keep their influence to a minimum, to prevent them from making a political come-back and also to prevent them from trying violent means, such as guerrilla warfare. Frankly, I don't think they will manage the second. They could be a nuisance but they would be isolated from outside assistance and our own army is too strong. People who talk about the invincibility of Mao's techniques forget that the Chinese communists had the Japanese invaders to help them demonstrate the impotence of the Kuomintang regime. In Vietnam you have a divided country, with the communist north physically backed by China. We in Indonesia are surrounded by *necolim*! From whom could the communist guerrillas get help? So, if we can feel confident that we won't have any invaders to repel, I think we can cope with the communist guerrilla bands. Their political challenge may be harder to meet, because it will be disguised. The party will not be allowed to operate openly. Everything depends on the success of our economic plans. Otherwise we may expect governments to come to power who are prepared to listen to the communists.

How do you see the role of the army in Indonesia now?

I represent, of course, the civilian side of what the foreign newspapers call—I hope accurately—the new regime. Our hope is that we will be able to reorganize the machinery of government, re-establish the political parties and resume elections, so that the link between people and government is constitutional, not just emotional. We have to move away from élitism, coups and factions, and we don't want government to become a prize of factional rivalry in the armed forces. But at the moment our need of the army is unquestioned. The army is essential to us for security and also for many services, such as transport and communication. We don't want to be run by the army but the best way of preventing that is to see that the army has a continuing role in government.

You will tame the army, as President Sukarno tried to tame the communists?

We are aware of the problem you raise. So are responsible army leaders like Nasution and Suharto. The difference with the communists is that the army does not have an ideology. Nasution and Suharto do not want political initiative. While we have this sort of army leadership, which blends with government rather than dominates it, we can protect the state from the angry young colonels of the future.

CHAPTER TEN

Foreign Policy

JAKARTA HAS BEEN a lively diplomatic centre since Indonesia first grasped its independence. By 1963, 55 countries had representation there, 43 of them at embassy level. By 1995, this had risen to 117, with 82 at embassy level. The political range in 1963 was wide, considering the constrictions of the Cold War. Communist China was there, which meant exclusion of Taiwan, and both North and South Vietnam maintained consulates, as did North Korea. East Germany had a consulate and West Germany an embassy. All the Soviet bloc countries except Albania were represented. Moreover, some of the missions were large. The United States embassy, housed in a modern building which was one of the sights of Jakarta when it was built, listed 53 diplomats, excluding clerical and other administrative staff. The number of diplomatic staff has risen to 72.

The USSR listed 35 diplomats in 1963. The Soviet Union having collapsed, its diplomatic numbers in 1995 were down to 22, although it has trade, military, cultural and information sections sited outside the embassy. The United Kingdom, whose new embassy opposite the Hotel Indonesia overlooking Friendship Square was destroyed by rioting in September 1963, and rebuilt, listed 20 (now 36), Australia (in a new embassy then, near the British, now in Kuningan in another new embassy) 18 (now 52), Japan 15 (now 49), China 15 (now 25), West Germany and India 9 (now 39 and 12).

Diplomacy is a sensibly slow-moving profession. The changes represent the ebb and flow of relationships and fortunes, in the midst of which Jakarta has continued to grow.

In keeping with its status as a key international city, Jakarta, whose name means 'glorious fortress', was given a face-lift in the 1960s and has been under the cosmetician's scalpel ever since. President Sukarno, an architect himself, got to work on the flat, sprawling, hot and terribly overcrowded city. Jakarta is described in the tourist books as the biggest metropolis in South-East Asia, which may literally be true. But it has the appearance from some perspectives of a sprawling Dutch provincial town, with its tiled roofs and canals. It is one of Indonesia's least attractive cities and, until June 1962, when Sukarno decreed that it should be rebuilt as 'an inspiration and beacon to the whole of struggling mankind and to all the emerging forces', there was speculation that Bandung might become the capital or that a Brasilia would be fashioned in the centre of Java, perhaps within sight of Borobudur.

Jakarta's name is not associated with the great exploits of Indonesian nationalism or with the ancient past. Its fame, as Batavia, is connected not so much with Indonesian history as with Dutch trading prowess. However, in 1928 the Indonesian youth made their famous declaration in Batavia calling for one nation, one flag, one language, and it was in Jakarta in 1945 that independence was proclaimed. In any case, it is conveniently situated for international traffic between Asia and Australia, the Indian and Pacific Oceans, and it has become the nation's business and media centre, as well as the centre of government and politics. The city has become the capital of Indonesia not by emotional preference or strategic choice but by the irresistible forces of inertia. It has become more politically intense under President Suharto because of the constraints he has placed (learning from Sukarno's failures) on political organization outside the national capital.

The fourteen-storey Hotel Indonesia (built with Japanese reparations) broke the skyline of old Jakarta in the 1960s, and some of the first edition of this book was written in one of its rooms. A six-lane highway from Merdeka Square to the outer suburb of Kebajoran ran past the Hotel Indonesia and the impressive sports stadia built (with Russian money and an Indonesian army work-force) for the Asian Games in August 1962. It has a clover-leaf overpass, which, second only to the hotel lit up at night, was one of the wonders of Sukarno's Jakarta. Another highway, providing a by-pass through the port of Tanjung Priok, was completed. The president had plans for a monument which would last a thousand years, a mosque which would be the biggest in the world, a department store modelled on one in Tokyo, a night-club, a supermarket and other projects designed to make Jakarta into the Cairo, Rome, Paris, Brasilia, of Indonesia.

Statues sprang up, designed in the heavy, exultant fashion of socialist realism. Jakarta was to be lifted into the cluster of symbols of the new Indonesia, alongside Manipol-Usdek, the biggest army in South East Asia, the fifth nation by population in the world, 'socialism à la Indonesie and the concepts of '*konfrontasi*' and revolutionary diplomacy. The old kampongs, once lost in the ever-growing greenery, began to be displaced by concrete and glass shops and office buildings. But, like the jungle, the ragged millions of crowded Java were hard to keep at bay. They blurred the lines of these grand structures, setting up their portable stalls along highways, next to a concrete pillar, against a wall.

The New Order government called a halt to Sukarno's dream. Above the heads of the squatters, the girders of half-completed buildings reared emptily for a while. Then, as the Asia-Pacific region became the production powerhouse of the world, Jakarta took off again. Not this time the socialist realism of non-alignment, but the universal architecture of corporate capitalism. Now there are half a dozen new hotels dwarfing the Hotel Indonesia. If you happen to arrive at night and drive from the subdued and sensible Sukarno-Hatta airport terminal, you can imagine as you approach the city proper, on a freeway slung like a highwire between monumental fantasies, all alight, that you are in New York or Tokyo. In daytime, it is obvious however that you are in an early stage of Bangkok. Cars jam the streets, public transport is poor.

Indonesian foreign policy during the first full years of independence had a decidedly pro-Western slant. Foreign policy was not a demanding priority; the nation was beset with domestic problems. Diplomatic relations were established with all major Western and non-committed countries, but no representatives were sent to communist countries except China. Indonesia sought and received Western economic aid, mainly from the Netherlands and the United States. It accepted Western sponsorship for membership of the United Nations and its bodies. It abstained on the vote in the UN to brand communist China as the aggressor in Korea. Efforts were made to establish friendly relations with the Dutch, no fuss was made over West Irian and nothing spectacular was attempted. In fact, the period of the first two cabinets was so unassuming that the parties in power came under attack, especially from the PNI, for failing to promote Indonesia's national interests. In Asia, Indonesia's closest relations were with India.

President Sukarno and Prime Minister Nehru exchanged state visits in 1950.

The Sukiman government (1951–52) was a Masjumi-PNI coalition. It continued the earlier pro-Western policies, under the colourful direction of Foreign Minister Subardjo, who had been one of the leaders in Tan Malaka's attempted coup of 1946, and in fact fell on the issue of an 'active and independent' policy. Two skirmishes preceded the collapse. The Sukiman government reacted against the assertive influence of Peking's ambassador in Jakarta by refusing sixteen Chinese embassy officials permission to land in Indonesia. Then the government became embroiled in a more serious dispute over the signing of the Japanese Peace Treaty in San Francisco. Its decision to attend the conference, although without committing itself in advance to signing the treaty, became for its left-wing critics in parliament and the press additional proof that Indonesia was settling down into a cosy corner in the Western bloc. Critics pointed out that India had refused to attend and that there was a close connection between the treaty and a proposed American military agreement with Japan. After a series of dramatic delays, the Indonesian government signed, but PNI pressure from within the cabinet was so strong that the treaty was never sent to the parliament and ratified. (A separate bilateral treaty on reparations was negotiated later in 1951 between Japan and Indonesia but it was not finally ratified by parliament until 1958). The government offset its pro-American leanings in foreign affairs by strenuous solidarity with the anti-colonialist movements in Indo-China, Malaya and North Africa, and it firmly supported mainland China and spurned Taiwan for membership of the United Nations. But it ran finally into trouble on a matter that seemed to be cut and dried—the acceptance of economic (including military) aid from America on the condition that Indonesia would make a 'full contribution' to the 'defensive strength of the free world'.

Under the United States Mutual Security Act of 1951, certain assurances, including the one mentioned, were required and the Sukiman cabinet, after deliberation—mainly, however, by Subardjo, as there appears to have been no formal cabinet discussion—accepted them. The deal was arranged in secrecy, Subardjo committing Indonesia in a note to the American ambassador (Merle Cochran) in January 1952. A month later the secret came out and, in the uproar that followed, both the Masjumi and PNI withdrew their support of the government, which collapsed within three weeks. There was a certain resentment of 'secret diplomacy', which savoured of colonialism, but the swift and strong reaction was primarily the obvious one—that Indonesia had strayed too far from the path of non-alignment. The retribution visited on the Sukiman government was not forgotten in the remaining years of cabinet responsibility and parliamentary government.

The Wilopo government (1952–53), a mixed PNI-Masjumi-PSI affair, quickly asserted that it would receive only economic and technical, not military, assistance from the United States, and a new agreement was negotiated. The cabinet was absorbed in domestic crises, especially legislation for elections and deteriorating relations with the army which culminated in the 'October 17th affair'. Relations with the Netherlands became sharper, after the new Dutch government set itself against any discussion on the status of New Guinea. Indonesia during this period forced the removal of the Dutch military mission.

The first government of Ali Sastroamidjojo (1953–55) was strongly PNI, with PKI support, and under the leadership of the ex-diplomat, Indonesia set out to impress the world with the activity, as well as the independence, of its foreign policy. The first meeting of the Colombo powers—India, Pakistan, Ceylon, Burma and Indonesia—occurred in April 1954, in an effort to bring the Indo-China war to a peaceful close. It was here that Ali Sastroamidjojo proposed the Bandung conference, which, held the following year, brought Indonesia into the forefront of world politics and into the leadership of the Afro-Asian bloc of nations. It was at the Bandung conference that Indonesia and communist China signed the Dual Nationality Agreement, which contained a major concession to Indonesia in China's waiver of the traditional claim that racial Chinese are national Chinese, wherever they are. Ali made a conscious effort to improve relations with China and with the USSR. Unsuccessfully, he proposed a non-aggression pact of China, India and Indonesia as a counter to the South-East Asia Treaty Organization (SEATO), formed in 1954. During this time, Indonesia also began its struggle for West Irian at the United Nations. It failed to gain the required two-thirds of the General Assembly vote at the 1954 session, but the issue was introduced into international diplomacy.

The Burhanuddin Harahap government (1955–56) was largely a caretaker government for the general elections, the first and last to be held in Indonesia. It corrected to some extent the strongly nationalist image created by Ali's strenuous foreign policy. It developed cordial contacts with Western countries, including Australia, and particularly it established with the Netherlands a fresh basis for talks on West Irian, which were held and failed. Its period was short and its authority refuted by the election results.

The second Ali Sastroamidjojo government (1956–57) was able to pick up the threads of militancy without dropping a stitch. Indonesia was a persistent critic of the British-French Suez action and was reserved in its comments on the Soviet suppression of the revolt in Hungary. It negotiated its first loan from the USSR. The Round Table Conference agreement with the Dutch in 1949 was revoked in stronger terms than previous governments had contemplated, and a large part of the debt Indonesia had accepted from the Netherlands was repudiated. Trade agreements with Czechoslovakia, Romania and North Vietnam were signed.

After an extended trip abroad, President Sukarno announced he had long been unhappy about the way political parties were being used in Indonesia and now he had seen in the USSR and China how development was rapidly taking place, he had decided to speak out. 'I do not want to become a dictator . . . I am really a democrat . . . But my democracy is not liberal democracy . . . What I would like to see in this Indonesia of ours is guided democracy—democracy with leadership, but still democracy.' He called for a *gotong royong* cabinet, including the PKI, and a national council of functional groups, headed by himself. Ali Sastroamidjojo returned his mandate to the president, who formed what he described as 'an emergency extra-parliamentary cabinet of experts' to introduce guided democracy. This was the so-called *kabinet kerdja* (working cabinet), with non-party Dr Djuanda, a veteran cabinet member, as prime minister, and Dr Subandrio, a diplomat, former ambassador in London and Moscow and secretary-general of the ministry of foreign affairs, as foreign minister. The cabinet, which comprised a balance of parties not unlike the last Ali cabinet, except for the inclusion of two ministers regarded as PKI sympathizers, lasted from April 1957 to July 1959. During its period regional elections were held in Java, with the PKI emerging as the island's strongest party.

The first priority in foreign affairs in 1957 was West Irian, and Dr Subandrio worked hard to build enough votes at the United Nations while President Sukarno threatened that if Indonesia were again defeated 'we will use a new way in our struggle which will surprise the nations of the world'. The two-thirds majority was not obtained, and tension rose quickly in Indonesia. Strikes and demonstrations against the Dutch took place, with the government taking over all Dutch enterprises, which were formally nationalized in 1959.

As the rebellious mood of army commanders in Sumatra and Sulawesi grew, Jakarta announced arms purchases from Poland, Czechoslovakia and Yugoslavia and criticized the United States and nationalist China, in particular, for assisting the rebels. When Washington formally denounced the rebels and released small arms and rice supplies to Jakarta, Indonesia continued to look elsewhere—scientific, educational and cultural co-operation with Czechoslovakia, trade with Bulgaria, an agreement with India on naval co-operation, a treaty of friendship with Malaya, and a cultural treaty with the Philippines. Tito and Ho Chi Minh paid state visits. Indonesia resisted Malaya's prodding to join ASA (Association of South-East Asia), which brought Malaya, Thailand and the Philippines into a loose association as a forerunner of ASEAN.

In 1960, Sukarno formulated a new conception of Indonesian foreign policy which grew steadily in emphasis—'the new emerging forces' versus 'the old established forces'. In his speeches at the Bandung conference in 1955, the Indonesian president had faithfully preached the precepts of non-alignment: the neutralist position as a rational brake on the power-maddened nuclear rivalries of the two world blocs, which was a continuous theme in early Indonesian statements about the world. But from 1960 this 'three world' theory was replaced by a 'two world' theory, in which the Afro-Asian nations were part of three-quarters of mankind—the new emerging forces—engaged in a deathly struggle with one quarter—the old established forces. Non-alignment should be based on a new approach that would 'startle mankind with its freshness'.

The New Emerging Forces was composed of the Asian nations, the African nations, the Latin American nations, the nations of the socialist (meaning communist) countries, and progressive groups in the capitalist countries. The old established forces (or order) was not defined, except by elimination. But it represented obviously the Western world, except for those 'progressive groups' which were in favor of its destruction. Central to the theory was conflict, which because 'one cannot escape history' would lead to the destruction of the 'old' and the establishment of a 'new' society. With this emerging ideology, there was emphasis under Sukarno's later leadership on status-symbols of the new Indonesian identity—a national monument supposed to last one thousand years, a mosque designed to be the biggest in the world—and on freeing Indonesia from its tainted Western colonial heritage by a mixed-bag ban on the Rosicrucians, Moral Rearmament, cha-cha and the twist. But it expressed itself most clearly in a more aggressive attitude on foreign affairs, especially 'confrontation' of the new state on its border, Malaysia.

The overlapping campaigns to take West Irian from the Dutch and to confront the proposed new state of Malaysia—both driven by a radical new ideology—gave Indonesian foreign policy in the early 1960s a decidedly aggressive momentum. At first it brought results. Secret talks between the Netherlands and Indonesia proceeded in Washington along lines suggested by an American diplomat, Ellsworth Bunker, and were eventually successful in reaching agreement on 15 August 1962. President Sukarno entitled his independence speech of 17 August 'A Year of Triumph'. The armed forces put on a model display in Jakarta to show that they were prepared for an assault on West Irian (under the command of one Major General Suharto) if diplomacy had not been successful.

Before Indonesia had taken over the administration of West Irian in May 1963, however, the country became heavily entangled in the issue of Malaysia. Indonesia had at first responded mildly. On 20 November 1961 Dr Subandrio, in an address to the United Nations General Assembly on the West Irian issue, observed that Indonesia had no territorial ambitions beyond the area once covered by the Netherlands East Indies and wished Malaysia well. However, the leader of the Brunei Party Rakyat, A. M. Azahari, who opposed Malaysia, made several secret visits to Jakarta and urged government leaders, including General Nasution, to support him. A base was set up in Malinau, in Indonesian Kalimantan, to train the nucleus of a guerrilla army. Azahari also made contact with anti-Malaysia groups in Singapore and Malaya and made several trips to the Philippines, which had publicly stated its claim to sovereignty over part of North Borneo in June 1962. When an armed rebellion took place in Brunei, it was from Manila that Azahari proclaimed himself 'Prime Minister of Kalimantan Utara'. It had never been clear what the rebellion hoped to accomplish politically. Azahari and his party had long sustained the dream of restoring

Brunei's ancient sultanate over Sarawak and Sabah. He had also spoken of a 'Greater Malaysia' including Indonesia and the Philippines. But it was clear that the immediate purpose of the rebellion was to forestall the plan for Malaysia. Within five days, British troops flown from Singapore had quashed the revolt in the major towns.

Indonesian support for the Azahari rebellion was widespread—not only from the PKI and the '1945 Generation', but from the PNI and eventually Sukarno and Nasution. Subandrio replied to what he described as 'offensive' statements from Kuala Lumpur linking Indonesia with the rebellion; he cited British army reports from Brunei that no evidence of Indonesian military intervention had been found. Diplomatic notes and protests were exchanged. Sukarno emphatically rejected the Malaysia concept, and Subandrio announced that Indonesia's patience was not inexhaustible and declared a policy of 'confrontation' toward Malaysia. Azahari came to Jakarta, where he set up a government-in-exile.

A period of intense diplomacy followed. The United Nations agreed to ascertain the wishes of the people of the proposed Malaysia. But it was evident that, whatever was said in public, the mechanics of confrontation were continuing. Joint navy and airforce manoeuvres were held in the South China Sea, involving some 50 ships and squadrons of MIG-21's and TU-16's. General Nasution visited Kalimantan and made several tough speeches, urging the frustration of Malaysia 'by force if necessary'. Guerrilla bands trained in Indonesia raided the Sarawak border.

When the secretary-general of the U.N. (U Thant) announced its team's finding, which was a strong endorsement of the wish of the majority of the people for Malaysia, Indonesia had an opportunity to step back without loss of face, as the conditions of her public concern for the wishes of the people of the non-independent territories had been met. But she chose otherwise. When Malaysia was proclaimed on 16 September 1963, Indonesia (and the Philippines) refused to recognize it and the new government of Malaysia broke off diplomatic contact, bringing political relations of the South-east Asian neighbours to the lowest point since they achieved independence.

From the end of 1963 the anti-Western and pro-Peking tendency of Indonesian policies strengthened. Once an active advocate of nuclear disarmament, Indonesia was one of the last of the 106 signatories of the nuclear test ban treaty. In November the Games of the New

Emerging Forces (Ganefo) were held in Jakarta. Ganefo had its origin
in the Asian Games, when Indonesia failed to issue visas to Israel and
Nationalist China and was suspended by the International Olympic
Committee. Although 51 countries were represented at Ganefo, those
interested in competing at the Olympics in Tokyo the following year
sent inferior teams to avoid disqualifying their best athletes. The
Philippines were beaten at basketball, Japan was defeated at judo and
the USSR had a hard time holding its own in gymnastics. But for
Communist China, disqualified from the Olympics in advance,
Ganefo was an opportunity to prove itself in both sport and diplomacy.

With Ganefo to be held every four years, President Sukarno set
about organizing the Conference of the New Emerging Forces
(Conefo). He ordered the construction in Jakarta of an enormous
complex of buildings, including an assembly hall to seat 2500, which
appeared equipped to rival the United Nations.

Throughout 1964 Indonesia's relations with the United States deteriorated. Sukarno, never popular with Congress, told the US to 'go
to hell' with its aid—and the Senate took him at his word. Washington
announced an agreement to train Malaysian troops in America.
Malaysia formally charged Indonesia before the UN Security Council
with aggression. The vote of 9 to 2 (only the USSR and Czechoslovakia supporting Jakarta) showed how isolated Indonesia had become from the non-aligned Afro-Asian countries. In January 1965
Indonesia withdrew from the United Nations when Malaysia was accepted as a member of the Security Council for that year. During the
year, President Sukarno spoke increasingly of Jakarta's close links with
Peking, and developed the idea of an axis linking Indonesia, North
Vietnam, North Korea, Cambodia and Communist China. (Cambodia, the only non-Communist nation included, declined the offer of
axis membership and showed its independence of Peking and Jakarta
that month by recognizing Singapore, which had separated from
Malaysia.) Peking's Foreign Minister, Marshal Chen Yi, visited
Jakarta. The two nations reaffirmed their common interest in excluding Western influence from South-East Asia. Following the visit,
Jakarta officials began hinting that Indonesia would soon have its own
atomic bomb, suggesting that Chen Yi had been pressed to provide
the nuclear facilities for an explosion in return for Indonesia's participation in a common military strategy for the region.

The dramatic course of Indonesian foreign policy came to a jarring
halt at the end of 1965, following the abortive coup. By April 1966

Peking and Jakarta were exchanging sharp and critical Notes, the Malaysia issue had been re-opened diplomatically and spokesmen for the foreign ministry were giving the impression that one of their main objectives in life was to be friendly with their neighbours, including Malaysia, and Western nations, like Australia.

It is fair to say that Indonesia in the preceding years had represented, to its neighbours, friends, and enemies, an unpredictable hazard. Dealings between countries are made easier by knowledge of two things—the definition of each other's 'vital interest', which is the area only to be disturbed in the expectation of serious trouble, and the certainty that the government is 'responsible', in the sense that it can be relied on to stand by whatever commitment its representatives make. In both these respects Indonesia created doubts in many chancelleries. It was acknowledged that Indonesia, a new nation, was still feeling its way in international politics, but a disturbing pattern could be seen: failure and tension at home deflected into action abroad. The system of government, which relied on President Sukarno's ability to satisfy the power groups surrounding him, seemed to be forcing, or enticing, him to devise increasingly abstract strategies of nationalist grandeur and aggrandizement abroad. Harold Crouch writes:

> Guided Democracy ... ultimately failed. Although all groups mouthed approval of the president's ideological precepts, his doctrines often became weapons in the hands of the army, the PKI, and other groups in their efforts to demonstrate each others' disloyalty. While political leaders in the capital behaved like traditional court advisers, the rival groups of courtiers were backed by nationwide organizations confronting each other throughout Indonesia.

The Suharto government had to reassure its neighbours and the wider world both that it knew what its real interests were and that it would stand by its commitments. It did this not by declaration, but by returning to a first principle of nationhood, which is that governments are responsible for the welfare of its people. It put national development, especially economic growth, first. Under three foreign ministers, Adam Malik (1967–78), Mochtar Kusumaatmadja (1978–88) and Ali Alatas (1988–   ), it restored Indonesia's credibility by concentrating on political stability and regional co-operation in order to ensure economic development.

Indonesian foreign policy has been dominated by two considerations. One is that Indonesia should not join any power blocs, describing itself sometimes as 'non-aligned' or 'neutral', sometimes as 'active and independent'. The other is fear for the territorial safety of the young Indonesian nation. From time to time other considerations have been apparent—that Indonesia should play a leading role in its region, for example, or contribute to a peaceful world order.

Because Indonesia straddles a waterway between the Pacific and Indian oceans, there will always be tension between, on the one hand, those powerful forces, whether they are states or commercial enterprises, which have an interest in seeing the traffic flow freely and, on the other, the desire of patriotic Indonesians to possess in their nation something distinctive and inviolate of their own. Java has been the dominant island under both Sukarno and Suharto, but when a nation is an archipelago, its heartland is in many places and it is vulnerable to pressure and blandishment from outside. Indonesian nationalism was born in the struggle against colonialism, but it was sharpened and refined in the complex politics of World War II and the Cold War. The stabilizing of Indonesia's immediate environment around the Association of South-East Asian Nations (ASEAN), the development of the wider region, especially through the inter-governmental forum Asia Pacific Economic Cooperation (APEC), and the end of the Cold War have helped to ease the tension between Indonesian nationalism and the outside world, but it will always be there. It will show in sensitivity by Indonesians to being lectured about human rights or in argument about the rights of international shipping to use the sea lanes over which Indonesia under the Law of the Sea, which it signed in 1994, claims sovereignty.

Indonesia's dramatic internal changes in 1965–66, at the height of the Cold War, might have seemed like an opportunity to break with 'non-alignment'. After all, Suharto was effectively reversing many of Sukarno's policies—on foreign aid, Malaysia, close links with China, just to mention a few. It was a time of grand gestures. Indonesia, like other colonial territories, arrived at centre stage in diplomacy when the romantic European trappings were still in vogue, although about to be replaced. Diplomacy was still like opera, full of voices, stances and effects. Instead, the Suharto government withdrew from centre stage and began rebuilding. It learned how to behave modestly, how to listen to others and accept their help, how to be patient when negotiating complex regional and multilateral arrangements. By doing so, it conscientiously prepared Indonesia, although perhaps at first not consciously, for the new world that was opening up in the late twentieth century.

The creation in 1967 of the Association of South East Asian Nations, ASEAN (Thailand, Malaysia, Singapore, Indonesia, the Philippines, and later Brunei) was the starting point of a more mature and constructive Indonesian foreign policy. Proposals for a small regional group had been around for some time, but Indonesia was suspicious. The 'Maphilindo' talks in 1963 had suggested a grouping of Malaya, the Philippines and Indonesia, as a way out of the Malaysia issue. The British view at the time was that the proposal went too far in Indonesia's direction. But Indonesia would have none of it, because the Philippines was a member of SEATO and a major base for US forces and Malaya was anti-communist (and involved with Britain, Australia and New Zealand in the Commonwealth Strategic Reserve). ASEAN, however, embodied two concepts which Indonesian nationalism valued above all.

The first was the notion of 'national resilience'. This has developed sophistication over the years but initially it simply meant that a nation's integrity and viability in the long run depended not just on a military capacity to ensure its physical security but on the nation's political, economic, social and cultural strengths as well. I do not know how or when this idea began: it seems always to have been there. (Some trace it back to a speech by Hatta in 1948). Closely associated, indeed sometimes interchangeable with it, were two other ideas—'self-reliance', meaning that for a nation to be independent it had to be prepared to look after itself, and 'comprehensive security', meaning that non-military strengths contributed just as much as military to the actual physical security of a nation. These were ideas which at the time seemed fuzzy, but have proved effective (and can be seen at work in Australian security thinking in the last decade). But in 1967 the important consideration for Indonesia was that ASEAN was not a military arrangement, so it did not conflict with Indonesia's 'non-aligned' or 'independent and active' foreign policy, and it did offer Indonesia the opportunity to spread the doctrine of resilience further. 'National resilience' became 'regional resilience'.

The other favoured concept was the need to keep outside powers from meddling in Indonesia. Its history as a colony, its early history as a nation and its strategic geography all made thoughtful Indonesians wary of the outside world, although at the same time they were fascinated by it and realized they needed its technology and its money for their own national development. By the time ASEAN was established, some of its members could see that the Americans were facing defeat in Vietnam. By 1971, ASEAN had developed the first outline of the Zone of Peace, Freedom and Neutrality (ZOPFAN), which was derided by Western strategists at the time but has survived in relevance. It recognizes three levels of relationships—among nations in the ASEAN region itself, between ASEAN and the major powers (especially China, Japan, Russia and the United States) and between the major powers themselves. It suggests ways of avoiding direct military intervention in the ASEAN region by the major powers and, conversely, ways of discouraging ASEAN states from inviting or provoking outside intervention. ZOPFAN's approach is not to try to exclude the major powers, but to include them—and all of them—on mutually agreed terms.

ASEAN thinking is essentially the same as Indonesian thinking. Economic development is the first priority. Economic development needs political stability, and not just for a year or two but for a quarter of a century at least. Political stability is mainly an internal matter, but it depends also on not being manipulated by outside powers. So, without changing its foreign policy principles, Indonesia changed markedly the way it puts these principles to work. It was a change which anticipated the end of the Cold War and is currently making a contribution to political stability and economic development in the Asia-Pacific region. The kind of thinking that has made ASEAN a modest success—inclusive, incremental, consultative, consensual, comprehensive—is the same kind of thinking behind Asia Pacific Economic Cooperation (APEC) and ASEAN Regional Forum (ARF) which are ASEAN-style forms of economic and security co-operation extended to the wider Asia-Pacific region.

Ali Alatas looks back on the last thirty years with satisfaction, but he is not the kind of man to be complacent. He has a well developed professional apprehension about the world. Ugly things are happening out there, he observed, in an interview for this book in his office in mid-1995. Fortunately, most of them were happening elsewhere, especially in Africa and Europe. He expressed a view which would also show up in Indonesia's first Defence White Paper published later that year: security in the Asia–Pacific was 'uncertain'. He did not agree that the Americans and the Russians would withdraw now that the Cold War was over, creating a 'vacuum' which would have to be filled, but he accepted that the region's nature—its physical space and its cultural and political diversity—made it difficult to manage as a 'community'. Indonesia was not working for a balance of military power in the region, which was impossible, but for a security equilibrium, with both military and non-military components. The UN exercise in Cambodia was an example of ASEAN and Indonesian thinking at work— all levels, local, regional and international meshing in an ambitious project to revive a 'failed state'. Disarmament was another area of Indonesian interest in new security thinking. Indonesia was active now on disarmament issues generally. 'As far as Indonesia is concerned, the lower the level of armaments needed for the equilibrium in the Asia–Pacific region to be stable, the better.'

In the context of this broad and flexible Indonesian foreign policy, Timor seemed like a relic of the Old Order. 'You can imagine that, for a government that had made the first priority of its foreign policy a spirit of non-assertive co-operation, there was nothing President Suharto wanted less than the kind of conflict the Portuguese handed us in Timor.' He agrees that what he once described as just a 'pebble in the shoe' had become a problem for Indonesia, but he was not prepared to apply Indonesia's new creative thinking to it. 'Decolonization has irrevocably taken place.'

Australia and Indonesia are as diverse a pair of neighbours as it is possible to find. One is a large, flat continent, thinly populated with, for the most part, Caucasians professing Christianity and individualism, essentially materialist and scientific in outlook, instinctively part of the Western world. The other is an archipelago of mountainous islands, populated with Asians professing, for the most part, Islam and communitarianism, essentially mystic and spiritual, instinctively wary of Western values. The effort each has made to get along with the other after Indonesia hurtled into the world in 1945 holds out some hope for the survival of reasoned self-interest in international relations.

There have been times when the cry has gone up in both countries for 'tough' attitudes to each other. But a broad, pragmatic interest in friendship has survived, supported sometimes by imagination, sometimes by prudence, sometimes by the sheer inertia of the irrevocable fact that the two countries were fated to be neighbours for ever. In the post-World War II decades, some Australians were interested in Indonesia as a career—as scholars, soldiers, diplomats, journalists, business and professional persons. The people seemed to like each other and the abstractions of race, religion and colour were often surprisingly melted in personal relationships of warmth and charm. Australians were not of the same interest to Indonesians, who could look north to a wider world. If positions for or against the West needed to be taken up, the United States was there for the asking. Radio Australia, with its popular musical requests, and the flow of Indonesian students to Australia, were more typical of the vague friendliness and neighbourliness of the two countries than disagreement or agreement over issues of foreign affairs.

Gough Whitlam, however, made a point of cultivating relations with Indonesia between 1972 and 1975, and this intensified after the Cold War. The official relationship became more intimate, first in a working partnership from 1988 between Alatas and Australia's Foreign Minister, Gareth Evans, and between defence officials, and in the 1990s between Suharto and the Australian Prime Minister, Paul Keating. This culminated in December 1995 in the announcement of a 'security agreement', in which the two countries undertook to consult regularly at ministerial level about matters affecting their common security and, in the case of 'adverse challenges' to either of them or to their common security interests, to consider 'measures' which might be taken.

It is sometimes said that Australia and Indonesia as neighbours have geography on their side and history against them, but in fact their historical relationship as nation-states has a sound beginning. Australia started out right with Indonesia by backing her in the early days when her independence of the Dutch was not assured. In spite of the long struggle over West Irian, the Malaysia issue, Timor and local irritants from time to time, the influence of this historical initiative has remained.

The nationalists who proclaimed Indonesian independence on 17 August 1945 quickly commanded respect in Canberra, which regarded them more favourably than did London or The Hague or, for that matter, Moscow. This support is surprising in retrospect. The Republic of Indonesia was an unknown quantity in Australia. The names of some of its leaders were known, but their pre-war record of nationalism against the Dutch had become confused with their deliberately misleading collaboration with the Japanese. The Dutch were allies in the global fight against German Nazism and Japanese Fascism, which was still an emotional issue although the war had technically ended. In addition, Australians, like other European-centred people, were not able to appreciate at that stage the long-range advantages of Asian nationalism. Few Australians had any interest in the Indonesian struggle against the Dutch. It seemed safer for the Dutch to return, as was their 'legal right', just as the British were expected to return to their colonial possessions in Asia.

On 24 September 1945, just five weeks after the proclamation of independence and a few days before the first British troops landed in Indonesia, the Brisbane branch of the Waterside Workers Federation took the initiative by announcing a ban on ships carrying arms to Indonesia. The decision had a startling effect, drawing attention not only to the issues involved, but to the political sophistication of the waterside workers. (Molly Bondan's personal account, *In Love With A Nation*, sheds light on how interested Australians were educated by some of the 600 political evacuees from Boven Digul, in New Guinea, including a number of communists under Sardjono, former chairman of the PKI, who took up wartime propaganda work in Brisbane.) Neither the Chifley government nor the Australian Council of Trade Unions supported the ban, but it drew attention to the cause of the Indonesian nationalists. In the prevailing sentiment of the times, which was hopeful and democratic, especially among Labor Party supporters, the union's actions made it difficult for the Labor government to oppose the nationalists on behalf of the colonialist Dutch, some of whom, coming to Australia from Indonesia during the war, had made themselves unpopular in official circles. Certainly, the ban was not lost on the Indonesians. The date—recorded as 28 September—has an honoured place in the diary of events in the official history of the revolution.

Looked at from the viewpoint of Australian security, which was at that time still recovering from the failure of the colonialists—Britain, France and the Netherlands—to hold South-East Asia against the Japanese, there was something to be said for the Indonesians if they could prove that they had popular support and real qualities of determination. This was shown during the battle against British and Indian troops in Surabaya in November. The Indonesians lost the battle but they showed, by bravely resisting superior forces, that their independence was not just a political stunt. They did not prove positively to the Australians by this that they were prospective allies, but they showed convincingly enough that the theoretical advantages of Dutch occupancy of the archipelago—commercial and defence arrangements—could not be guaranteed. A government less inclined to be guided by ideals on foreign affairs than was the Chifley administration (with Dr H. V. Evatt as Minister for External Affairs) might not have been moved to support the Indonesians. Subsequent events showed, however, that Australia's role in the period of the 1945–49 conflict between Indonesians and the returning Dutch was correct.

The first Dutch 'police action' on 21 July 1947 brought a sharp international reaction, removing some of the caution in Canberra's mind during 1946, when the British were engaged in the thankless business of restoring order and trying to bring the Dutch and Indonesians together. Australia and India each brought the matter before the Security Council and Australia was nominated by Indonesia to the three-man United Nations' Committee of Good Offices. (Belgium was the Netherlands' representative and the United States took the decisive third place.) For the next two years, Australian diplomats and military officers attached to the committee played an important part in the complicated negotiations leading, after the second Dutch 'police action' in December 1948 (which brought open Australian criticism of Netherlands' duplicity), to the transfer of sovereignty and international recognition of Indonesia one year later. During this time Australia was active in supporting Indonesian independence, despite European backing for the Dutch and growing United States concern over the uncertain place of Indonesia in the approaching Cold War. Australia took part in the 1949 New Delhi conference—otherwise entirely Asian—to discuss the Indonesian conflict. J. A. C. Mackie, in his chapter on Australian–Indonesian relations in *Australia in World Affairs, 1956–1960*, notes that Australia had a moderating influence on the resolution finally passed, and prevented a non-white alignment. But the decision to attend was opposed within the Labor Party and attacked by Liberals.

The Labor government was replaced by Menzies' Liberal and Country Party coalition in December 1949, too late to change Australian policy toward the transfer of sovereignty to the Indonesians, if that—suggested by Liberal Party sympathies with the Dutch—were wanted. However, some reaction against the Evatt policies became evident. The new Minister for External Affairs, Percy Spender, visited Jakarta in January 1950 and the Indonesian government learned, apparently with surprise, that Australia did not look kindly upon its claim to New Guinea. One field correspondent, Arnold Brackman, claims that 'baited by the nettled press' on the White Australia policy as well as on West Irian, Spender 'within two days had drained the store of good will that Australia had accumulated during the Indonesian revolution'.

As the year progressed, with an attempted armed uprising led by Captain 'Turk' Westerling, which received a lot of attention in Australia, proclamation of the unitary state on 17 August, and various extravagant statements by non-government nationalists like Mohammed Yamin, opinion in Australia began to harden against Indonesia. Some members of the Labor Party, especially Arthur Calwell, criticized the government for not being tough with the Indonesian leaders over West Irian. The government's view, which had the official support of the Labor Party, was put by Spender on several occasions throughout 1950. These reasons, in varying emphasis, were to dominate Australian thinking on this issue during the next decade. First was the fear, that if Indonesia were given West Irian 'it would be but a matter of time . . . when the claim will be pushed farther so as to include the Trust Territory of Australian New Guinea and its people'. Second was the determination to keep communism, which was believed to be rising in Asia as shown by the war in Korea, from gaining a foothold among the New Guinea people. Third was the belief that New Guinea was 'an absolutely essential link in the chain of Australian defence'. Self-determination, which became a frequently used argument later, was not prominent at this stage.

When R. G. (later Lord) Casey became Minister for External Affairs in 1951, he urged that the West Irian question be kept 'in cold storage' as a means of damping down emotions. By this time, however, opinion was hardening in both Jakarta and The Hague and, when the succession of moderate Indonesian governments ended in 1953 with the first Ali Sastroamidjojo cabinet, the prospect of putting the issue on ice had become remote. Whatever flimsy basis the Indonesian claim had in the eyes of anthropologists, historians and Western defence experts, its source in popular Indonesian sentiment and international politics was not neglected under Ali, who had strong nationalist and

communist support in parliament. This was the period of the abro-
gation of the Netherlands–Indonesian union, the first appeal to the
United Nations on Irian (1954) and the Bandung conference (1955).
Australia opposed the Indonesian request at the UN to place the West
Irian issue on the agenda. The assembly agreed to the request, but the
resolution, which asked no more than that the two parties should get
together, did not gain the necessary two-thirds majority. The following year, Casey visited Jakarta, during the office of the caretaker
Burhanuddin Harahap government, which was a temporary reversion
to moderation pending the election. Casey announced Colombo Plan
aid, and a communique urged the 'greatest possible degree of co-
operation' between the two countries, while maintaining their respec-
tive views on the West Irian issue.

Australia continued to oppose Indonesian efforts to bring West
Irian before the United Nations. Despite the admission of new members, especially from the so-called Africa-Asian bloc, Indonesia's vote
did not show a marked improvement, due mainly to strong lobbying
by Australia and the Netherlands' Nato allies, which had success in
Latin America. Indonesia's political instability began to alarm Canberra. In 1956, when the second Ali Sastroamidjojo government was
installed, regional dissatisfaction with the central government in Jakarta
was becoming evident. Hatta's resignation reinforced Canberra's belief
that a showdown was imminent.

With hindsight (and the benefit of several decades of peaceful
neighbourly co-existence), Australia's reluctance to accept that West
Irian was part of Indonesia seems politically grudging and diplomatically short-sighted, especially as Australia had no practical alternative to
offer. The fact is that Australia was slowly preparing itself to accept
what was inevitable, as was shown by Subandrio's 1959 visit. This was
effectively the first visit to Australia by an Indonesian foreign minister
(Subardjo having unexpectedly dropped in when returning from his
controversial visit in 1951 to San Francisco to sign the Japanese peace
treaty). For all the mixed public reception Subandrio received, a growing official respect for Indonesia's position showed through. Subandrio
maintained a radical stance, telling the Australian cabinet, 'Your ancestors could have understood Indonesia better than you do'. Yet the
five-day visit was capped by a joint announcement which contained an
important qualification, suggesting that Canberra was shifting—'that if
any agreement were reached between the Netherlands and Indonesia
as parties principal, arrived at by peaceful processes and in accordance

with internationally accepted principles, Australia would not oppose such an agreement'. The government ran into heavy criticism from newspapers and some of its members, notably Sir Wilfrid Kent Hughes, for appearing to provide Indonesia with an incentive to put pressure on the Dutch for a settlement. Both Menzies and Casey denied a change in policy, and pointed to Subandrio's acceptance of peaceful means for the settlement of the issue. If the Dutch and Indonesians did in fact reach agreement without duress, Australia had no alternative but to accept the agreement, it was said—but the situation was claimed to be hypothetical, and it was specifically denied that Australia had any intention of urging the Netherlands to negotiate.

The sophistication of this position, which had some difficulty in being interpreted by press and parliament, was the basis of the visit by Menzies to Jakarta later that year. Menzies extracted assurances from Sukarno about the use of force and laid emphasis on self-determination for the Papuan people. But it was becoming obvious that Australia had little influence on Indonesia, which was acquiring arms from Moscow to take West Irian by force if necessary, nor on the Dutch, who announced a decision to strengthen their defences. Australia's influence in Washington also proved to be weak. President Kennedy took a 'fresh approach', telling Sukarno that he would be assisted by a 'calm atmosphere' and urging him to 'maintain tranquillity' in the region during a six-month period of mediation.

From this time until 15 August 1962, when the Netherlands and Indonesia, under firm American control, finally signed a treaty, there was an air of unreality in Australia's calm response to the mounting tension in its near north. Mobilization on all sides was now widely reported. Volunteers to liberate West Irian were pictured enlisting from all corners of the republic. An Indonesian motor-torpedo boat was sunk by the Dutch south of the disputed territory in January 1962. A week later, some sections of the Australian press, following a visit to Melbourne by senior officials of the external affairs department, began speaking of a change in Australian policy, which was denied officially in Canberra. (In December 1961 the Menzies government had been returned with a much reduced majority of two after a campaign in which an unusual combination of the Labor Party and the *Sydney Morning Herald* had protested against what was described as appeasement of a dictator, drawing lessons from Hitler's expansion in the 1930s.) Australian press comment became increasingly sharp as the Indonesians announced parachutist landings on islands off the West

Irian coast, and finally on the territory itself. The Dutch rushed re-
inforcements to the territory and Indonesia used diplomatic pressure
on Japan and the United States to prevent landing and transit rights for
Dutch planes in the airlift. A fifth assassination attempt was made
on Sukarno, amid United Nations appeals to both countries to stop
hostilities.

The treaty was not warmly received in Australia, although it was
recognized as having brought to an end a long and bitter argument
which had affected relations with Indonesia. It was realized that
although technically the agreement had been gained by diplomacy and
that the rights of self-determination for the indigenous people of West
Irian were explicitly safeguarded in the agreement by United Nations'
participation in the 'act of choice', Indonesia had gained occupancy by
a mixture of diplomatic bluff and military threats.

In the files of the US embassy in Jakarta, the following item
appeared in a list of countries whose relations with Indonesia were
assessed in 1963:

> Australia: relations with Indonesia are best characterized as civil.
> They are marked by a growing, if grudging, recognition by
> Australia that it has an important role to play in Asia. The sudden
> realization that the insular dominion now shares a common bor-
> der in New Guinea with the biggest and most populous South-
> east Asian country is an important factor in this awakening.

To any who followed the anguish behind the private and public
debates in Australia over West Irian, the truth in this appraisal will
seem irritatingly detached. It was the Kennedy administration's decision to help Indonesia which shifted the ground under Australia's
feet. Yet it was not before time that the ground shifted. The Australian
government had dallied for years, hoping against hope that the Dutch
could hold on, nervous about public opinion, aware that militarily
Australia depended on the United States. There was some public sympathy for Indonesia's claim and a tendency to regard her patriotic ex-
travagances over West Irian as a special case. West Irian was formerly
Dutch territory and therefore part of the Indonesian successor state.
Australia, in any case, did not want the territory herself and was not
prepared to fight for the Dutch to have it. She was not able to dissuade
the United States from a tolerant interest in an Indonesian victory and
did not have the military capacity to support an independent policy

herself. Juggling all these factors, the Australian government had no alternative than to accept the US-brokered agreement.

The way Australia handled the Malaysia issue showed that something had been learned from the West Irian experience. It seemed that Indonesia was now as determined to remove the British from South-East Asia as she had been to remove the Dutch. As far as Australia was concerned, this was too high a price to pay for a new friendship that had barely been tested and was unstable. The traditional links with Britain, the Commonwealth defence arrangements with Malaya and the general support for Malaysia as a solution to the political future of the peoples of Singapore, Sarawak and Sabah, made Australia's choice inevitable, although not easy to make when the time came.

Indonesia's immediate neighbours—Australia, Malaysia and the Philippines—were faced with a simple problem of balance of power in the region. Whatever reservations were held in Kuala Lumpur and perhaps even in Canberra about Britain's position in the region in the long term, neither country was able to match Indonesia militarily and neither wanted Indonesia to be dominant militarily in South-East Asia. Manila was dependant on the Americans, whose attitude to Indonesia (at least while Kennedy was president) was ambivalent. The British naval, air and military bases in Singapore, and the American air base in the Philippines, as well as the roaming presence of the American seventh fleet, might be seen by Indonesia as a threat, but to others in the region they were reassuring.

Australia managed the Malaysia issue more deftly than it did West Irian. It sided with Kuala Lumpur and, to a lesser extent, Britain, while keeping open its lines to Jakarta. In the event, everyone was saved the consequences of Sukarno's determination to live dangerously ('*vivere pericoloso*' was his phrase) by the upheaval in Jakarta which unbalanced and then unseated him. Indonesia's accommodating regional policy since then has made life for Australia distinctly more comfortable.

The East Timor issue continued, however, to cause tension. There have been three discernible phases in Australian policy. In 1974–75 (from the coup in Lisbon to the coup in Canberra), Australia wanted integration of East Timor with Indonesia, but she also wanted integration to take place through a process of peaceful self-determination. These two objectives proved irreconcilable in a fast-moving drama in Timor (and a political crisis in Canberra). It is also clear now that Defence (preferring independence) differed with Foreign Affairs (which differed within itself) and Whitlam took a strong personal leadership role in favour of integration. Whitlam believes now that Suharto's undertaking to him not to use force (reminiscent of Sukarno's undertaking to Menzies over West Irian) lapsed when the Whitlam government was dismissed by the governor-general on 11 November, 1975.

The second phase, 1975–88, shows Australia accepting the Indonesian annexation, sometimes grudgingly. The Fraser-Peacock government did so formally in January 1978. The Hawke-Hayden government accepted what had been done, but was wary of developing the relationship. The third phase, from 1988 to the present, began with Gareth Evans and Kim Beazley, as Minister for Defence, taking the initiative over a wide range of foreign policy, trade and defence activities. The Australia-Indonesia Institute was established to revive people-to-people contact, Indonesian troops were invited to exercise in Australia and the Timor Gap Treaty was completed, enabling oil exploration to continue in an area in dispute. The idea behind these initiatives was not to make the 'relationship' more important, but to give it content as ballast, so that it would not be upset when the inevitable jolts occurred. The perception at the time was that, while East Timor might have been handled better and needed attention by Indonesia as a matter of human rights and economic development, it could not be allowed to operate as a veto over the relationship as a whole.

In mid-1995 an incident occurred which showed that despite the broadening and deepening in the relationship since 1988, serious misunderstandings could still happen. Indonesia nominated Lieutenant General Herman Mantiri as its ambassador in Canberra, despite indications from Australia that because of remarks he had made in support of the army at the time of the massacre in Dili in 1991, his appointment was not welcome, if for no other reason than that it would create persistent security problems for the Australian authorities. Why the Indonesians persisted in the appointment when there were other candidates more acceptable, such as another civilian to follow Sabam Siagian, a former editor whose appointment had been in tune with the new, open flavour of the relationship, was never satisfactorily explained. Australia kept up the pressure, and Indonesia eventually withdraw the nomination, showing its displeasure by pointedly leaving the post in Canberra vacant for a few months. Nevertheless, when Jakarta finally made the appointment, it was a strong one—a senior professional who was a civilian.

The incident showed how easily things can go wrong in an intense and sensitive relationship. At both ends there are live loose wires and faulty power points. In Indonesia, policy-makers and decision-takers have to work in an intricate and volatile political culture, where decisions such as the appointment of an ambassador risk being entangled with the higher politics of the day. Several explanations did the rounds during the Mantiri affair. One was that ABRI had taken a stand on appointments to missions in the South-East Asian region, which, because of security implications, should, it argued, be military. In consequence, Washington and London, which it had always prized, could become civilian, and Australia, which it had lost when Siagian was appointed, should return to the fold. Another explanation was that Feisal Tanjung, leader of the so-called Green or Islamic faction, wanted Mantiri, who is a Catholic and close to Benny Moerdani, out of the way. Another explanation was that Suharto went along with the appointment on the assumption that the anti-Timor sentiment in Australia could be controlled, or certainly weathered.

In Australia, political leaders have to live with the fact that, however important the relationship with Indonesia may be from a foreign affairs, trade and defence point of view, the military regime in Indonesia is not popular in the electorate and sympathy for the East Timorese is widespread. Some of this tension is simply an unbridgeable cultural divide. It cannot be bridged yet because it is too wide and deep, but it can be traversed, as it has been since Indonesia's independence, by individuals and groups, official and non-official, who make an effort to understand.

The security agreement of 1995 is an important development. It represents a new stage in relations between the two unlikely neighbours. For Australia, it signals (once again—the signals have been frequent recently) that the 'insular dominion' has come out. Australia is more confident politically and militarily than it was when it first contemplated a relationship with Indonesia. The security agreement is also recognition that any role Australia might play in its region cannot avoid or ignore Indonesia—by going over its head, as it were, to the major players in the northern hemisphere. For Indonesia, the agreement is less important. It is easier for Indonesia to ignore or avoid Australia. No doubt, the agreement owed something to Suharto's personal appreciation of Keating. But it is also evidence that Australian influence and material support is worth having, and that a degree of trust has developed between Jakarta and Canberra.

CHAPTER ELEVEN

Future

Contemporary history is hard to write with assurance. The history of Hitler's Germany or Stalin's Russia—to take two dramatic examples—are today deceptively simple, filled with the anguish and knowledge of later events. But at the time people were confused about what was happening; one of the confusions was their hope that it would not turn out the way it did. From the time Indonesia entered the world as a new nation, it attracted hope and sympathy. Does it still?

The future is brighter for Indonesians now than when this book was first published. Their standard of living is higher, and seems likely to continue to improve. They have adjusted their nationalism to the region and the world in order to encourage peace and prosperity. Domestically, they have established firmly under two contrasting presidents a national ideology, *Pancasila*, which, while inevitably mis-used as ideologies always are, contains seeds of hope for Indonesia in the twenty-first century. As ethnic and religious fault-lines open up around the world, Indonesia is living, or is trying to live, according to an official standard of racial and cultural tolerance and co-operation.

The bleak future predicted in the earlier edition was influenced by the assessment that Sukarno had embarked on a dangerous course for Indonesia of provoking trouble abroad in order to distract attention from failures at home. But there was concern at a deeper level too, and in that respect the bleak future turned out to be uncomfortably close. What was called then the Politics of Ecology is even more demanding in Indonesia now that the country has had thirty years of political stability and rapid economic growth. In 1965 it was possible to be philosophical and detached about the environment. Now it is just as pressing for Indonesia to find a way of enhancing its environment by development, rather than destroying it, as it is to find a way of giving its people human rights and real as distinct from formal democracy.

The environment has begun to show up on the danger screen in at least three respects. Unrestrained urbanization, especially in and around Jakarta but also in general on the island of Java, is creating a range of familiar problems, including air and water pollution, but also some not familiar, such as salinity. The salt-water level in low-lying Jakarta is rising as land is converted from agricultural to urban usage and pressure on natural water supplies increases. Industrial development has proceeded at such a pace that it is difficult to monitor for its environmental impact, even if that were the government's intention. The Suharto administration's record is spotty. In the early years of rapid economic growth, it tended to ignore environmental issues which were in any case usually seen as political issues or quantified as the necessary costs that economic development inevitably brought. An energetic minister, Emil Salim, sensed the dangers of unrestrained and unthinking economic development, but in the competitive global market place (and with countries like Vietnam and China offering investment opportunities without environmental considerations) Salim was more successful in getting Western countries, especially the United States, to become aware of the effort Indonesia was making to adopt sensitive environmental policies than in implementing the policies. The third concern is the rundown of natural resources, especially timber, and the effects of extensive mining. When the first edition of this book was prepared, it was estimated that nearly one quarter of Java's forest area remained: the figure now (a more scientific assessment, admittedly) is 3 per cent. While other regions are less depleted, Indonesia's economy is still heavily dependant on natural resources and the process can be expected to continue. The extensive removal of timber has brought not only the familiar effects of erosion, but landslides annually in the wet season.

Thirty years ago, the prediction that population would have doubled by now rang with a kind of clarion anxiety. Now that the prediction turns out to be precisely true, it is surprising how calmly it can be received. Have we become immune to Malthusian pessimism? In the case of Indonesia, there are two mitigating factors. Family planning has been taken seriously and its effect is expected gradually to show. Also, the economy is moving into industry, which has the potential to meet numerical needs more effectively than agriculture alone. Population pressure is still a problem for Indonesia, however, because it is so unevenly spread. Java has about 5 per cent of Indonesia's land area, but it has 60 per cent of its population. It has always been heavily populated because of the fertile soil, but now political and industrial concentration on Java, especially Jakarta, leading to rapid urbanization, is creating a second wave of immigration.

Under Sukarno, Indonesia took a deliberate step away from the Politics of Ecology, of which some of the early Indonesian leaders seemed aware. It engaged itself, rather, in the Politics of Psychology. Here, the indices of population and production have not been as compelling a reality as the measure of the notice one can attract—the extent to which one's identity is recognized by others. Sukarno even created for Indonesians a new ideology, which idealized their suffering, identified their enemies and channelled their energies into revolutionary tasks directed away from the failures and compromises of the government.

Politicians are still finding it difficul to operate in the impersonal, statistical, slow-motion framework of the Politics of Ecology. The myth-makers must first work the long-term interests of the land and the people into symbols as urgent and compelling as those which represent the short-term interests of the state and the nationalism it expresses. There has not yet been time for this in Indonesia, or in many other countries. The history of the modern world has shown that nationalism unifies the will of a people more emphatically than any other cause, including those extremes of human self-interest, economic welfare and religion. Nationalism exists today as a force in countries as disparate as the US, Japan, France and China, and even Australia, which must be among the least provocative nations in the world. In new nations, like Indonesia, nationalism is not just a super kind of patriotism. Nationalism is the process by which the nation is created after it has become a sovereign state, so it continues to be strong after independence.

The Nation is a hard master. It demands a loyalty above all others —those of religion, politics, social or economic class, and certainly ecology. Its demands are both urgent and fundamental; if your country is conquered, it says, you become someone else's property, whatever your beliefs, wealth or social standing. When editorial writers describe an action by one of their country's leaders as 'statesmanlike' they mean that it is above self-interest, but if the action were so elevated as to be above the national interest, he or she would be condemned as a traitor.

Thirty years ago, I made this judgment:

> ... the chances for democracy in Indonesia are slight, while tyranny's chances are excellent. An underdeveloped country with a high population growth can hold off catastrophe by wise policies, hard work and population control. With luck—I don't think anyone knows the answer to these problems of the future—it might win through and its large population become a symbol of strength, as it is in developed countries. Population control is costly, but not nearly as costly as battleships and jet bombers. There seems little prospect while Sukarno remains, and even beyond him, that this approach will be taken by Indonesia. How the dangers of this can be brought home to the Indonesian people, without inflaming suspicion, is one of the major hazards of responsible diplomacy.

It could be said that 'wise policies, hard work and population control' have done all this for Indonesia. Certainly they have 'held off catastrophe'. But are democracy's chances any better? The other side to the coin of anxiety about Sukarno's leadership was an assumption that if Indonesia had political stability and steady economic progress for thirty years, democracy would be stronger and tyranny weaker. Indonesia has had that stability and that progress and yet democracy is not stronger. Some would say it is even weaker than in Sukarno's day. At least then there was still the hopeful pressure of the early days of independence, when the outcome for democracy was still uncertain. Official wisdom now is that those days were chaotic, but those who live in the perpetual flurry of democratic systems will read the signs more sympathetically.

What can be said now about the future of Indonesia as seen from the vantage point of the Suharto era? Can we assume that as economic development continues, as more Indonesians enter the historic middle class, which provides them with the material comforts and the intellectual inclination towards a less authoritarian society, that Indonesia will become more democratic? Or should we be wary of such an assumption, noting that it has not been borne out so far by the Indonesian experience, nor by the experience of others, such as China or

Singapore? Should we assume rather that the peculiar political animal
that is Indonesia—the personal, authoritarian military regime that at
present exists—is here to stay?

The political leaders of Indonesia have all the power they want in
their hands now, as they did thirty years ago—the power of the armed
forces and police to prevent an uprising, the power of censorship and
propaganda to convince the people that the reasons for their predica-
ments, whatever they are, lie elsewhere and, above all, the authority of
the state and the mystical appeal of the nation. Why should they give
it up for democracy, which they would say is as relentless in its cruelty
as capitalism or the jungle—undermining the state with its endless
bickering, its many ambitions ceaselessly struggling for supremacy,
tearing down leaders, demeaning age and authority. Democracy is not
the only system of government known to humankind, they might say,
and even in the West its shortcomings are showing. In any case, it was
tried in Indonesia and failed. Indonesia has its own indigenous system
of politics, which may not be democratic according to the experience
of the West, but it works. There is force in this argument, although it
is self-serving for those presently in power.

The case for democracy rests ultimately on grounds that are not
simply political, but moral and practical as well. No-one should be
surprised that Indonesians do not want to follow the adverserial style
of party politics which they observe at work in Australia or the high-
powered, high-cost electoral system of the United States. But does
their own system deliver what it claims? That is the practical test.

The moral ground for democracy is that people have the right to
choose those who have power over them. Some Indonesians say that
this is done in their country, even if the elections seem to Western
democrats to be contrived, but others are just as sure that the system
does not provide the Indonesian people with a real choice. The practical argument for democracy is that it is the best political system for
management of a market economy, because its transparency acts as a
check on the excesses and subterfuges of capitalism. Some Indonesians
claim they are on the way to effective economic management, even if
the transparency is not as clear as Western free marketeers want, but
others are just as convinced that the market is being manipulated and
distorted, not in the national interest but in the personal interest of a
group in power. The issue is not whether there should or should not
be intervention by the state in management of the economy. State-

managed capitalism is a fact of life in Indonesia, as it is in most Asian countries. The issue is whether the intervention is strategic or haphazard, productive or ineffective.

These are not issues which are being forced on Indonesians by outsiders, nor are they issues which arise from theoretical speculation about politically correct forms of democracy or pure models of the free market. They are issues which arise naturally from Indonesia's stage of economic and political development, and they will have to be resolved by this generation of Indonesians. So what are democracy's prospects in today's Indonesia? Even to begin to answer that question, one must examine, not the Politics of Ecology or the Politics of Psychology but the Politics of Succession. This requires a big leap from the general to the particular. At least in the foreseeable future, the fate of democracy in Indonesia depends on how a successor to President Suharto is found.

Thirty years ago, there was a sense of mounting crisis surrounding Sukarno's leadership. No such feeling is present today, either inside Indonesia or outside. Rather, there is an atmosphere of resignation. The gossip runs about the latest ups-and-downs and ins-and-outs in the political stakes, but expectation of a change in the present system is slight. Some idealism can be detected among students and intellectuals, but the professional and middle classes seem to have accepted the status quo, opting for peace and quiet rather than democratic reform.

When Suharto became president of Indonesia (he was acting president from 8 March 1967 and president from 27 March 1968), de Gaulle was still president of France, the Shah of Iran was still on the peacock throne, Chairman Mao ruled in China, Lyndon Johnson was president of the United States and Indira Gandhi had just become prime minister of India. Of Indonesia's neighbours, only Lee Kuan Yew in Singapore had comparable staying power, and he eventually voluntarily stepped down. In democratic Australia, with elections every three years, the Indonesian leader has seen prime ministers come and go—Holt, Gorton, McMahon, Whitlam, Fraser, Hawke, Keating, and now Howard. Of world leaders, Fidel Castro of Cuba is the only one to have been in power longer than Suharto. Another comparable public figure to match Suharto's longevity is not an elected politician, which technically Suharto is, but Queen Elizabeth, an hereditary monarch, which Suharto sometimes appears to be, or would like to be.

Suharto has become such a fixture of the nation's official life that the politics of succession is a barely discussable subject, a reticence encouraged by his natural secrecy and the timidity of officials who fear that an interest in the subject might be construed as political opposition. Still, Indonesians being human, the discussion goes on and, listening to it, the visitor might deduce that there are four possibilities.

The first is that Suharto has a successor in mind and will reveal the name in time for the proper procedure to be followed. Considering the president's great authority, especially with the military and in Golkar, this would mean a unanimous appointment of his chosen successor by the MPR in 1998, following the elections in 1997 which would have brought Golkar's usual victory. That is the theory. The difficulty with it is that Suharto does not appear to have chosen a successor, or even to have shown an inclination to want to do so. He certainly has shown a fondness for Habibie, but he has also placed his daughter Sitit Hardianti Rukmana (Tutut) in a political role as vice-chairman of Golkar and his son-in-law Brigadier General Prabowo Subianto is known to be ambitious. Without a crowned prince or princess, Option One looks shakey. The death in April 1996 of Mrs Siti Hartinah (Tien) Suharto strengthened the claim of Mrs Rukmana to be groomed for the presidency at her father's side, possibly as vice-president, but this would also magnify the prospect of Option Four.

The second possibility is that he will announce his retirement and leave it to the system to produce his successor. This theory has two sub-plots. One is that he will genuinely leave it to the system, the other that he will only appear to do so, but will in fact have a candidate who for all the reasons advanced in Option One will be successful. Putting this aside (as really belonging to the 'crown prince/princess' option, although there are tactical differences) the question is whether Suharto is likely to leave to the contingencies of politics a matter so important to him personally. He has already had a rebuff from the system, when the military forced Try Sutrisno on him as vice-president when he was intending to bring in Habibie. In retrospect, the appointment of Habibie could have been Suharto's way of indicating his choice of a successor. The vice-president is a natural, although not inevitable, successor and it would have been an opportunity for Habibie to have grown in stature under the president's wing, as it were.

Option Two is marginally less plausible than Option One. It has been noted that Suharto has contrived such a finely balanced and tightly structured form of government, with himself at the centre, that any crack in the system, no matter how small, threatens the whole. Also there would be no guarantee of protection for himself or his family with this method of choosing a successor. Suharto knows that the dangerous period is when he leaves office and relinquishes the power that now protects him, his family and those who have worked the system for him. That is when records become available, inquiries are held, grievances aired, revenge plotted. He has before him not only the example in several Third World countries of disgraced former leaders, but the example in several former communist countries of personal security files of those considered *persona non grata* being revealed.

Option Three is that he stays in office for at least another five-year term, which would take him to 2003. Because of the difficulties inherent in Options One and Two, Option Three is considered more likely. It is also more popular because it requires no decision now, leaving Indonesians with the devil they know (and some would say he is a devil who has served Indonesia well) rather than one they have to get to know, who may not be as successful as Suharto and whose policies are unknown or untried. His age, which would be approaching seventy-seven on reappointment in 1998, does not seem to Indonesians to be a handicap. Indeed, many see it as an asset, providing experience and wisdom. Suharto seems to be in good health, enjoying the work. Let him guide Indonesia into the twenty-first century, advocates of Option Three say: Why change a winning rider just for the sake of changing riders?

Option Four is the dark side of the Indonesian political process. In it, Suharto dies, is incapacitated or is forced from office. Suddenly, he no longer controls the system. Who does? In the event of his death, the vice-president takes over. For incapacitation, there is no constitutional clarity, which is not peculiar to Indonesia, and much would depend on common sense. In the event of forced retirement, it would obviously depend on circumstances. In the case of military pressure, for example, including a coup, the proposed candiate would most likely be the vice-president, Try Sutrisno, although with the army's track record one can never be sure. Needless to say, the visitor hears many versions of Option Four in the hothouse of Jakarta political gossip. They range from a repeat of the upheaval of 1965–66 to a surgical palace coup which leaves the surrounding political landscape unharmed. However, it is not as probable as Option Three, the most popular of the options, except of course that at Suharto's age an illness is always possible and this itself can fuel speculation about a successor, as it did in Sukarno's case. Its improbability lies in the tight watch which Suharto keeps on those near and around him. There would need to be a defection from either family or close associates for Option Four to be feasible.

Some important differences between the Sukarno era and the Suharto era suggest that the transition this time could be orderly. One is the obvious improvement in living conditions, which makes politics less volatile. For Indonesia's élite, there are more alternatives to being involved in politics as the economy expands. Another difference is that *Pancasila* has become the state ideology, whereas in Sukarno's time it was only a declaration which acknowledged the need for several ideologies to coexist in Indonesia. The result is that political correctness has been strengthened. In the short term, this provides stability. Also, there is much less inclination on the part of outside powers, especially the United States, China and Russia, to interfere in Indonesian politics. This inevitably meant a high level of political activity in Sukarno's time, persistently testing the nationalist credentials of the government. All these differences make it more likely that the succession will be managed without the upheaval of 1965–66.

Against this, the army now is not led by someone like General Nasution who was always respectful to the civilian political leadership which the president represented. The turnover of leadership in the army has been excessive and factionalism is intense. Nor was there in Sukarno's time a presidential family to contend with, not just in the way it now permeates the business community but in its political ambitions as well. Also, Cold War coinage had two sides. There is less political interference from outside now, but there is also more room to move inside. If it becomes clear that the president is not prepared to accept Try as his successor, the forces of politics combined with resentment and factionalism within the army might well seek a way to stop him.

None of the four options contains a bright democratic prospect. An alarming thought is that the best prospect lies in a dramatic break with the present, suggested in Option Four, which almost certainly contains also the worst prospect. It is this deadlock in the Politics of Succession that creates the eerie atmosphere of resignation in Indonesia at present. The President will not decide, and he will not allow others to decide for him.

It is hardly surprising that increasing numbers of the political élite in Indonesia are putting their faith outside politics in what is called a 'civil society'. Unable to influence the presidential succession, they are spending their time fashioning the elements which will provide checks and balances to the inner political core, no matter who is president—building independence from government in business, political and community organizations, the law, universities and the media, establishing better quality in hospitals, schools and libraries. These are the people on whom an improvement in recognition of 'human rights' depends.

Like democracy, the concept of human rights can be endlessly argued about—while little is done to stop abuses so fundamental that there can be no argument about them. Killing or imprisoning people without trial *are* universal abuses, whatever the cultural context. Yet, while it is sometimes useful for foreign governments to draw attention to shortcomings, the effect is often inconclusive. The reason is obvious—governments are themselves the chief abusers of human rights, and government-to-government dialogue on relevant issues can easily degenerate into exchanges between pots and kettles. All the experience since human rights was put on the agenda by governments in the 1975 Helsinki Accords is that while international monitoring is valuable, persistent pressure needs to be applied to governments and state authorities from within the society itself. Those who are turning away from politics to social construction in Indonesia are therefore helping to build a framework for democracy.

Government is so important in Indonesia, however, as it is in most developing countries, that the task of building a civil society is likely to be protracted. It might become increasingly attractive to be a private citizen in Indonesia, enjoying the comforts of rising living standards in a secure society without the hassle of activist politics, but being a public citizen, which is what a civil society requires, could present you with the worst of both worlds—the wrath of government and a shortage of comforts.

Building democracy is hard work—and hazardous. It is particularly dangerous in a country in which the military occupy an emotionally strategic position. The rising middle class of Indonesia, on which the hopes for a civil society depend, sees the military at present as its protection against the populist politics of resentment, yet the task of creating a civil society in Indonesia is also irrevocably the task of disengaging the military from politics. World-wide this has proved to be quite a task, even when the middle class is a prime mover.

Let me borrow, however, not from thoughtful Indonesians who may feel despondent about the prospect, but from their president. 'Don't be easily surprised, don't be overwhelmed by anything, and don't overestimate your own position.' Modesty and perseverance are useful attributes at this stage of Indonesia's history. In the Asia-Pacific, there are two contending triumphs at the moment—the Western triumph, celebrating victory in the Cold War, and the Asian triumph, celebrating the economic transformation of a region from seamless poverty to production powerhouse of the twenty-first century. Indonesia does not readily celebrate either of these triumphs. Just as in the Cold War it sought, for the most part, to keep its distance from the contending ideologies, so it is not today wholeheartedly with the value-adding, prudent savers on the Confucian bandwagon. Indonesia has its own way of doing things. It instinctively mixes and balances old and new, traditional and modern, foreign and local. The fusion is never simple and the result not easily predictable.

Indonesians as people are as concerned about human rights as Americans or Australians are. They need, however, to discover for themselves the best way in their own political environment to protect and nourish these rights. They have to find a way of retiring their presidents without inviting coups and bloodbaths for everyone else. They need to find a technique for disengaging, if not the army, its guns. If Indonesia cannot manage these things, it has potential to be a problem state. It's size, its resources and its strategic location, straddling the waterway between the Pacific and Indian oceans, ensures that its future in these circumstances will always concern its neighbours.

If it can do these things, while continuing to build on the achievements of the last thirty years, Indonesia will be on the way to becoming a great nation. It will indeed (as its first president always said it would) 'dazzle the world with its freshness.'

Glossary

ABRI   the armed forces

adat   gradually developed body of customary law; like common law

agama Jawa   'religion of Java'; a syncretic blend of religious beliefs

CSIS   a political and economic think-tank

DPR   the parliament

dwifungsi   the dual role—civil and military—of the armed forces

Golkar   the political organization supported by the Suharto government and the military

gotong royong   traditional village practice of mutual assistance

ICMI   an association of Muslim intellectuals attached to the Suharto government

Manipol-Usdek   manipol stands for 'political manifesto' and usdek is an acronym of the five points of the manifesto: return to the 1945 constitution; socialism; guided democracy; guided economy; Indonesian identity. The slogan was coined by President Sukarno in 1960.

marhaen   literally 'proletariat' but used by Sukarno as the basis of a 'little people' kind of socialism

Masjumi   created in 1943 by the Japanese to represent Muslims, it was active in the Sumatran and Sulawesi uprisings. Banned by Sukarno, it has been recently revived.

MPR   the body which elects the president every five years. In Sukarno's time it was the MPRS.

mufakat   consensus; agreement; unanimity

musjawarah   mutual discussion

Nasakom   an abbreviation of Nas (nationalist) A (*agama* or 'religion') and Kom (communist), indicating the three political streams supporting Sukarno's government

Pancasila   the five principles enunciated by Sukarno in 1945 to provide the philosophical basis of the Republic

Peta   the home defence corps formed by the Japanese in 1943, which became an agent of nationalism.

PKI   Indonesian communist party, formed in 1920, destroyed in 1965–66.

PNI   the main nationalist party (led by Sukarno), created in 1927, merged today with other nationalist parties in the PDI

priyayi   old Javanese official class; now used to describe a cultured person or cultured behaviour

PRRI   the revolutionary government in the Sumatra uprising of 1958

PSI   small, influential, anti-totalitarian party founded by Sjahrir, banned by Sukarno

santri   devout Muslim

wayang   theatre either of human actors, puppets or shadow images

Bibliography

Abdulgani, Ruslan, *The Bandung Spirit and the Asian-African Press*. Department of Information, Jakarta, 1963.

Aidit, D. N., 'Dare, Dare and Dare Again!' (Report to PKI central committee), *Harian Rakyat*, 11 February 1963.

Anderson, B., *Tolerance and the Mythology of the Javanese*. Cornell Modern Indonesia Project monograph series, Ithaca, NY, 1965.

Ardjasni, 'My Life', *Eastern Horizon*, January, February, March 1962.

Australia Di Mata Indonesia: Kumpulan Artikel Pers Indonesia 1973–1988. Gramedia, Jakarta, 1989.

Barlow, Colin and Hardjono, Joan (eds), *Indonesia Assessment 1995*, Institute of Southeast Asian Studies, Singapore, 1996.

Bell, Coral, 'Non-Alignment and the Power-Balance', *Australian Outlook*, August 1963.

Bourchier, David and Legge, John (eds), *Democracy in Indonesia: 1950s and 1990s*, Monash Asia Institute, Melbourne, 1994.

Boyce, P. J., 'Canberra's Malaysian Policy', *Australian Outlook*, July 1963.

Brackman, Arnold C., *Indonesian Communism*. Praeger, New York, 1963.

Calder, Ritchie, *The Inheritors*. Heinemann, London, 1961.

Calhoun, John B., 'Population Density and Social Pathology', *Scientific American*, February 1962.

Cantril, Hadley, 'A Study of Aspirations', *Scientific American*, February 1963.

Chase, Robert S., Hill, Emily B. and Kennedy, Paul, 'Pivotal States and U.S. Strategy', *Foreign Affairs*, vol. 75, no. 1, 1996.

Clancy, G. B., *A Dictionary of Indonesian History*, Sunda Publications, Sydney, 1992.

Clark, C. M. H., *A History of Australia*, vol. 1. Melbourne University Press, Melbourne, 1962.

Compulsory Education in Indonesia. Ministry of Education, Jakarta, 1961.

Cribb, Robert (ed.), *The Indonesian Killings 1965–1966*, Centre of Southeast Asian Studies, Monash University, Melbourne, 1991.

Crouch, Harold, *The Army and Politics in Indonesia*, Cornell University Press, Ithaca, NY, 1988.

Crozier, Brian, *The Rebels.* Chatto and Windus, London, 1960.

Cunningham, K. S., 'Final Report of UNESCO Mission to Indonesia on Teacher Training and Educational Research' (mimeographed paper), 1957.

'Diplomatic and Consular List', Department of Foreign Affairs, Jakarta, 1963, 1996.

Dobby, E. H. G., *Southeast Asia.* University of London Press, London, 1958.

Evans, Gareth and Grant, Bruce, *Australia's Foreign Relations.* Melbourne University Press, Melbourne, 1995.

Far Eastern Economic Review Yearbook. Hong Kong (annual)

Feith, Herbert, *The Decline of Constitutional Democracy in Indonesia.* Cornell University Press, Ithaca, NY, 1962.

——, 'President Sukarno, The Army and The Communists: The Triangle Changes Shape', *Asian Survey*, August 1964.

——, 'Symbols, Ritual and Ideology in Indonesian Politics' (paper presented to the Australian Political Studies Association conference), August 1962.

Feith, Herbert and Lev, Daniel S., 'The End of the Indonesian Rebellion', *Pacific Affairs*, Spring 1963.

Fischer, Louis, *The Story of Indonesia.* Hamish Hamilton, London, 1959.

Fish, Hamilton, 'The Troubled Birth of Malaysia', *Foreign Affairs*, July 1963.

Freedom House, *Freedom in the World: The Annual Survey of Political Rights and Civil Liberties 1994–1995*, Freedom House, New York, 1995.

Fukuyama, Francis, *Trust*, The Free Press, New York, 1995.

Geertz, Clifford, *The Religion of Java.* Glencoe Free Press, Illinois, 1960.

Gorer, Geoffrey, *Bali and Angkor.* Michael Joseph, London, 1936.

Grant, Bruce, *The Crisis of Loyalty.* Angus & Robertson, Sydney, 1972.

——, *What Kind of Country?* Penguin, Melbourne, 1988.

Greenwood, Gordon, and Harper, Norman (eds), *Australia in World Affairs 1956–1960*. Cheshire, for Australian Institute of International Affairs, Melbourne, 1963.

Gunn, Geoffrey C., *A Critical View of Western Journalism and Scholarship on East Timor*, Journal of Contemporary Asia Publishers, Manila, 1994.

Gunther, John, *Inside Asia*. Hamish Hamilton, London, 1939.

Haar, B. ter, *Adat Law in Indonesia*. Bhratara, Jakarta, 1962.

Handbook on the Political Manifesto: two executive directions of Manipol. Department of Information, Jakarta, 1961.

Hanna, Willard A., *Bung Karno's Indonesia*. American Universities Field Staff, Inc., New York, 1961.

Hardjono, Joan (ed.), *Indonesia: Resources, Ecology and Environment*, Oxford University Press, Oxford, 1991.

Hardjono, Joan and Warner, Charles (eds), *In Love With A Nation: Molly Bondan and Indonesia*, Warner, Picton, 1995.

Harris, Richard, 'Communism and Asia: Illusions and Misconceptions', *International Affairs*, January 1963.

Harsono, Ganis, *Recollections of an Indonesian Diplomat in the Sukarno Era*, University of Queensland Press, Brisbane, 1977.

Higgins, Benjamin, *Indonesia: The Crisis of the Millstones*. Van Nostrand, Princeton, NJ, 1963.

Hill, Hal, 'Survey of Recent Developments', *Bulletin of Indonesian Economic Studies*, Australian National University, Canberra, 1992.

Hill, Hal and Hull, Terry (eds) *Indonesia Assessment 1990*. Australian National University, Canberra, 1990.

Hindley, Donald, *Communist Party of Indonesia 1951–1963*. University of California Press, Berkeley, Calif., 1964.

——, 'Foreign Aid to Indonesia and its Political Implications', *Pacific Affairs*, Summer 1963.

The History of the Armed Forces of the Republic of Indonesia. Ministry of Information, Jakarta, 1958.

Huxley, Aldous, 'The Politics of Ecology' (paper), Center for the Study of Democratic Institutions, Santa Barbara, Calif., 1963.

Indonesia. Cornell Modern Indonesia Project monograph series, Ithaca (bi-annual).

'Indonesia Today', special issue of the *Bulletin*, Sydney, 14 December 1963.

Jervis, Robert, 'The Future of World Politics: Will it Resemble the Past?', *International Security*, vol. 16, no. 3, 1991.

Johnson, John J. (ed.), *The Role of the Military in Under-developed Countries*. Princeton University Press, NJ, 1962.

Kahin, George McTurnan, *Nationalism and Revolution in Indonesia*. Cornell University Press, NY, 1952.

Kroef, J. M. van der, 'Two Forerunners of Modern Indonesian Independence: Imam Bondjol and Thomas Matulesia', *Australian Journal of Politics and History*, November 1962.

Legge, J. D., *Sukarno: A Political Biography*, Allen Lane/Penguin, London, 1972.

——, 'Indonesia since West Irian', *Australian Outlook*, April 1963.

Leur, J. C. van, *Indonesian Trade and Society*. Sumur, Bandung, 1960.

Lev, D., 'Indonesia 1965: The Year of the Coup', *Asian Survey*, February 1966.

Lockhart, R. H. Bruce, *Return to Malaya*. Putnam, London, 1938.

Lubis, Mochtar, *Twilight in Djakarta*. Hutchinson, London, 1963.

Macdonald, Malcolm, *Angkor*. Jonathan Cape, London, 1960.

Mackie, J. A. C., 'The Indonesian Economy 1950–1963', *Schriffen des Instituts Fur Asienkunde in Hamburg*, vol. 16, 1964.

——, *Konfrontasi: The Indonesia-Malaysia Dispute 1963–1966*, Oxford University Press, Kuala Lumpur, 1974.

McVey, Ruth (ed.), *Indonesia*. Human Relations Area Files, Inc., New Haven, Conn., 1963.

——, 'Faith as the Outsider: Islam in Indonesian Politics' in Piscatori, James (ed.), *Islam in the Political Process*, Cambridge University Press, Cambridge, 1985.

Mahbubani, K., 'The Pacific Way', *Foreign Affairs*, vol. 74, no. 1, 1994.

Makka, A. Makmur, *BJH: Bacharuddin Jusuf Habibie*, CV. Cipta Kreatif, Jakarta, 1989.

May, R. J. and O'Malley, William J., *Obverving Change in Asia*, Crawford House Press, Bathurst, NSW, 1989.

Modelski, George, *The New Emerging Forces: Documents on the Ideology of Indonesian Foreign Policy*. Australian National University, Canberra, 1963.

Moerdowo, R., *Reflections on Indonesian Arts and Culture*, Permata, Surabaya, 1959.

Mohamad, Goenawan, *Sidelines: Writings from Tempo*, Hyland House, Melbourne, 1994.

Myrdal, Gunnar, 'Economic Nationalism and Internationalism' (Dyason Lectures for 1957), *Australian Outlook*, December 1957.

Nasution, A. H., *Fundamentals of Guerrilla Warfare*. Indonesian Army Information Service, 1953.

Njoto, 'Develop the Manipol-Offensive in the Field of the Press' (speech on twelfth anniversary of Harian Rakyat), *Harian Rakyat*, 8 February 1963.

Palthe, P. M. van Wulfften, *Psychological Aspects of the Indonesian Problem*. Brill, Leyden, 1949.

Pauker, Ewa T., 'Indonesia: the Year of Triumph', *Current History*, November 1962.

Pauker, Guy J., 'Indonesia's Eight-Year Development Plan', *Pacific Affairs*, Summer 1961.

Ricklefs, M. C., *A History of Modern Indonesia since c.1300*, Stanford University Press, Stanford, Calif., 1993.

Robison, Richard, *Indonesia: The Rise of Capital*, Allen & Unwin, Sydney, 1986.

Rose, Saul (ed.), *Politics in Southeast Asia*. Macmillan, London, 1963.

Schwarz, Adam, *A Nation In Waiting: Indonesia in the 1990s*, Allen & Unwin, Sydney, 1994

Selosoemardjan, *Social Changes in Jogjakarta*. Cornell University Press, New York, 1962.

Sheridan, Greg (ed.), *Living with Dragons*, Allen & Unwin/Mobile Oil Australia Ltd, Sydney, 1995.

Shrieke, B., *Ruler and Realm in Early Java*. W. van Hoeve Ltd, The Hague and Bandung, 1957.

Sjahrir, Sutan, *Out of Exile*. John Day, New York, 1949.

Subandrio, *Indonesia on the March* (collection of speeches, 1957–63). Department of Foreign Affairs, Jakarta, 1963.

Suharto, *Suharto: An Autobiography* (as told to G. Dwipayana and Ramadhan K. H.), Citra Lamtoro Gung Persada, Jakarta, 1989.

Sukarno, President of Indonesia. Ministry of Information, Jakarta, 1958.

Tamara, M. Nasir, *Indonesia in the Wake of Islam: 1965–1985*, Occasional Paper, Institute of Strategic and International Studies, Kuala Lumpur, 1988.

Thio, *Indonesian Folk Tales*, Tunas, 1962.

Tjoa, Marianne, Survey of the History of Java and Sumatra (private paper), Jakarta, 1963.

Tregonning, K. G., 'Australia's Imperialist Image in South-east Asia', *Australian Quarterly*, September 1961.

Turner, Michele, *Telling: East Timor Personal Testimonies 1942–1992*, New South Wales University Press, Sydney, 1992.

Vakikiotis, Michael R. J., *Indonesian Politics Under Suharto*. Routlege, London, 1994

Veur, P. W. van der, 'The Irian Changeover', *Australia's Neighbours*, July–August 1963.

Vlekke, B. M. H., *Nusantara: A History of Indonesia*. W. van Hoeve Ltd, The Hague and Bandung, 1959.

Wedding Ceremonials. Prapantja, Jakarta.

Wertheim, W. F., *Indonesian Society in Transition*. W. van Hoeve Ltd, The Hague and Bandung, 1959.

——, *Moslems in Indonesia: Majority with Minority Mentality*, Occasional Paper, James Cook University of North Queensland, Townsville, 1980.

Woodman, Dorothy, *The Republic of Indonesia*. Cresset Press Ltd., London, 1955.

Index

Abdulgani, Ruslan, 26, 49
ABRI—Angkatan Bersenjata Republik Indonesia (Armed Forces of the Indonesian Republic), 87, 88, 91–4, 100, 105, 106, 108–9, 112, 155, 217; see also Armed Forces; Army
Aceh, 9, 69, 143, 163; early history, 11, 12, 13, 15, 16; l953 rebellion, 128; Acehenese, 143–4
adat, 4, 125, 126, 127, 134, 143, 174, 184, 185
Africa, 2, 19, 38, 129, 200; nationalism, 51, 197
Afro-Asian bloc, 198, 200, 203, 212; see also 'new emerging forces'
agama, see religion
agriculture, 2, 4, 111, 114, 115, 116, 123, 126, 134, 143, 145–50, 152, 219
Aidit, D. N., 29, 74, 75, 77, 78, 98; 1965 coup, 74, 77, 104, 163
Aidit, Sobron, 136
AJI—Asosiasi Journalis Independen (Association of Independent Journalists), 68
Alatas, Ali, 65, 206–7, 208
Albuquerque, Alfonso de', 11
Algeria, 109
Alimin, 50
Alisjahbana, Takdir, 135, 137, 143
All-Indonesian Youth Congress, 135
alus, 131, 133
Ambon, 32, 94, 148; see also Moluccas
amok running, 14, 140
Anderson, Benedict, 62
Angkor, 1
animism, 4, 125, 133, 146, 160; peoples, 140, 144, 148, 150; politics, 24, 54

Anwar, Chairil, 135, 136, 137, 143; poem, 136–7
APEC—Asia-Pacific Economic Cooperation 65, 123, 204, 206
Apodeti—Timorese Popular Democratic Association, 39; see also Timor
Arabia, 144; trade, 6, 9, 12, 15, 153
Arena, The (Gelanggang), 135, 136
ARF—ASEAN Regional Forum, 65, 206
Arismunandar, Wismoyo, 108; see also Rainbow Coalition
armed forces, 35, 40, 42, 64, 72, 73, 74, 79, 87, 89, 91, 99, 103, 104, 107, 108, 113, 114, 129, 140, 141, 200, 201, 205, 215, 216, 222, 224, 227–8; see also ABRI
arms and equipment, 12, 99, 221; disarmament, 207; foreign, 36, 100, 196, 199, 202, 207, 213; see also Waterside Workers Federation
army, 34, 35, 37, 39, 67, 68, 71, 73, 75, 76, 77, 78, 93, 99, 103, 106, 144, 155, 158, 159, 160, 161, 163, 165, 166, 171, 192, 194, 199, 226, 228; factions, 74, 78, 90, 95, 96, 192, 226; history, 94–6; 1955–61 rebellion, 97–8; 1965 coup, 37, 73, 163, 187; politics, 58, 75, 81, 83, 89, 90, 159; see also ABRI; corruption
Arndt, Heinz, 110
art, 5, 52, 135, 160
ASA—Associaton of South East Asia, 199
ASEAN—Association of South-East Asian Nations, 65, 196, 199, 205, 206, 207
Asia, 2, 4, 18, 19, 38, 93, 223; Communism, 79–81; nationalism, 18, 51–2, 79, 121, 209; Pacific region, 64–5, 206–7, 228; see also South-East Asia

Asian Development Bank 114
Asian Games, 43, 194, 202
Association for the Integration of Timor into Indonesia, 39; *see also* Apodeti
Australia, 2, 10, 19, 31, 51, 77, 93, 111, 123, 127, 129, 130, 133, 139, 167, 170, 191, 193, 198, 203, 205, 207–17, 220, 222, 223; industry, 146, 189; Malaysia, 215; Mantiri affair, 216–17; military, 30, 37, 214, 215; security agreement, 65, 72, 166, 208, 217; Timor, 39, 150, 151, 215–16; West Irian, 211–15
Australia-Indonesia Institute, 216
Australia in World Affairs 1956–60, 210
Australian Labor Party, 209, 210, 211, 213
Azahari, A. M., 200–1
Azahari rebellion, 201; *see also* Malaysia

Babad Tanah Djawi, 14–15
Bahasa Indonesia, 22, 25, 45, 135; *see also* languages; Malay–Polynesian language group
Bakorstanas—Badan Koordinasi Bantuan Pemantapan Stabilitas (Body for Co-ordinating National Stability), 88; *see also* ABRI
Bali, 7, 8, 15, 124, 126, 149–50, 152; the Netherlands, 12, 15, 16, 17, 150
Bandung, 30, 50, 51, 54, 59, 95, 101, 106, 152, 167, 194
Bandung conference, 197, 199, 212
Bangladesh, 38, 111
Banjarmasin, 145; war, 16
Bantam, 12, 14, 24
Bantenese, 153
Bapakism, 60, 127–8, 160
BAPPENAS—Badan Perencanaac Pembangunan Nasional (National Development Planning Agency), 122–3
Barisan Pelopor (Pioneer Legion), 101; *see also* Japan, Occupation
Baru, Pudjangga, 135
Bataks, 93, 101, 104, 144
Batavia, 13–14, 17, 21, 24, 26, 51, 153, 194; *see also* Jakarta
batik, 133–4, 184
Beazley, Kim, 216
Belgium, 15, 210
Bencoolen (now Bengkulu), 51
BIA—Badan Intelijian Negara, 88; *see also* ABRI

Blitar, 42, 49; 1944 revolt, 26
Bogor, 152, 153; palace, 52, 61, 76, 106, 163
Bondan, Molly, 45, 209
Borneo, *see* Kalimantan
Borobudur, 1, 2, 6, 194
Boven Digul, 23, 24, 209; *see also* New Guinea
BPKI—Badan Penjelidik Kemerdekaan Indonesia (Body for Investigation of Indonesian Independence), 28
Brackman, A. C., 29, 211
Britain, 2, 12, 13, 16, 18, 19, 20, 30, 65, 100–1, 139, 145, 149, 193, 205, 208, 215, 217, 223; military, 29, 30, 37, 201, 209, 210, 215
Brunei, 28, 69, 145, 200–1, 205
Brunei Party Rakyat, 200
BTI—Barisan Tani Indonesia (Indonesian Peasant Front), 80
Buddhism, 1, 2, 4, 5–6, 10, 13, 63, 94, 125, 130, 160, 175; peoples, 140, 150
Budi Utomo, 21; *see also* nationalism
Buginese, 13, 16, 147
Bulgaria, 199
Bulletin of Indonesian Economic Studies, 110
Bunker, Ellsworth, 179, 200; *see also* West Irian
Bumi Manusia (This Earth of Mankind), 137
Burhanuddin Harahap government (1955–56), 197–8, 212
Burma, 13, 94, 108
Buru, 164, 166
Burung-Burung Manya (The Weaver-Birds), 137

Caetano, Marcello, 38
Calwell, Arthur, 211
Calvinism, 20, 148, 175; *see also* Christianity
Cambodia, 1, 9, 203, 207; Pol Pot, 139
capitalism, 100, 118, 119, 122, 177, 178, 182, 189, 195, 222–3; 'crony capitalism', 112, 113
Casey, Lord R. G., 211, 212, 213
Catholicism, 11, 20, 33, 38, 81, 105, 106, 137, 148, 159, 174, 175, 217; *see also* Christianity; Partai Katolik
Celebes, *see* Sulawesi
censorship, 68, 88, 98, 136, 137, 222
Chifley government, 209–10
Chile, 108

China, 5, 9, 37, 70, 79, 80, 81, 83, 111, 120, 124, 178, 188, 191, 195, 196, 198, 199, 201–3, 204, 206; Mao Tse Tung, 102, 191, 223; nationalism 18, 220; trade 5, 9, 12, 15, 145; relations with Indonesia, 9, 193, 195–8, 202, 203, 204, 226; see also Communism; ethnic Chinese

Christianity, 13, 18, 62, 63, 64, 84, 94, 97, 98, 100, 125, 146, 173, 174, 175, 185, 190, 207; peoples, 130, 144, 147, 148, 149, 174; see also Calvinism; Catholicism; Protestantism; religion

CIA—US Central Intelligence Agency, 75, 107, 113, 159, 166

CIDES—Centre for Information and Development Studies, 85–6, 159; see also Habibie, B. J.; ICMI; Islam

civil service, 81, 88, 165, 175; women, 184

civil war, 34, 35, 77; '1955–61 rebellion', 97–8, 99

Clark, Manning, 10, 20

Coen, Jan Pieterszoon, 13–15

Cold War, 17, 37, 41, 69, 78, 79, 93, 110, 121, 122, 129, 159, 193, 204, 210; collapse, 81, 206; post, 87, 207, 208, 226, 228

Colombo Plan, 43, 212

Colombo Powers, 198

Commonwealth Strategic Reserve, 205

Communism, 7, 22, 24, 35, 61–2, 67, 72, 79–80, 87, 89, 93, 101, 102, 118, 121, 122, 137, 156, 167, 171, 172, 174, 175, 178, 179, 182, 188, 190, 191–2, 199, 209, 211; 'Indonesian', 29; military, 76, 81, 83, 98, 100; national, 89; '1965 coup', 37, 74, 138–41, 187, 188; Suharto, 59; Sukarno, 31, 76, 77, 83, 98; see also Gerwani; Marxism; PKI

Conefo—Conference of the New Emerging Forces, 202–3; see also 'new emerging forces'

'Confrontation', 36, 37, 40, 65, 195; Malaysia, 37, 99, 199, 200, 201, 202; West Irian, 179

Confucianism, 94, 228

Congress of Permuda Indonesia (Young Indonesia), 22

Constitution, 28, 118, 156; '1950', 32, 35; '1945', 35, 177

corruption, 53, 59, 69–70, 77, 82, 83, 104, 115, 120, 160, 180, 222; military, 87, 91, 92, 98–9, 112; see also elections; army; Suharto, family

Cribb, Robert, 141

Crouch, Harold, 59, 203

CSIS—Centre for Strategic and International Studies, 60, 84, 85–6, 106, 108, 159

Cuba, 39, 171, 223

Czechoslovakia, 198, 199

dalang, 45, 126, 133; see also wayang kulit

Darul Islam (Islamic State), 140; '1949–62 rebellion', 153; see also Islam

The Decline of Constitutional Democracy in Indonesia, 33

defence and security, 65, 80, 100, 107, 108, 191, 192, 195, 206; the West, 101, 177; see also territorial boundaries

Dekker, F. E. Douwes, 21, 23

democracy, 40, 67, 68, 71, 72, 76, 82, 85, 86, 102, 103, 126, 127, 156, 157, 198, 219, 221–3, 226, 227; national, 79, 80; see also elections

Democracy Forum, 85, 156; see also Wahid, A.

deregulation, 112

Dhani, Air Marshall Omar, 74, 81

dictatorship, 67, 68, 96, 171, 175, 198, 213

Dini, N. H., 137

diplomacy, 80, 89, 193, 195, 196, 200, 204, 214, 221; Malaysia, 202, 203

diplomats, foreign, 177, 193, 197

Diponegoro, Prince, 15–16, 24, 57

Djojohadikusomo, Dr Sumitro, 34, 105

Djuanda, Dr, 36, 198

DPR—Dewan Perwakilan Rakyat (People's Representative Council), 68, 82–3; see also elections

Dual Nationality Agreement, 197; see also China; ethnic Chinese

dukun, 54; see also animism; mythology and magic

dwifungsi, 90, 104, 107, 158

East Indies, 9, 17, 18, 19, 20, 28, 200

East Timor, see Timor

Eastern Indonesia, 151; see also Irian Jaya; Maluku; Sulawesi; West Irian

ecology, politics of, 218–20

economic development, 32, 37, 40, 42, 48, 55, 56, 60, 64–5, 69, 70, 73, 86, 87, 111,

121, 122, 128, 137, 203, 206, 216, 219, 221, 223; *see also* ASEAN

economic mismanagement, 87, 108, 110, 115, 120, 190; *see also* corruption; Pertamina scandal

economic reform, 70, 71, 80, 110, 112, 114, 115, 116, 117, 123, 181, 189, 192

education, 21, 70, 85, 94, 106, 116, 119, 125, 134, 144, 148, 158, 168, 172, 179, 186, 191; *see also* nationalist movement; women

Eight-Year Plan, 116–17

elections, 33, 63, 68, 71, 76, 77, 83, 186, 192, 197, 212, 222; government, 72, 82

'ET'—Ex-Tahanan Politik (Former Political Prisoner), 81, 164; *see also* human rights; internal security

ethnic Chinese, 9, 11, 13, 19, 84, 112, 113, 114, 123, 144, 145, 149, 155, 197

etok-etok, 132, *see also* philosophy, ethics

Europe, 9, 13–17, 18, 20, 24, 52, 210

Evans, Gareth, 208, 216

Evatt, Dr H. V., 210, 211

exports and imports, 34, 56, 99, 110, 111, 115, 116, 120, 121, 143, 145, 146, 148, 149, 152

family planning, 65, 185, 190, 219, 221

family system, 118, 185; *see also* social structure

Fatmawati, 54, 55

fauna, 142, 145, 146, 148, 150, 151, 153

Feith, Herbert, 20, 32, 96

financial system, 111

Flinders, Matthew, 10

flora, 142, 145, 149, 150, 151, 153

foreign aid, 76, 80, 110, 111, 120, 121, 123, 178, 188, 191, 196, 197, 198, 202, 204

foreign debt, 55–7, 110, 111, 115, 121, 198

foreign investment, 111, 115, 117, 158, 189, 194; environment, 219

France, 18, 21, 45, 158, 159, 209, 220, 223

Fraser-Peacock government, 216

Freedom House, 69; *see also* human rights

Freeport-McMoRan, 149; *see also* United States of America

Fretilin—Frente Revolucionaria de Timor-Leste (Revolutionary Front for an Independent East Timor), 38, 39; *see also* Timor

Fundamentals of Guerrilla Warfare, 102

Gajah Mada, 8–9; university, 16

Gama, Vasco da, 11

Ganefo—Games of the New Emerging Forces, 202; *see also* 'new emerging forces'

Geertz, Clifford, 125, 127, 131, 132, 133

geography, 1, 124, 128, 142, 146, 148, 149, 151–2, 178, 206, 208, 228

Gerindo—Gerakan Rakyat Indonesia (Indonesian People's Movement), 25; *see also* nationalism

Germany, 21, 24, 25, 28, 30, 73, 193, 209

Gerwani, 139

Gestapu—Gerakan September Tiga Puluh (Movement of September 30th), 139; *see also* '1965 coup'; '30th of September movement'

Gibbon, Edward, 5

Ginanjar, Kartasasmita, 73

Golkar—Golongon Karya (Functional Group), 63–4, 68, 81, 83, 88, 91, 161, 224; *see also* elections; government, system of; political opposition; political parties

Golongon Merdeka (Freedom Group), 23

gotong royong, 36, 47, 118, 126, 127, 128, 198; *see also* government, system of

Gorer, Geoffrey, 19

government, system of, 6, 7, 19, 25, 32, 35, 36, 40, 42, 55, 63–4, 67, 68, 69, 71, 76, 155, 156, 157, 160, 171–2, 186, 192, 198, 203, 227; elections, 80–2; military, 87, 88, 90, 192; *see also* ABRI; army; elections; '1965 coup'; Suharto; Sukarno

Grant, James P., 65; *see also* United Nations

Greece, 5, 6

Group of Fifty, 104; *see also* Nasution, A. H.

guerrilla warfare, 26–7, 30, 31, 32, 101, 102, 106, 128, l36, 149, 191, 200, 201; Communist, 191, 192; military, 88–9, 102

'guided democracy', 33, 67, 71, 97, 103, 126, 186, 187, 189, 198, 203

Guruh, 92

'Gus Dur', *see* Wahid, A.

Habibie, Dr B. J., 73, 81, 85, 91, 108, 112, 116, 159; family, 58; ICMI, 84, 92; Suharto successor, 224; *see also* Golkar; Wahid, A.

Halim, 61; air force base, 73, 76, 163; Luang Buaya (Crocodile Hole), 138, 139; *see also* '1965 coup'

Harahap, Burhanuddin, 34
Harian Rakyat, 77, 98; *see also* PKI
Hariati, 55
Harmoko, 81, 91; *see also* Golkar; Wahid, A.
Harsono, Ganis, 74
Hartini, 54, 55, 185; marriage to Brig. Gen.
   Moerdani, 106
Hartono, General Rahid, 91, 92; Rainbow
   Coalition, 108
Hasan, Bob, 59, 113
Hatta, Mohammed, 23, 29, 31, 35, 49, 51,
   52, 117, 212; collaboration Japanese, 25,
   26; military, 25, 26
Hawke-Hayden government, 216
Hefner, Robert, 68
Heiho, 94; *see also* Japan
Heroes' Day, 42, 181
Hinduism, 1, 2, 6, 10, 13, 24, 63, 125, 130,
   157, 160, 175; Brahmin priests, 5, 6, 150;
   peoples, 140, 150
HIP—Humbungan Industrial Pancasila
   (Pancasila Industrial Relations), 92, 93
*History of the Armed Forces of the Republic of
   Indonesia*, 89
HMI—Himpunan Mahasiswa Islam (Islamic
   Students Union), 74; *see also* Islam; '1965
   coup'; Student Action; youth
Ho Chi Minh, 199
Hotel Indonesia, 47, 182, 193, 194, 195
Houtman, Cornelius de, 12
human rights, 68, 69, 86, 87, 98, 107, 160,
   184, 204, 216, 219, 227, 228
Humardhani, Sudjono, 60–1, 104, 158
Huntington, Samuel, 38
Husein, Colonel, 97

Ibu Inggit, 54
ICMI—Ikatan Cendekiawan Moslem se
   Indonesia (Indonesian Association of
   Muslim Intellectuals), 73, 84, 158, 159,
   160; rival to CSIS, 84; rival to NU, 84–6;
   rival to ABRI, 92
Idrus, 135, 137, 143; *see also* literature
independence, 69, 210, 217, 220, 221;
   proclamation, 29, 117, 194, 208;
   Sukarno, 52
India, 4, 5, 6, 10, 19, 31, 38, 67, 70, 88, 94,
   111, 120, 124, 144, 193, 195–6, 197, 199,
   210, 223; literature, 7, 127; nationalism,
   18, 21; Nehru, 53, 196; trade 5, 9, 12, 15,
   153; military, 30, 209

Indian Party, 21, 23
Indies Social Democratic Association, 21
'Indonesian identity' (à la Indonesie) 117,
   172, 176, 183; 'socialism à la Indonesie',
   195; *see also* philosophy, ethics
Indonesian Killings 1965–1966, The, 141
Indonesian Legal Aid Foundation, 93; *see
   also* law
'Indonesia Raya' (Greater Indonesia), 22, 25
industry, 73, 83, 92, 93, 111, 116, 125, 143,
   145, 151, 152, 184, 219, 220; *see also*
   strikes; ecology, politics of
inflation, 110, 111, 114, 115, 120, 181, 186,
   190
In Love With a Nation, 209
internal security, 87, 107, 129, 188, 189
International Court of Justice, 151
International Olympic Committee, 202; *see
   also* Ganefo
invulnerability, belief in, 14, 53
IPKI (League of Upholders of Indonesian
   Independence), 33, 102, 81; *see also* PDI
Iraq, 74
Irian Jaya, *see* West Irian
Ishak, Josef, 74, 75
Islam, 2, 4, 9, 10, 11, 13, 21, 26, 27, 38, 55,
   63, 68, 71, 92, 94, 97, 98, 100, 105, 106,
   108, 125, 130, 143, 145, 146, 155–61;
   163, 173, 174, 176, 182, 207; Koran, the,
   15, 57, 157; military, 83, 94; Mohammed,
   22, 62, 85; nationalism, 18, 21, 129; peoples 144, 148, 149, 153; politics, 24, 51,
   64, 78, 83–6, 108, 140, 175, 217; *santris/
   abangan*, 84, 125, 140; women, 184, 185;
   see also ICMI; nationalism
Israel, 88, 102
Istora Sports Palace, 74; *see also* '1965 coup'
Italy, 16, 70
I-Tsing, 6; *see also* China

Jakarta, 5, 8, 26, 29, 34, 37, 43, 47, 48, 52,
   64, 66, 73, 77, 79, 83, 93, 96, 97, 100,
   103, 106, 120, 124, 140, 143, 153, 155,
   162, 163, 164, 169, 175, 176, 181, 182,
   186, 195, 199, 201, 202, 203, 212, 213,
   219–20, 225
Japan, 7, 13, 18, 25, 28, 49, 52, 70, 88, 95,
   101, 111, 114, 123, 166, 170, 189, 191,
   193, 202, 206, 209, 214, 220; Indonesian
   collaboration, 22, 25, 26, 51, 209; introduction of elections, 126; occupation, 8,

23, 25–6, 27, 51–2, 58, 94, 105, 126, 127, 185; peace treaty, 197, 212; surrender, 29

Java, 1, 2, 5, 7, 9, 10, 12, 13, 14, 15, 19, 21, 24, 30, 41, 52, 71, 72, 73, 94, 100, 102, 116, 120, 124, 126, 131, 132, 134, 135, 142, 143, 145, 148, 151–4, 157, 160, 172, 173, 176, 194, 198, 219, 220; '1965 coup' aftermath, 140, 163; oil, 152, 153; revolts/rebellions/wars, 9, 15–16, 22, 26

Java Sea, Battle of, 4

Javanese, 180, 181, 186, 190; civilization, 2–4, 15, 76, 98, 128; culture, 7, 47, 54, 57, 60, 65, 70–1, 84, 104, 127, 130, 131, 153, 174; *see also priyayi*

Jayabaya, King, 7

'Jogja Charter', 96, 97

'Jogja Days', 30

Jogjakarta, 8, 10, 16, 42, 57, 58, 59, 96, 101, 119, 134, 141, 144, 153; Diponegoro, 15–16; national capital, 30–1, 34; sultan, 110, 111, 134, 153

Jonge, Jonkheer de, 24

'July 3rd affair', 31

'July 27th affair', 97

kabinet kerdja (working cabinet), 35, 198

Kadiri, 7

Kahin, George McTurnan, 26, 27, 89

Kalimantan, 5, 8, 15, 16, 28, 129, 145–6, 151, 200, 201

KAMI—Kesatuan Aksi Mahasiswa Indonesia (Indonesian Student Action Front), 103; *see also* student action

Kartini, 21, 22, 57, 186

kasar, 131, 133

Kawilarang, Colonel, 97

Keating, Paul, 208, 217

Kedah, 5

Kemusuk, 57

Kennedy, J. F., 213, 215; administration, 214

Kerakjatan, 118

Khmers, 1

Khruschev, Nikita, 48, 99

'Konfrontasi' *see* 'Confrontation'

Komodo, 151

Kompas, 85

Kompassus—Komando Pasukan Khussus, 105

Kong Le, 77

Kongress Wanita Indonesia (Indonesian Women's Congress), 184, 186; *see also* women

Kopkamtib—Komando Operasi Pemulihan Keamanan dan Ketertiban (Law and Order Restoration Command), 88

Korea, 88, 106, 195; North, 81, 202; South, 70, 94, 108, 165

Kostrad—Komando Candangan Strategis Angkatun Darat (Army Strategic Reserve Command), 38, 59; *see also* ABRI; armed forces; army

Kusumasumantri, Iwa, 97

Lajar Terkembang (*Unfurled Sails*), 135

Laksar Rakyat (People's Army), 94

land ownership, 126, 140, 144

land reform, 140, 152

languages, 105, 153; nationalism, 22; peoples, 132, 144, 148, 149, 153; Sukarno oration, 44–5

Laos, 77

Latin America, 38, 199, 212; *see also* Afro-Asian bloc; 'new emerging forces'

law, 68, 69, 70, 90, 172, 185, 227; and order, 88, 91, 107, 141; government, 68, 82, 88; women, 184–5

Law of the Sea, 204

Leimena, Dr Johannes, 36, 75

Lekra—Lembaga Kebudayan Rakyat (Peoples Cultural Institute), 136; *see also* censorship; literature

Lemhannas—Lembaga Pertahanan Nasional (National Defence Institute), 88

Leur, J. C. van, 4, 6

Liberal Party of Australia, 210

Liem Sioe Liong, 113

Linggadjati Agreement, 31

literature, 133, 134–8; censorship, 136, 137; women, 135, 137

living standards, 64

Lockhart, Bruce, 24

Lombok, 8, 15, 51

Lubis, Mochtar, 32, 137, 138

Lubis, Zulkifli, 97

Lukman, 61, 78, 79, 163

Mackie, J. A. C., 210

McVey, Ruth, 84

Madiun Revolt, 31, 35, 51, 78, 79, 89, 101, 187

Madura, 12, 15, 151, 153

Magsaysay Prize, 138

Mahabharata, 7, 127
Majapahit, 8–9, 27, 28, 127
Makassar (now Ujung Padang), 10, 15, 24, 32, 147
Malacca, 6, 10, 11, 12, 28; Strait of, 6, 142, 143
Malaka, Tan, 22, 26, 89, 95, 196; *see also* 'July 3rd affair'
Malari Affair, 91, 158
Malay-Polynesian language group, 2, 130, 144, 148, 153; Malay as national language, 18, 22, 105, 132, 134; *see also* Bahasa Indonesia; languages
Malaya, 24, 28, 170, 173, 196, 199, 215
Malayan Peninsula, 5, 10, 37, 142
Malaysia, 37, 40, 65, 69, 77, 94, 99, 100, 106, 111, 129, 130, 181, 188, 200, 201, 202, 203, 204, 205, 208, 215; 'Confrontation', 200, 201; *see also* Azahari rebellion
Malik, Adam, 81, 143; *see also* Partai Murba
Mallaby, Brigadier General, 30
'Maphalindo' talks, 205
Manila, 13, 35, 200
Manipol-Usdek, 177, 195
Mantiri Affair, 216–17
Mantiri, Lieutenant General Herman, 216–17
Marga T, 137
marhaen, 35, 50, 57, 80, 83, 89, 107, 119, 120, 124, 131, 152; *see also* BTI
Marsinah case, 91, 92, 93, 169
martial law, 88, 90
Marxism, 22, 27, 53, 54, 79; *see also* Communism; Sukarno
Masjumi, 33, 34, 35, 81, 85, 140, 196, 197–8; *see also* elections; NU; PSI
Mataram, 6, 7, 9, 10, 14, 127
Max Havelaar, 21
Mecca, 46
media, 18, 56, 57, 59, 70, 71, 75, 77, 85, 93, 98, 181, 194
Menzies, Robert G., 213, 215
Menzies government, 210, 213; *see also* Australia
Merdaka Utara, 52, 75, 193
Mesopotamia, 7
Mexico, 70, 111
Minahasa, 94, 148, 173, 174
Minangkabau, 8, 15, 24, 135, 144, 181; revolt, 22
Middle East, 10, 94, 120, 130; *see also* Arabia; Islam

Moerdani, General Benny, 39, 105–8, 159, 217; *see also* Timor
Mohamad, Goenawan, 68, 136; *see also* censorship; *Tempo*
Mohammadijah, 21, 58, 140
Moluccas, 8, 9, 10, 12, 20, 23, 77, 148, 164
Monitor, 85, 156
Mordiono, State Secretary, 65, 82
MPR—Majelis Perwakilan Rakyat (People's Consultative Assembly), 76, 82, 103, 224
MPRS—Majelis Permusyawaratan Rakyat Sementara (Provisional People's Consultative Assembly), 35
mufakat, 36, 118, 126, 127
Murba, *see* Partai Murba
Murtopo, Major General Ali, 36, 60, 104, 106, 158
music, 80, 133
musjawarah, 36, 54, 118, 126, 127
Musso, 31, 50, 51; *see also* Communism
mysticism, 24, 58, 60–1, 84, 125, 131, 133, 134, 140, 157, 160, 172, 207, 222; Sukarno and Suharto, 41, 46
mythology and magic, 14, 127, 133, 147; Java, 47, 54, 130; Sukarno, 53, 54

Nasakom cabinet, 47, 78, 83
Nasser, Colonel, 77, 79
Nasution, Abdul Haris, 30, 35, 59, 74, 76, 81, 94, 95, 96, 97, 98; Malaysia, 99, 201; 'middle way', 89, 104; military in politics, 102, 104; '1965 coup', 74, 75, 104, 163
Nasution, Adnan Buyung, 68
national Communism, *see* Communism
national democracy, *see* democracy
National Front, 36, 80, 120
National Over-All Development Plan, *see* Eight-Year Plan
'national resiliance', 205
national unity, 34, 55
nationalism, 4, 11, 18, 42, 94, 124, 128–9, 135, 137, 142, 169, 170, 171, 174, 194, 204, 205, 209, 218, 220–1; *see also* independence; Nationalist movement; Republic of Indonesia; RUSI
Nationalism and Revolution in Indonesia, 26
nationalist movement, 7, 8, 17, 18, 21, 22–4, 25–6, 27, 28, 29, 31, 32, 51, 83, 84, 89, 90, 100, 106, 208; *see also* independence; nationalism; Republic of Indonesia; RUSI

nationalization, 90, 99, 199

Nato, 212

Natsir, Mohammed, 34

natural forces, 124–5; rainfall, 125, 145, 149, 152

natural resources, 34, 112, 115, 116, 118, 120, 124, 143, 145, 146, 148, 149, 153, 219; see also oil

Necolim, see neo-colonialism

Nehru, Jawaharlal, 79, 184

Nemoto, Naoka, 55

neo-colonialism, 69, 129, 189, 191

nepotism, 69, 70, 72, 83, 107; see also Suharto family

Netherlands, The, 2, 4, 7, 8, 11, 12, 15, 17–25, 30, 31, 32, 34, 36, 38, 52, 54, 58, 59, 69, 84, 90, 94, 101, 102, 105, 117, 123, 125, 127, 128, 129, 132, 143, 145, 153, 166, 176, 180, 181, 194, 195, 197, 198, 200, 208, 209, 210, 215; Batavia, 13–14, 17, 194; Dutch East Indies Company, 13, 15, 148; Hague, The, 15, 25, 32, 95; peoples, 143–4, 145, 147, 148; revolts, supression, 13–16, 31, 83, 136, 210; Renville Agreement, 89; Round Table Conference, 32, 198; Sukarno, 49–51; West Irian, 179, 200, 212–14

neutrality, non-alignment, 72, 129, 173, 177, 178, 195, 197, 199, 203, 205

New Delhi conference, 210

'new emerging forces', 99, 171, 172, 179, 199; see also Afro-Asian bloc; Conefo; Ganefo

New Guinea, 10, 23, 24, 28, 148, 198, 211, 214; Papua, 65, 111, 124, 142, 149; Papuans, 69, 128, 129, 213, 214

New Order, 41, 60, 65, 71, 79, 82, 83–4, 103, 104, 105, 106, 107, 111, 137, 138, 155, 156, 195; see also Golkar; '1965 coup'; Suharto

New Zealand, 37, 205

Nigeria, 108

'1950 revolt', 128

'1965 coup', 7, 37–8, 53, 59, 61, 73–9, 103, 104, 162–3; aftermath, 138–41, 150, 156, 163–4, 168, 187; as half-coup, 75, 78; Pramoedya, 137; Revolutionary Council, 75, 77, 78; see also Halim

Nitisastro, Widjoyo, 112

NU—Nahdatul Ulama (Muslim Teachers Party), 33, 83, 155, 156, 157, 159; ICMI rival, 84–6; membership, 85, 140; PPP

withdrawal, 84, 155; 29th Congress, 91, 92; see also elections; political opposition; political parties

Nyoto, 61, 74, 78, 79

'October 17th affair', 96, 102, 197

oil, 70, 83, 114–15, 118, 143; ABRI, 93; location, 143, 146, 149, 151, 152, 153; Timor Gap Treaty, 216

'openness', 68, 72

OPM—Organisasi Papua Merdeka, 149; see also New Guinea

OPSUS—Operasi Khusus (Special Operations Group), 39

Out of Exile, 8, 23

Pancasila (The Five Principles), 27, 28, 62, 118, 122, 157, 160, 162, 172, 173, 218, 226; Islam, 84, 160; state, 64

Pakistan, 94, 130

Palembang, 11

Palembang River, 6

Pane, Sanusi, 135, 143

Pangestu, Prajogo, 113

Parkindo—Partai Kristen Indonesia, 33, 81; see also Christianity; PDI; political parties

Parmusi, 81

Partai Katolik, 33, 81; see also Catholicism; PDI; political parties

Partai Murba, 33, 81; see also PDI; political parties

Partindo—Partai Indonesia, 23

Pauker, Guy J., 95

PDI—Partai Demokrasi Indonesia (Indonesian Democratic Party), 54, 64, 81, 83, 157, 161; interference, 82, 88, 92; see also DPR; elections; political parties

Pendidikan Nasional Indonesia (Indonesia National Education Group), 23

Peoples Democratic Front, 89; see also armed forces

Perdang, 34

Perhimpoenan Indonesia (Indonesian Union), 22, 23

Perlak, 9

Permesta (overall struggle), 34, 106

Persarikatan Nasional Indonesia (Indonesian Nationalist Organization), 50; see also nationalism; nationalist movement

Persia, 6, 10, 12; see also Arabia, Middle East

Pertamina scandal, 70, 93, 114–15; see also corruption

Perti, 81; *see also* human rights

Peta—Soekarela Tentara Pembela Tanah Air (Home Defence Corps), 26, 94, 95, 96

petrus incident, 106, 141

Philippines, 69, 70, 77, 94, 101, 108, 130, 165, 199, 200, 201, 202, 205, 215

philosophy, ethics, 57, 70, 130–4, 160, 190

PJP—Pembangunan Jang-ka Panjang (Long Term Development Plan), 116

PKI—Partai Kommunist Indonesia (Indonesian Communist Party), 22, 26, 29, 37, 61, 74, 75, 80, 81, 84, 88, 91, 93, 98, 99, 100, 102, 103, 121, 136, 138, 140, 162, 163, 164, 165, 187, 197, 198, 199, 201, 203, 209; banning of, 61, 78–9; Biro Khusus, 74, 78; '1965 coup', 74, 77, 78; aftermath, 79, 139–41; Sukarno/military, 76, 83; *see also* Aidit, D. N.; Communism; '1965 coup'; political parties

PNI—Partai Nasional Indonesia (Indonesian Nationalist Party), 22, 23, 33, 50, 51, 54, 64, 81, 83, 84, 98, 195, 196, 197, 201; *see also* nationalism; nationalist movement; PDI

poetry, 133, 135, 137

political opposition, 33, 34, 35, 68, 70, 71, 84, 106, 156, 195, 196, 224; lack of, 81–2; *see also* elections

political parties, 33, 35, 54, 63–4, 67, 85, 92, 96, 98, 161, 192; interference, 75, 81, 82, 83, 88, 198; *see also* democracy

political prisoners, 187–8

political system, *see* government, system of

pollution, 219

Polo, Marco, 9, 11, 142

population figures, 34, 65, 108, 116, 120, 124, 160, 190, 219–20, 221; birthrate, 111; specific, 143, 145, 146, 148, 149, 151, 152, 153; *see also* family planning

Portuguese, 11, 12, 18, 20, 38, 146, 148; Timor, 17, 38, 40, 128, 150, 207; *see also* Timor

Powell, Colin, 58

PPP—Partai Persatuan Pembangunan (United Development Party), 64, 83, 155, 159, 161; interference, 82, 88; NU, 84, 92; *see also* elections; government, system of; Islam; political parties

PPPKI—National Union of Political Associations, 51

Pramoedya Ananta Toer, 74, 137–8, 164

Prawiranegara, Sjafruddin, 34

privatization, 56

priyayi, 131–2, 133, 134, 165; *see also* philosophy, ethics

Protestantism, 11, 33, 81, 144, 173, 175; *see also* Christianity, Parkindo

PRRI—Pemerintah Revolusioner Republik Indonesia (Revolutionary Government of the Republic of Indonesia), 34, 106, 143; *see also* nationalism; nationalist movement

PSI—Partai Socialis Indonesia (Indonesian Socialist Party), 33, 34, 35, 197

Pudjangga Baru (*The New Writer*), 135

Putera—Pusat Tenaga Rakyat (Peoples Manpower Centre), 52

Raffles, Sir T. Stamford., 2

Rainbow Coalition, 108; *see also* ABRI

Ramayana, 127

Ratna Sari Dewi, *see* Nemoto Naoka

Recollections of an Indonesian Diplomat in the Sukarno Era, 74

'Red' Saraket Islam, *see* Saraket Islam

regional co-operation, 65–6, 107, 122, 203, 208, 215; *see also* ASEAN; APEC; ARF

regional security, 72, 107, 191, 208, 217

regionalism, 34, 65, 128, 195; '1955–61 rebellion', 97–8, 99, 128

Reksosamudro, Pranoto, 75

religion, 63, 69, 70, 116, 124–5, 129, 130, 143, 156, 158, 160, 161, 172, 174, 177, 220; Sukarno, 46–7, 54; tolerance, 62, 122, 175; *see also* animism; Buddhism; Calvinism; Catholicism; Christianity; Hinduism; Islam; mysticism

The Religion of Java, 125

Renville Agreement, 31, 89

Repelita I–VI (Five Year Development Plans), 114–16, 123; *see also* economic development

Republic of Indonesia, 8, 17, 29, 31, 41, 48, 89, 143, 208; *see also* independence; RUSI

Republika, 85, 158

resentment, politics of, 69

Robison, Richard, 15

Round Table Conference, 32, 95, 102, 198

Royal Netherlands Indies Army, 94, 101

Royal Netherlands Military Academy, 101

RTZ corporation, 149
rubber, 34, 143, 146
Rudini, Major General, 109
Rukmana, Hardijanti (Tutut), 73, 81, 91, 224
Rusli, Marah, 134, 143
Russia, 15, 18, 36, 45, 81, 108, 128, 207; *see also* Soviet Union

Sabah, 201, 215
Sadli, Mohammad, 112
Saleh, Chairul, 26, 36, 38, 76, 81; *see also* Partai Murba
Salim, Agus, 22, 50, 143
Salim, Emil, 219
Salim, Natsir, 143
Salim, Sudono, *see* Liem Sioe Liang
Samual, Colonel, 97
sandang pangan, 37, 118–19
Sarawak, 28, 201, 202, 215
Sardjono, 209
Sarekat Islam, 21, 22, 50, 81; *see also* PSI
Sasono, Adi, 86; *see also* CIDES
Sastroamidjojo, Ali, 97, 198, 211; governments, 198, 211, 212; *see also* PKI; PNI
Schwarz, Adam, 71
science, 116, 125, 134
SEATO (South-East Asian Treaty Organization), 197, 205
security police, 81, 88, 93, 108, 181, 222
Selasih, 135
Selosoemardjan, 7, 119, 120
Semar, 7, 130; *see also* Wayang Kulit
Semarang, 153, 162
Shell Oil Company, 55; *see also* oil
Shrivajaya, 6, 17, 27, 28
Siagian, Sabam, 216, 217
Siam, 9
Simatupang, Major General T. B., 95, 96
Simbolon, Colonel, 97
Sinar Harapan (*Hopeful Beam*), 174; *see also* Protestantism
Singapore, 2, 16, 35, 69, 101, 111, 123, 188, 200, 201, 202, 205, 215, 221, 223; *see also* ASEAN
Siti Nurbaja (*Miss Nurbaja*), 134
Situmorang, Sitor, 143
Sjahir, Sutan, 8, 23–5, 33, 35, 49, 51, 89, 143; as prime minister, 29, 31, 186; Tjipanas 26, 27
Sjam, 74–5; *see also* PKI, Biro Khusus
Sjarifuddin, Amir, 25, 26, 89; as prime minister, 29, 31, 186

Sky Above and the Mud Below, The, 129
slogans, symbols, 43–8, 96, 98, 117, 118, 124, 137, 142, 163, 170, 172, 180, 194, 195, 200, 220, 221
smuggling, 34, 59
Sneevliet, Henrik, 21; *see also* Indies Social Democratic Association
SOBSI—Sentral Organisasi Buruh Seluru Indonesia (Central All-Indonesia Workers' Organization), 80
Social Change in Jogjakarta, 7
Social Democratic Labour Party, 22
social justice, 80, 118, 123
social structure, 120, 126, 127, 128, 132; peoples, 144, 147, 150, 154; *see also* family structure; philosophy, ethics
socialism, 117, 118, 122
Soedjatmoko, 138
Solo, 2, 7, 15, 153
South-East Asia, 6, 37, 121, 176, 194, 200, 214, 215, 217; *see also* Asia
Soviet Union, 31, 36, 79, 80, 110, 121, 124, 178, 179, 193, 202, 206; Communism, 79, 80, 188; relations, 34, 100, 194, 197, 198, 202, 208, 213, 226; *see also* Russia
Spain, 18
Spender, Percy, 211
Spice Islands, *see* Moluccas
'spirit of 1945', 35, 102
SPSI—Serikat Pekerja Seluruh Indonesia (All-Indonesia Workers' Union), 92, 93
Sri Lanka, 111
strikes, 92, 98, 199
student action, 23, 27, 29, 103, 137, 158; '1965 coup', 38, 74
students, 43, 103, 181, 208, 223; *see also* youth
Subandrio, Dr, 26, 36, 38, 61, 74, 75, 81, 129, 198, 200, 201, 212
Subardjo, Foreign Minister, 196, 197, 212
Subianto, Brigadier General Prabowo, 73, 81, 105, 108; Suharto, succession, 224
Subroto, Gatot, 97
Sudirman, General, 89, 94, 96, 101, 102
Sudrajat, General Edi, 92, 108
Suharto, 17, 40, 41, 42, 55–66, 59, 67, 69, 70, 84, 85, 88, 91, 92, 100, 103, 104, 105, 107, 108, 109, 123, 151, 155, 156, 163, 165, 166, 167, 194, 204, 219; achievements, 62, 64–5, 114–16, 122; army, 36, 38, 58, 59, 75, 192, 200; Australia, 65, 208, 216, 217; democracy, 71, 82; era, 72, 74, 76, 79, 90, 128, 221, 223, 226, 228;

ethnic Chinese, 11, 113; family, 63, 70, 72, 73, 83, 107, 108, 112, 113, 114, 155, 165, 166, 224, 225; '1965 coup', 59, 73, 75, 76, 138, 163; personality, 55–7, 58, 62, 59–60, 62, 134; quotes, 58, 60, 62, 63, 90, 141; succession, 71 72, 72, 107, 139, 141, 223–6, 227; and Sukarno, 61–2; Timor, 39, 207; youth, 57–8, 63

Suharto, Mrs Siti Hartinah (Tien), 59, 224

Sukarni, 25

Sukarno, 8, 17, 22, 23, 26, 27, 28, 29, 30, 31, 32, 33, 36, 37, 38, 40, 41, 42–55, 58, 59, 61, 64, 65, 66, 67, 69, 70, 71, 75, 79, 81, 83, 84, 94, 95, 98, 99, 100, 102–3, 104, 106, 110, 117, 120, 121, 129, 162, 163, 169, 171, 173, 178, 180, 182, 185, 187, 189, 190, 191, 192, 194, 198, 202, 203, 204, 213, 216, 218, 220, 221; childhood, 26, 49–50; Communism, 53, 54, 76, 77, 80, 83, 97; era, 33, 34, 35, 55, 74, 116, 122, 170, 171–2, 173, 214, 220, 226; jailed, 23, 51; Japanese collaboration, 25, 51; Malaysia, 201, 215; nationalism, 18, 50–1, 53; 'new emerging forces', 199; '1965 coup', 74, 76, 77–78, 139, 163; oration, 43–8, 96, 124, 200; personality, 41, 46, 51, 52, 53, 54, 134, 175; succession, 38, 76, 90, 223, 226; and Suharto, 61–2; Sukarnoism, 42, 78, 189, 190, 191; quotes, 1, 17, 44, 45, 46, 47, 48, 51, 118, 119, 26, 198; see also 'guided democracy'; 'new emerging forces'

Sukirman government, 196

Sulawesi, 8, 10, 15, 16, 17, 23, 24, 34, 58, 77, 98, 100, 106, 146–8, 164, 173, 174; '1955–61 rebellion', 97, 128, 173, 198

Sumarlin, 112

Sumatra, 4, 5, 6, 8, 9, 11, 12, 16, 22, 34, 51, 54, 77, 81, 101, 104, 106, 124, 125, 126, 142–5, 151, 152, 176; '1955–61 rebellion', 97, 128, 173, 199

Sumbawa, 8, 151

Sundas, the Lesser, 149–51

Sundanese, 153, 179, 180

Supeno, Colonel Bambang, 95, 96, 97

Supersemar, 7, 158; see also '1965 coup'

Supreme Advisory Council, 35

Surabaya, 21, 30, 50, 105, 153, 209

Sutowo, Ibnu, 115; see also Pertamina scandal

Sutrisno, Tri, 71, 72, 104–5, 107, 108, 166, 224, 226

Sydney Morning Herald, 213

Taiwan, 70, 193, 197; Nationalist China, 202

Taman Siswa (Garden of Pupils), 22

Tanjung, General Feisal, 91, 92, 108, 217

Tanjung Priok, 106, 194; riots, 91, 158, 166

tariffs, 112, 115, 123

taxation, 34, 123

technology, 84, 94, 111, 116, 134, 167, 206

Tempo, 69, 73; see also censorship; Mohamad, Goenawan

territorial boundaries, 28, 32, 35, 38, 40, 87; see also defence and security

Thailand, 69, 94, 111, 199, 205

Thamrin, Mohammed, 25

'30th of September Movement', 74, 75, 77; see also Gestapu; '1965 coup'

Timor, 38–40, 150, 207, 208; Dili, 39, 40, 71, 90, 91, 216; East, 17, 40, 66, 69, 105, 106, 144, 141, 215–16, 217; Portuguese 28, 129, 150; see also Apodeti, Fretilin, UDT

Timor Gap Treaty, 216

Timorese Social Democratic Association, 38

Tjokroaminoto, Umar Said, 21, 22, 50, 54; see also Sarekat Islam

TNI—Tentara Nasional Indonesia (Indonesian National Army), 94; see also ABRI; armed forces; army

Toraja, 147, 174

Tordesillas, treaty of, 18

tourism, 116, 150

trade, 5, 6, 9, 10, 107, 120, 122, 145, 147, 148, 153, 171, 198; see also exports and imports

trade unions, 22, 80, 92; see also strikes

transport, 18, 104, 192, 195

Trikora, 46

TRIP (Tentara Republik Indonesia Pelajar), 30, 105

Tutut, see Rukmana Hardijanti

Turkey, 12, 21

Twilight in Djakarta, 32

The Twilight of Majapahit, 135

UDT—Uniao Democratica Timorese (Timorese Democratic Union), 38, 39; see also Fretilin; Timor

underground, anti-Japanese, 25, 26, 27, 29

United Nations, 30, 36, 37, 39, 40, 95, 114, 129, 151; Committee of Good Offices, 210; Declaration of Human Rights, 184; Security Council, 37, 89, 202, 210; Unicef, 65

United States of America, 16, 31, 45, 58, 65, 68, 69, 70, 78, 79, 80, 84, 93, 106, 124, 139, 149, 159, 167, 170, 171–2, 178, 191, 193, 196, 197, 199, 200, 206, 207, 208, 210, 213, 214, 217, 219, 220, 223; aid, 195, 196, 197; relations, 202, 215, 226; South-East Asia, 100–1, 215; Vietnam, 37, 206; West Irian, 200, 213; see also Kennedy, J. F.
United States Mutual Security Act, 196
Unity in Diversity, 30, 128–9, 151
Utojo, Colonel Bambung, 97
Utusan Hindia (Indies Messenger), 50

Venezuela, 108
Vietnam, 9, 29, 52, 102, 111, 121, 190, 191, 193, 219; North, 67, 79, 81, 197, 202; United States, 37, 206
volcanoes, 1, 124, 142, 146, 148, 149, 151
Volksraad (Peoples Council), 24, 25
Vow of Youth, 22, 194

Wahid, A., 84, 85, 91, 92, 107, 155, 156, 157, 159; see also NU
Wallace, Alfred Russel, 20, 151
Wallace Line, 151
Wardhana, Ali, 112
Warouw, Colonel, 97, 98
Waterside Workers Federation, 209; see also West Irian
wayang kulit, 7, 45, 49, 127, 130, 133, 172; see also dalang
Weber, Max, 4
West Timor, see Timor
West Irian, 32, 36, 37, 40, 46, 48, 59, 77, 99, 124, 125, 128, 129, 148–9, 151, 164, 167, 174, 176, 179, 195, 200, 208, 211–14, 215; United Nations, 198, 199, 212; see also New Guinea
Westerling, Captain 'Turk', 30, 211
Western bloc, 171, 177, 178, 179, 188, 190, 191, 195, 196, 199, 207, 208, 228
White Australia Policy, 211
Whitlam, Gough, 208; East Timor, 215, 216; government, 216
Widjaya, Eka Tjipta, 113
Wilopo government, 33, 197
women, 21, 35, 55, 128, 135, 137, 139, 160, 184–6
World Bank, 111, 112, 114, 123
World War II, 4, 19, 20, 25, 41, 51, 204, 209

Xavier, St Francis, 11

Yacatra, 13–14
Yamin, Prof. Mohammed, 25, 28, 117, 211
Yani, Lieutenant General Achmad, 74, 94
Yavadvipa, 5
YLBHI—Yayasan Lembaga Bantuan Hukum Indonesia (Indonesian Legal Aid Foundation), 68
Young Java, 50
youth, 22, 30, 43, 63, 89, 102, 137, 138, 163, 183, 194, 201; see also student action; students
Yugoslavia, 129, 178

ZOPFAN—Zone of Freedom and Neutrality, 206; see also ASEAN